For
GRA

POCKET ANNUAL 2000

Bruce Smith

6th Year of Publication

Virgin

Formula 1 Grand Prix Pocket Annual 2000

Copyright © Bruce Smith – Author 2000

ISBN: 0-7535-0431-6

Disclaimer: In a book of this type it is inevitable that some errors will creep in. While every effort has been made to ensure that the details given in this annual are correct at the time of going to press, neither the authors, editor nor the publishers can accept any responsibility for errors within. If you have any comments or ideas for future editions of this annual you can E-mail the author at: SmithBruce@Hotmail.com

First published in March 2000 by *Virgin Publishing*.

Virgin Publishing Ltd
Thames Wharf Studios
Rainville Road
London
W6 9HA

Typeset by Bruce Smith.

Edited by Mark Webb.

CONTENTS

3

A-Z Formula One Drivers

Team Directory

Circuit Directory

Race 2000

Introduction

WELCOME TO THE sixth edition of the *FORMULA 1 POCKET ANNUAL*. You will notice a number of, what I hope you will consider to be, improvements to the information collated here. I have tried where possible to take note of suggestions that many of you have made and hope that you feel that the new features are of benefit. The most significant of these can be found in the Drivers' section, which now lists the final classification of each of the drivers in detail for every single Grand Prix they have taken part in. There is a bit more about this, and other notes concerning the content, towards the end of this introductory section.

As for the 1999 season it had just about everything. From the brilliant to the boring, from the clear-cut to the muddy-watered. The cynics had opportunities to get their claws into the sport, but it was a season where they were mostly kept quiet.

One thing that does become clear with each year that passes is the significance of pole position. It doesn't decide the race winner (in fact only three wins came from pole in 1999) but in 1999 every pole driver who finished the race did so with a podium position. Another interesting statistic was the fact that out of the 16 races, the pole driver retired on an amazing seven occasions and several of those were down to driver error, especially in the case of Mika Hakkinen.

Probably the most exciting race of the season came at Magny-Cours and the significance here was that it became so because the grid, courtesy of the changing and worsening weather, was almost turned on its head. We had, after all, Barrichello and Alesi on the front row, with Hakkinen and Irvine sharing the seventh and eighth rows, but fighting in brilliant style to gain points. It set me thinking on a train of thought that would never be contemplated. But just suppose there were a few wild card races selected in secret at the start of each season, that were only announced after qualifying at each particular race and which effectively meant that the grid was re-ordered from back to front. Crazy maybe, but exciting yes. Now I find myself with my fingers crossed for the onset of rain during qualifying sessions.

Something that we certainly don't need is the confusion that surrounded the Malaysian Grand Prix with the disqualification of the Ferrari drivers Schumacher and Irvine a couple of hours after the event. F1 is a technical sport and the legitimacy of cars must be of paramount importance to ensure a level racing field. But in recent years, in the majority of cases, the infringements that have produced disqualifications could have been identified had the post-race scrutineering been undertaken prior to the race itself. This creates complications I know, but for the credibility of the sport it must be implemented. In much the same way as a team must provide samples of its fuel before a race, and against which a race sample is also compared after the event, then a car could be checked and passed. Should the post-race check show up any physical changes, other than those from wear and tear, then a disqualification could be effected and without appeal.

Call me cynical, but I wonder if the Ferrari appeal would have been upheld had it occurred in the first half of the season. For the sake of fair play I hope so, but I wonder…

Another item of fall-out from the Malaysian Grand Prix centred on tyres. After the race, McLaren boss Ron Dennis contemplated an official complaint over the finishing condition of the tyres on Michael Schumacher's Ferrari. In fact pictures showed that they were virtually bald, with the grooves worn away, so much so the indication was that they were effectively slicks, that used to be in operation up to the 1997 season.

The FIA do not police the condition of tyres after a race, only before. Bridgestone had always stated that the tyres would run slower when the grooves were worn away but on some circuits this does not seem to be the case. No doubt it is something that will have been addressed by the tyre manufacturers during the lead-up to the 2000 season.

Whoever said that rules were rules? At the French Grand Prix both Arrows' drivers were placed ahead of the Minardi drivers on the grid despite the fact that neither Arrows' man made it inside the 107% rule. In fact they hadn't qualified for the race, but the Minardi duo had. The reason for the decision – the Arrows' drivers had been quicker in practice!

Damon Hill

Although he may have retired from the F1 cockpit I am sure that England's favourite sportsman will be a familiar sight around the F1 paddocks, or at least the TV studios, in the months and years ahead. Looking back over his career, there is much to remember, indeed many incidents are difficult to forget. The despair when he was shoved out of contention for the Drivers' Championship by Michael Schumacher in the final race of 1995. The joy when he put that behind him and took his championship in 1996 and the blubbering of Murray Walker as he did so (supported by millions watching). Then there was that first victory for Jordan in 1998.

But to my mind the most memorable Damon moment came on 10th August 1997 at the Hungaroring when in a totally uncompetitive Arrows car he came within a whisper of a win. Leading into the final lap and then into the final corner victory was within his grasp until a 50p washer that had been failing in the final minutes of the race finally proved critical and the loss of speed allowed Jacques Villeneuve to pass the Arrows just yards from the line. Had Damon won it could have been regarded as one of the greatest wins in F1 history. Nevertheless to my mind that was the ultimate Damon moment.

Book Changes 2000

The most significant change comes in the Drivers' section. Each Grand Prix in which a driver has started is listed on an annual basis but now their classification is signalled after the race. For example:

> San 3

signifies the driver finished third in San Marino, while:

> Mon r

indicates that the driver retired at Monaco.

In previous editions of the Annual a number after the race venue indicated the number of points, if any, won by the driver at the meeting.

DNS: Another bone of contention has been the DNS or did not start rule. This has led to some confusion both here and in a number of other publications. However, the following 'standard' has now been adopted for these pages.

A driver is deemed not to have started a race if he is not on the grid for the start which becomes the race. For example, if a driver suffers a problem on the formation lap and is therefore not lined-up on the grid and does not take part in the start and therefore race, he is recorded as a dns. Equally, if a race is stopped and the driver, who originally started the race, is unable to take the restart, he is recorded as a dns.

The significance of this is that a dns does not count towards a driver's total number of GPs for the stats in this book. Thus, although Michael Schumacher took part in the first start at the British Grand Prix in 1999, because he did not take part in the second start (following his accident) this does not count towards his total number of GPs. However, for the sake of completeness such dns are listed within the driver details in the Drivers' section and are presented in brackets, ie:

> (GB dns)

Formula 1 Web Site

Check out the web site at:

> www.formula-1.co.uk

to keep up to date with the latest news, views and stats.

The cut-off date for completion of this year's annual was 12th January. There were still some questions to be answered at that point, not least in the final calendar of races for the season and the appointment of a few drivers. However, all the proposed circuits have been included.

Thanks 2000

I would like to thank all the Formula One teams for their co-operation in producing this annual. Thanks also to Mark Webb who proof read these pages and Benetton Formula for some of the additional circuit information.

If you have any comments or ideas for future editions of this annual you can E-mail me at:

SmithBruce@Hotmail.com

RULE CHANGES 2000

Aggregate Rules

The 2000 season sees a tweak in the F1 rules in that races that are stopped and restarted will no longer be decided on aggregate times. Previously, if a race had gone two laps but less than 75% of the distance, drivers had their times for the two 'halves' added together. The placings were then decided in order of the quickest aggregate times. This last decided a Grand Prix in Japan in 1994 when Damon Hill beat Michael Schumacher. From now on if a race is halted, the cars will reform on the grid and start again for the remaining laps – just as if they had been running behind the safety car. The idea here is that it will make the end result easier to follow, although probably not as exciting as having to race against the clock.

Formation Lap

Another change is that drivers who are temporarily delayed on the formation lap will be allowed to overtake to regain their grid position in the formation so long as they do not put the other cars in danger.

Grand Prix Review 1999

Pre-Season

The pre-season testing got underway with four teams carrying their 1998 line-up into 1999. Continuity has always been a card that the current big two have supported and both McLaren and Ferrari remained unchanged in monocoque personnel. World champion Mika Hakkinen and David Coulthard would be piloting the McLarens, with Michael Schumacher and Eddie Irvine behind the controls of the F399. The Ulsterman would be starting his third season as the contractual number two at Ferrari. Looking to build on youth, and take the debut form they showed in 1998 with them, both Giancarlo Fisichella and Alexander Wurz were contracted to Benetton the year 2000. The fourth unchanged line-up was at Prost where second year driver Jarno Trulli would partner Olivier Panis, entering his fifth year with the team. Prost did have one major change though, running the Peugeot V10 for the first time, with Mugen Honda making the reverse journey to Jordan.

Eddie Jordan raised a few eyebrows when he signed German Heinz-Harald Frentzen to partner Damon Hill in the Buzzin Hornets – a move that was to prove an outstanding success by the end of the season. Johnny Herbert gave up the Swiss countryside of the Sauber team for the roundabouts of Milton Keynes, joining Rubens Barrichello at the Stewart-Ford set-up. Pedro Diniz filled the vacancy left by Herbert to join Alesi.

Williams, Minardi and Arrows all introduced new line-ups. Ralf Schumacher and Alex Zanardi had a season's worth of F1 experience between them, and Sir Frank Williams continued with his habit of employing American CART champions by taking on Zanardi. The Italian based Minardi team partnered Ferrari test driver Luca Badoer with F1 rookie Marc Gene. Arrows picked up the highly rated Takagi from the defunct Tyrell team and introduced Spaniard Pedro de la Rosa. The grid line-up was completed by the arrival of new team British American Racing (BAR) who were optimistic going into the season with the 1997 champion Jacques Villeneuve at the wheel and supported by Brazilian rookie Ricardo Zonta.

By the time the smaller outfits had declared their line-ups, the March 7th start to the 1999 season was upon us; but only after a dispute between the new BAR team and the FIA, in which the new boys looked set to take the legal action that would allow them to run their cars in different liveries. The FIA stood firm, however, and after arbitration BAR were forced to back down on what they were proposing to do. Despite boasting they would win in their first year, number one driver Jacques Villeneuve hit the nail on the head when he announced that the 1999 season would represent his biggest ever challenge. How right he would be.

Late pre-season testing was plagued by a succession of rear-wing failures, the most spectacular of which came when Johnny Herbert had a 190 mph crash at Barcelona during pre-season testing. Talk of flexible wings dominated the paddock and the FIA moved to quell this by introducing new load tests in time for the Brazilian race.

March

The 118,000 people packed in and around the Albert Park circuit witnessed an incident-packed **Australian Grand Prix**. Such was the McLaren domination in the practice and qualifying sessions, it looked as though we were going to have a repeat of the processional bore that saw the 1998 season off to a start in Melbourne 12 months earlier. Not so. The other contenders to their crown weren't even close to the McLarens in qualifying, but in the post-race brush down it was their reliability that was being brought into question.

In qualifying the Silver Arrows pulverised the rest of the field and there were worried looks on the faces of the Ferrari officials, who had seen the gaps between the teams seemingly get bigger rather than narrower after thousands of close-season miles testing. As the red lights were extinguished for the start, the Mercedes-powered cars simply disappeared into the distance, leaving all in their wake. The clear track they left behind them multiplied as cars fell out of the race – by half-distance fewer than half of the 22 starters were running and by its completion only eight had survived to finish. They had been helped when Michael Schumacher, only being able to select first gear at the start, was forced to take the inevitable re-start from the back of the grid. After ten laps the McLarens led Irvine's third-placed Ferrari by 18 seconds. But by the time the leading Hakkinen had doubled that distance, Coulthard was out with a gear selection problem and the Finn was having throttle problems. When the yellow flags that had held the race in place for two laps disappeared, so did the chances of the World Champion, who could not accelerate and was out of the race.

Irvine took the lead and stayed there despite being hard pressed by Heinz-Harald Frentzen, whose debut for Jordan, running the Mugen Honda power pack for the first time, was somewhat overshadowed because it was Damon Hill's 100th Grand Prix. Irvine flashed over the finish line ahead of Frentzen by a second while Hill had spun-off after he had been shunted by Jarno Trulli's Prost on the opening lap. Amazingly it was Irvine's first ever F1 victory and came in his 82nd Grand Prix.

Ralf Schumacher, in his first race for Williams, was a very strong third, whilst the BAR cars failed to last the course. Reigning CART champion Alex Zanardi fared little better when he lost control of his Williams and crashed. Giancarlo Fisichella ran home fourth in the Benetton, while Rubens Barrichello was fifth for Stewart Ford in his spare car, his original having erupted in flames which helped cause the original start to be aborted. Spanish rookie Pedro de la Rosa was sixth for Arrows. The joy of a point for Arrows – which was more than they had managed in 1998 – was made all the sweeter by the sight of Torao Takagi following de la Rosa home in the second Arrows, ahead of Michael Schumacher. However, Schuey still managed to record the race's fastest lap as he closed on the pack!

April

It seemed like an eternity for the **Brazilian Grand Prix** to come round, with a five-week gap between the first two races of the season after the Argentinean race had been scrapped from the diary. Qualifying didn't indicate that the other teams had made much progress with Mika Hakkinen a second ahead of Schumacher as the McLarens had the front row to themselves for the second successive race and with the Finn producing his first finish and first win of the season. Although both McLarens looked by far the most competitive cars at the Interlagos circuit, it was circumstances rather than car power that produced the victory. Indeed it was the dramas that occurred at the very start that set the tone of the afternoon.

As the red lights went out to signal the start, David Coulthard in the number two car stalled on the front row. This upset him and the Ferrari of Michael Schumacher who worked miracles to get out from behind him and into the stream of passing traffic. Home driver Rubens Barrichello had the best start and eventually took the lead as things settled down. Hakkinen's sticky gearshift problems disappeared within a couple of laps and he was soon on the tail of Schuey. Barrichello though was flying at the front looking for a first Stewart win and sending the home crowd of almost 80,000 wild as he led for the next 22 laps of the race.

In this time Coulthard retired with a gearbox problem and Herbert in the other Stewart suffered an engine failure which had the Stewart mechanics holding their breath as Barrichello continued in the lead. Schumacher took the lead, however, when Barrichello pitted but the German was unable to stop Hakkinen regaining his lead when he made a very slick pit stop to rejoin at the front on lap 38. Hakkinen drove to the chequered flag to take the 10th win of his career, some five seconds ahead of the German's Ferrari. Elsewhere Frentzen made it two out of two podium finishes, coming home third, while Ralf Schumacher took fourth for Williams and Eddie Irvine's fifth place was enough for him to keep the lead in the Drivers' Championship. The combined Ferrari points extended them to an eight point lead in the Constructors' Cup.

In the lead-up to the first European race of the season the news came that 55-year-old Harvey Postlethwaite had died. He had suffered a heart attack while working for Honda as part of their F1 development team. Postlethwaite had been involved in much of the F1 development down the years and spent much of the last decade with Tyrrell.

May

As the teams arrived in Imola for the **San Marino Grand Prix**, the Stewart team were given a huge boost when Ford confirmed that they would be channelling all their resources into an exclusive technical partnership with the team. The also added that they would be vacating their position as the sport's major off-the-shelf engine suppliers from the end of the season. This statement left many of the smaller teams immediately seeking new engine partners for the 2000 season and started the rumours, later to be founded, that the Stewart team would run under the name Jaguar Racing after 1999.

The San Marino meeting produced Ferrari's first win at Imola for 16 years. This is an amazing statistic considering it is their home Grand Prix and the circuit carries the name of their founder – the Autodromo Enzo e Dino. Victory was taken by Michael Schumacher – his first of the season – but for the second race in a row, it was a winner who built on the misfortunes of another, in this instance, David Coulthard.

Again the McLarens were strong, very strong. But this time it wasn't so much reliability as bad luck that posed the problems. For the third time in three races the silver arrows occupied the front row. Hakkinen had a third successive pole position and from there the Finn lead until, with 17 laps completed, the champion erred and found himself crashing into the barrier wall, right in front of his disbelieving team. DC happily accepted the role of race leader. Dominating from the front, it looked certain that the Scot would be claiming his first win for over a year. But when he pitted on lap 35, he swapped the wide open spaces of the front for the traffic of the back ranks and, without the ability to see them off quickly, he lost vital seconds and with it the race.

With Coulthard in traffic the Ferraris took over but were disappointed when Irvine faded out with engine failure 15 laps from home. Schumacher held on for the win, with DC coming in second. Barrichello and Hill fought out a battle for the final podium position which the Stewart driver won, with Fisichella and Alesi making up the final placing. The Sauber driver's sixth place was fortunate in that it came about after the luckless Zanardi spun out after skating on oil when he looked certain to collect his first point.

Schuey's victory propelled him into the Drivers' Championship lead, in the process consolidating and stretching Ferrari's lead in the Constructors' Cup to 12 points over McLaren.

The streets of Monte Carlo were as hot as they had ever been for the **Monaco Grand Prix**. Those who came and sweated also witnessed another type of heat as Michael Schumacher turned up the championship cooker. His pace off the grid and his domination from the front on the street circuit left him as the most successful driver Ferrari have ever had, thundering as he did to his 16th win inside the scarlet cockpit and his fourth win in six Monaco races. Both Ferrari cars ran home together to earn maximum points and, amazingly, their first ever one-two at Monaco.

With Hakkinen securing yet another pole position Schumacher pulled another text-book start out of his bag and immediately took back the pole position as he swept through Ste Devote from the start. By the time the cars headed up the hill towards Casino Square he had cemented his lead as Irvine followed the German's lead and produced a carbon-copy move on Coulthard. By the time they exited the square, both Ferraris were at the front. Schuey Senior produced a succession of fast laps and by lap 21 was almost 15 seconds ahead of Hakkinen, back in second place, and Irvine. Coulthard, in the other McLaren, retired from fourth place with mechanical problems. Irvine was able to take second place when Hakkinen made a mistake at Mirabeau, losing his back end, and with it some 18 seconds of track time. The Finn took time to take his pit stop but Irvine's two-stop strategy worked in his favour to ensure he maintained that second place.

Frentzen took advantage of Barrichello's suspension failure to move up into fourth place to record his third points-scoring finish in four races for Jordan, a result helped by the German staying out for 57 laps before re-fuelling. A happy Benetton team took the final two places with Giancarlo Fisichella and Alexander Wurz taking the flag in fifth and sixth places.

With Ferrari netting maximum points, they extended their Constructors' Cup lead to 24 points ahead of McLaren, with Jordan closing to within four points of second placed McLaren. Frentzen moved to within a point of Hakkinen who trailed Irvine by four points and Schumacher by 12 points.

For the fifth time in succession, Mika Hakkinen stood without peer at the end of the qualifying session for the **Spanish Grand Prix**. And for the first time his and DC's McLarens looked the part for the race. The domination they had threatened at the start of the season bore home in full in the industrial hinterland of Barcelona as they dominated from the front to secure McLaren's first one-two finish of the season. Indeed as a race this was almost a non-event and left those who preach that F1 is a bore with plenty of ammunition. Indeed there was only one passing movement of note – that when Damon Hill sneaked past Rubens Barrichello to take seventh place, just two laps from home.

Hakkinen had needed another last gasp run to secure pole position but the surprise in qualifying was Jacques Villeneuve's sixth place, one behind a resurgent Alesi. Villeneuve continued his form at the start and thrust his car into third place ahead of both Ferraris until his rear-wing collapsed and forced him to pit where he couldn't engage first gear and was forced to retire. Pedro de la Rosa utilised a three-stop strategy that allowed him to finish 11th in front of his home fans from 19th place on the grid, and in a Minardi which was proving very reliable, if not overly competitive.

With McLaren taking maximum points, they were able to reduce the gap in the Constructors' Cup to 15 behind Ferrari's tally of 51. Hakkinen's win also bit into Schumacher's Drivers' Championship lead, trailing the German by six points (30 to 24). Coulthard's second place put him within one point of Frentzen's fourth place position.

June

Formula 1's jaunt to North America for the **Canadian Grand Prix** produced a notable first for the sport in that it was the first time ever a race had been won from behind the Safety Car. The driver to set that particular record was Mika Hakkinen, who recorded his third win of the season, and with it moved ahead of Michael Schumacher in the Drivers' Championship. The race was almost dominated by the Safety Car which made no less than four appearances as the spins and collisions happened at regular points throughout a race that was run in dry conditions, although anyone looking at its story might have thought there had been a torrential downpour throughout.

It was Hakkinen's first win in Canada and it denied Schumacher a third successive victory on the circuit after he lost the lead he had had from the start, sliding into the wall as he exited the final corner on his way to start lap 30. It was a mistake by the German and after the race he acknowledged it. It wasn't a total loss for the Ferrari team, however, as Irvine took third and ensured that Ferrari's lead in the Constructors' Cup wasn't slashed but merely eroded to nine points (55 points to 46).

In qualifying Schumacher had taken pole with his very first flying lap. It must have come as a shock for the Finn who found himself off pole for the first time in the season! Schuey made the perfect start, but mayhem developed behind him as Trulli lost control of his Prost going into the first curve and he took out Alesi's Sauber and Barrichello's Stewart with him. Trulli's car lost its right rear wheel and left the others badly damaged. Wurz suffered a mechanical failure on the same lap and out came the Safety Car for the first time. After the Safety Car had re-appeared for a second time, when Zonta spun off, Schumacher timed everything right to streak away from Hakkinen.

When the German made his exit from the race via the wall the Safety Car came back out as Hakkinen took over at the front. At the restarts Coulthard and Irvine locked wheels, losing places as they regained control of their cars. Irvine was incensed and drove brilliantly to get himself back up to third by the finish. Almost unnoticed, Fisichella took advantage and was elevated to second when Frentzen, who looked to have secured six points, had a disk brake failure and was thrown off the road with five laps to go.

The German reigned supreme at Magny-Cours. Not Michael this time but Heinz-Harald Frentzen, who secured his first victory in a Jordan at the **French Grand Prix** despite being in pain ever since hurting a leg in an accident that put him out of the Canadian race in Montreal two weeks earlier. Heinz-Harald's win helped shake up the championship battles and provided the first inkling that he too wouldn't be that far off the race for honours when the season reached its final shake-down. The Jordan driver used just one pit stop during the race, coming in with the rest of the pack when the rain started a third of the way into the race. From thereon he remained in third or fourth place until the final set of pit stops by the other front runners saw him take advantage and then move into the lead when Hakkinen made his final stop seven laps from the chequered flag.

The weather conditions during qualifying produced a rather different looking grid, indeed it had Hakkinen in 14th place, Irvine in 17th place and a front row containing Barrichello and Alesi! Rubens' first pole for Stewart was achieved largely because he got in an early fast lap before the heavy rain hit – a tactic used by the Sauber and Prost teams to good effect.

Barrichello led for most of the race's 72 laps but had to settle for third place in the end. Jean Alesi, normally so dominant in the wet, lost control and spun-off after the rain set in. Storming from the back was Mika Hakkinen and he took over the lead on lap 60 – this after having spun on an earlier charge! His front running lasted just five laps though when he pitted for his second stop, coming out in second place where he remained. Ralf Schumacher was fourth in his Williams, brother Michael came fifth in his Ferrari and Eddie Irvine finished sixth. Frentzen though took advantage for his first Jordan win.

While one Jordan driver was celebrating, the other was in reflective mode and contemplating his future in the sport. Damon Hill only qualified after a successful appeal to the stewards got him past the 107% rule. He then faded out of the running when his engine started to misfire at the midway point, this following a pit-lane collision, with Pedro de la Rosa, in which he picked up a puncture.

The **British Grand Prix** at Silverstone produced a pivotal moment in the Drivers' Championship. In the Northamptonshire sunshine Michael Schumacher suffered a first lap accident that effectively ended his championship challenge for the season. Indeed, as his Ferrari ploughed into the tyre wall at Stowe, it came close to ending his life. If this accident had happened a few years earlier it certainly would have. The German went to turn out of the Hanger Straight at 145 mph when he suffered a brake failure as he continued in a straight line, skimming the gravel and into the wall – nose first. It left him with a double fracture of his lower right leg.

Schumacher's accident rather overshadowed David Coulthard's victory on home turf. It was DC's first win since Imola in 1998 – 20 races before – and it pushed him back into championship contention, especially as teammate Hakkinen had an enforced retirement on lap 36 when his left rear wheel flew off and bounced around the circuit. So much for the wheel ties introduced at the start of 1999, that were supposed to stop this happening!

For the third race in a row the Safety Car had its part to play in a race that had five different leaders through its 60 laps. Qualifying had seen Hakkinen re-establish himself as the pole king with his sixth pole in eight races. Damon Hill, in what was being sold as his final British GP, pulled out an emotional performance to qualify in a season's-best sixth place.

When the race restarted Hakkinen duly took the lead and stayed there for the first 25 laps, before Irvine and then Coulthard took to the front as the Finn and Ulsterman took their pit stops. Frentzen and, to the raptures of the crowd, Hill also led briefly during the second round of pit-stops before DC took control again on lap 46 and the Scot held on for a win by 1.8 seconds.

Ralf Schumacher took third place to claim his first podium finish since joining Williams, while another solid performance by Frentzen saw him home in fourth place, just over 10 seconds ahead of fifth placed Hill – his best finish of the year. Brazilian Pedro Diniz finished in sixth place.

In the championships, Ferrari's lead over McLaren was down to just two points, while Irvine's six points took him on level points with his team-mate.

In the days following the race, the talk was all about who would replace Schumacher at Ferrari and of course when the German could be expected to return. The early suggestions were that test driver Luca Badoer, who finished among the also-rans driving for Minardi, would take over. In the end Ferrari plumped for the more experienced Mika Salo. Meanwhile the first rumours concerning the possible move of Irvine from Ferrari to the Ford-backed Stewart team for the 2000 season started to circulate.

For the first time in a long time, a Grand Prix had a close finish. Eddie Irvine, now playing the role of team leader for Ferrari, flashed across the finish line just three-tenths of a second ahead of David Coulthard's McLaren to win the **Austrian Grand Prix**.

The race had started with the first all-McLaren front row since Imola. Irvine lined up third with his new team-mate, Mika Salo, a creditable seventh given the small amount of testing time he was able to put in. The race though was thrown open when DC managed to send his team-mate spinning out of the lead as they came together at the second corner of the first lap. Hakkinen gathered his composure and car well and set about reclaiming the places he had lost. Coulthard was now heading the race, followed by Barrichello – who had taken advantage of the incident – and Irvine. Despite all the front runners racing on a one-stop strategy, the refuelling stops turned matters around. Coulthard, Hakkinen and Barrichello pitted and Irvine remained out to take the lead and build a big enough gap to ensure he kept it when he came in five laps after them, re-emerging less than two seconds ahead of DC. The Scot pushed him hard but Irvine held out for the closest race since Monaco in 1992.

Heinz-Harald Frentzen continued his vein of good form by finishing fourth, ahead of Alexander Wurz's Benetton, and Pedro Diniz, who finished sixth for Sauber, for his third point of the season.

Irvine's success brought his points tally to 42, just two behind Hakkinen who had now scored only four points in two races, contrasted to Irvine's 16 points. Frentzen moved to within three points of acquiring third place from Michael Schumacher. Ferrari maintained their two point lead over McLaren in the Constructors' Cup.

August

The **German Grand Prix** was supposed to have been where Schumacher supporters paid homage to the senior brother on his charge for what they hoped would be a Ferrari win. Well, they got the latter, but with Schuey still sidelined it was Irvine who bagged full points with his second successive win, something that well and truly blew the championship wide open and had the onlookers talking of him as a potential winner. Not only did Irvine race home but he did it in tandem with stand-in Ferrari man Mika Salo who produced the race of his life and, but for team orders to allow Eddie through, would have deservedly recorded his first Grand Prix win – something that Irvine was quick to acknowledge after the race. It was the second Ferrari one-two of the season and secured Irvine a position eight points clear at the head of the Drivers' Championship and gave his team a 16-point lead in the Constructors' Cup.

Irvine's win was achieved from a fifth place on the grid. Hakkinen, who along with Coulthard had signed again for McLaren for the year 2000 in the lead-up to the race, was back in the frame with his eighth pole of the season, which was McLaren's 100th pole overall. He was joined on the front row by the increasingly impressive Frentzen – another German pleasing his home crowd.

Salo had a great start thrusting into second place past DC, while at the same time Irvine lost a place. The Ulsterman was the first of the leading pack into the pits, a manoeuvre that ultimately got him into the front after Salo allowed him through. Hakkinen might have retained the lead after the round of pits but a problem with his refuelling rig meant he was standing still for 24 seconds and on the very next lap his left rear tyre blew-out and spun him off the road and out of the points.

Coulthard had a torrid time, which included a 10-second Stop-Go penalty. Amazingly though he managed to drive aggressively in the final stages and finished fifth. Ralf Schumacher, finished fourth in the Williams while Panis provided Coulthard's sandwich by finishing sixth.

The **Hungarian Grand Prix** was a big race for McLaren and its drivers and they responded in superb style as they took maximum points for the fourth time in the season, thus closing the gap on Ferrari and its drivers to within a handful of points in both championships. As far as races go, this was another of those processional affairs with little incident, but that in itself was probably just what McLaren were hoping for.

Yes, again Hakkinen had taken pole position – number nine in the year – but was only the merest fraction of seconds ahead of Irvine, who produced one of his best qualifying sessions of the season. Irvine though would have been disappointed. He had looked set to take second place until he ran wide on lap 63, struggling to cope with his tyres that were going 'off' with every lap, and DC seized the initiative to overtake him. The Ulsterman had to settle for third – his first points in Hungary. With Mika Salo finishing a lowly 12th, the Ferrari championship lead was cut to just four points. Heinz-Harald Frentzen finished fourth, a result that took him joint third with Coulthard in the Drivers' Championship.

The **Belgian Grand Prix** had the usual look of familiarity about it – a McLaren front row with Hakkinen, who else, taking pole position. The second row was a little different. It burgeoned with the yellow of Jordan with Frentzen in third and a rejuvenated Hill in fourth place. Everything had been decided in the last seconds of qualifying, where Hill had in fact held the number one starting position with but a handful of seconds to go.

The championship battle looked to be narrowing down to Hakkinen and Irvine. David Coulthard sat on the grid with the realisation that he needed a win to maintain his championship hopes. He responded brilliantly by producing perhaps the best drive of his career to date, coming home over 10 seconds ahead of Hakkinen for a second successive McLaren one-two – a result that put them back on top of the Constructors' table with a nine-point margin.

Hakkinen's second and Irvine's eventual fourth had seen the Finn regain the Drivers' Championship initiative but by just a point. Team orders might have produced a different story had they favoured the Finn who found himself trailing DC at the first corner, where he stayed for the rest of the race, bar a few laps between pit stops that briefly elevated Ralf Schumacher. Heinz-Harald Frentzen finished a distant third for Jordan, ahead of Irvine's Ferrari. Ralf Schumacher's Williams maintained fifth and Damon Hill, in the second Jordan, claimed a second successive point – edging the Jordan team into an increasingly secure third place in the Constructors' title race.

September

Just when it looked a straight battle between the McLarens and Ferraris, Heinz-Harald Frentzen, for the second time during the season, popped up to throw the cat among the pigeons as he flew his Jordan home to victory at the **Italian Grand Prix**. Frentzen had signalled his intent in qualifying when he split the McLaren drivers on the grid where, once again, Hakkinen secured pole. The Finn must have been happy, with Irvine slumping to eighth behind Salo, who recorded a sixth. The surprise contender was Alex Zanardi in fourth, edging out team-mate Ralf Schumacher. It was to prove a short dawn for the Italian, however.

Hakkinen shot off at the start and was producing a typically dominant race from the front. He had established a lead of 10 seconds when, unchallenged, he spun off on lap 30. Driver error. It was a lapse in concentration as he selected first instead of second to negotiate another corner, stalling the engine in the process. Few will forget the sight of the Finn sobbing, head in hands, in among the trees. Heinz-Harald took over and remained there through the pit stops to take the full quota of points available to him.

Frentzen's win was his second of the season and the third of his career and thrust him firmly into the title fight with 50 points, in third place, behind joint leaders Hakkinen and Irvine. Irvine scored the single point he needed to draw level with Hakkinen on 60 points. But the Finn retained the lead because he had scored four wins this year to Irvine's three.

Heinz-Harald began the **European Grand Prix** where he left off in Italy – at the front. The Jordan driver took his second career pole position ahead of the two McLarens. He made the perfect start to maintain his lead and was in charge until lap 32 when he suffered an electrical problem that forced him into retirement and effectively out of the Drivers' Championship race. What followed was a chaotic race and, given events, it was quite fitting that the winner should come from the back ranks in the guise of Johnny Herbert. The Englishman, who had suffered such bad luck in the early part of the season, took advantage of mistakes around him to provide a jubilant Stewart-Ford team with their maiden Grand Prix victory, in which their other driver Rubens Barrichello joined him on the podium in third place.

Mika Hakkinen swept home fifth but those two points were enough to move him two points in front of Irvine in the Drivers' Championship. The McLaren and Ferrari teams both made costly mistakes with tyres in a race affected by rain as the two other title contenders lost vital ground. Irvine finished seventh.

Thirty-five-year-old Herbert inherited the lead 17 laps from the finish of a race re-started after Minardi's Marc Gene had a problem and further marred by a horrific first-corner crash involving Sauber's Pedro Diniz. Herbert gambled on wet-weather tyres in the changing conditions and it proved the perfect choice. Jarno Trulli scored a surprise second place position in the Prost – his best ever placing in F1.

With only Hakkinen scoring, McLaren extended their lead to eight points in the Constructors' Cup with 110 points, while Stewart moved to within two points of Williams in fifth place.

October

The **Malaysian Grand Prix**, the penultimate race of the season, and the week following it, smacked of farce as Eddie Irvine secured the victory he needed to put him into a four-point Drivers' Championship lead, with one race remaining. Then two hours after the podium celebrations had finished, both Ferraris were disqualified from their one-two because of an illegal barge board on the cars, which was found during the after-race scrutineering checks. Mika Hakkinen was elevated from third to first place and his lead of 12 points became effectively unassailable, to provide him, in theory at least, with the Drivers' Championship.

Having first admitted their mistake, Ferrari appealed the decision on the basis that subsequent re-checks on the barge boards showed that they were within tolerances. And so six days later the Ferraris were re-instated, Hakkinen was relegated to third and once again Irvine had a four-point advantage going into the final race. This was the first time ever that a team appeal following disqualification had been successful.

The lead-up to the first race at the new Sepang circuit, just outside of KL was all about the reappearance of Michael Schumacher as a support driver to Irvine in a bid to help the Ulsterman and Ferrari towards both championships. Schumacher, still with a 10-inch plate in his leg, was in typically sensational form to secure pole position – the 22nd of his career – and then provide the perfect support drive, twice allowing Irvine to pass to ensure the Ulsterman drove to victory. Schuey continually backed up Hakkinen, and settled for second place.

Johnny Herbert was fourth and his Brazilian Stewart team-mate Rubens Barrichello was fifth, edging them in front of the Williams team and into fourth place in the Constructors' Cup. Meanwhile Jordan secured a magnificent third place in the Constructors' Cup.

A week after he had been crowned Drivers' Champion on a technicality, and then had it taken away from him on appeal, Mika Hakkinen drove a perfect **Japanese Grand Prix** to secure victory and his second successive Drivers' Championship – only the seventh driver to achieve the feat. It was an immaculate performance from the Finn who, just as 12 months earlier when he took the 1998 crown, drove a peerless race that was about as near to perfection as possible. It was an incident-filled race, which saw the two Ferrari drivers come in second and third, points enough to earn the Italian team their first Constructors' Cup since 1983.

The two key stages in the defining race of the season were the final qualifying run and the start to the race. In qualifying Hakkinen edged out Schumacher and Irvine fell to fifth when Frentzen produced another powerful performance to edge the British driver down the order after he had spun late in the session. Coulthard was third.

Irvine needed Schumacher to get ahead at the start and win the race. Instead, it was Hakkinen who produced a blistering get-away as Schuey was curiously lethargic in his start. Surprise second place at the start was taken by Panis who shot up from sixth. Coulthard ran third and did his best to hinder Irvine until he spun off and damaged his car's nose after 34 of the 53 laps. After completing one more lap, in which Schuey later accused him of dirty tricks by zig-zagging in front of him, he retired.

As soon as the Finn took the lead, Irvine had to hope for driver error or a reliability problem to help him, as his car was uncompetitive for all of the race. Neither materialised, and nor did the sort of charge from Schuey one would have expected had he been in the running for the drivers' title.

Behind the front trio, Frentzen confirmed his and the Jordan team's brilliant year by securing third place in the Drivers' Championship. His fourth place was ahead of fellow-German Ralf Schumacher, in a Williams, and sixth-placed Jean Alesi in his last drive for the Sauber team. Williams couldn't secure the points they needed to edge them back in front of Stewart, who achieved fourth place in the Constructors' Cup in just their third year. Damon Hill had a disappointing final Grand Prix. He spun off and finally decided to call it a day after 21 laps, when he returned to the pit lane for the last time.

The accusations continued to fly between Coulthard and Schumacher senior after the race, with DC threatening legal action in relation to some of the comments. It was a sad way to end the final weekend of the championship which, when added to the debacle after the Malaysian meeting, brought a rather unsatisfactory curtain down on proceedings.

Close Season

The close season saw the final driver changes start to fall into place. Several teams were continuing with their 1999 line-ups, in particular McLaren, Williams, Benetton and BAR. Ferrari and the new Jaguar (Stewart) Racing team effectively swapped Irvine and Barrichello while Jarno Trulli left Prost to take the place left by the retiring Damon Hill, partnering Heinz Harald Frentzen at Jordan. Another Prost casualty was Olivier Panis who took his considerable experience to McLaren as test driver. Another McLaren man and reigning F3000 champion, German Nick Hedfield, teamed up with Jean Alesi at Prost, while Mika Salo's reward for some oustanding stand-in performances with BAR and Ferrari was a contract with Swiss team Sauber.

Benetton had a minor upheaval when Chief Designer Nick Wirth resigned from the team, while in mid-January the future of Alex Zanardi was still clouded in mystery. ■

ANNUAL KEY

The Formula 1 Grand Prix Pocket Annual is divided into several clear sections that arrange information, statistics and reviews in relevant sections which are clearly defined in the Contents list on pages 3 and 4.

At the start of each section you may find a small guide or key to specific information and abbreviations used.

Country abbreviations are used and the key to these is listed below.

Arg	Argentina	GB	Great Britain	Pes	Pescara
Aus	Australia	Ger	Germany	Por	Portugal
Aut	Austria	Hol	Holland	SA	South Africa
Bel	Belgium	Hun	Hungary	San	San Marino
Bra	Brazil	Ita	Italy	Swi	Switzerland
Can	Canada	Jap	Japan	USA	United States
Dal	Dallas	Mal	Malaysia		of America
Esp	Spain	Mex	Mexico	USAE	USA (East)
Eur	Europe	Mon	Monaco	USAW	USA (West)
Fin	Finland	NZ	New Zealand		
Fra	France	Pac	Pacific		

RACE PROCEDURES

There is a strict timetable laid down by the FIA for the build-up and start of each Grand Prix race. This set of procedures ensures that no team is favoured when it comes to circuit time, qualifying, warm-up and the actual race. Details of these are given below – all times are local. Note that what follows is a general guide only and liable to change.

Circuit Practice

There are four sessions of free practice. These take place on the Friday and Saturday, except for the Monaco Grand Prix when the Friday practice is held on the Thursday. The two sessions on the Friday last for one hour each and are held from 11.00 to 12.00 and 13.00 to 14.00. The two sessions on the Saturday last for 45 minutes each and are held from 9.00 to 9.45 and 10.15 to 11.00. A change from the 1998 season is that there is no limitation on the number of laps permitted. Prior to this, there had been a limit of 30 laps across the two sessions.

Qualifying Session

A single one-hour session is held for qualifying (prior to 1996 there used to be two sessions). This takes place on the Saturday from 13.00 to 14.00. Since 1997, each driver has been limited to a maximum of 12 qualifying laps, and a lap will count towards the qualifying laps provided the driver has started it before the expiry of the 60-minute clock. The 12 laps are normally performed by teams as three- or four-lap sessions. This is at the discretion of teams and drivers – the usual scenario is an 'out' warm-up lap, where the tyres are brought up to race temperature, two flat-out laps, where drivers go all out for a fast time, and a final 'in lap' as drivers come back into the pits.

The fastest lap out of those registered will count as the qualifying time. To qualify for a race, all drivers must establish a lap time that is within 107% of the time set by the fastest driver in the qualifying session. Drivers with times outside this limit will not automatically qualify for the race – the FIA have the right to admit a driver to the race. The driver's grid position is determined by his time. Thus the fastest qualifying time earns the driver the first or pole position on the starting grid. A spare car may be used in the qualifying session in case of accident or mechanical problems. Indeed, some teams even use a special qualifying engine.

From the 1998 season, any car that is given assistance, after stopping, to get back to the pits, will have its fastest lap time of the session deleted.

Warm-up Session

A 30-minute warm-up session is held on the Sunday of the race, and this normally starts four and a half hours before the start of the race. If, after this, rain occurs, then an extra 15-minute session may be sanctioned to allow teams to make wet-weather changes.

The Start

The race follows a set countdown to the start. Thirty minutes prior to the race the pit lane is opened for just 15 minutes. During this window all cars must leave their paddocks and make their way to the starting grid. A horn is sounded two minutes prior to the pit lane closure and 15 minutes prior to the start of the race, the pit lane is closed. Any cars not out of the paddocks must now start from the pit lane – this effectively places the car at the back of the grid.

Once all cars are formed on the grid, a series of time boards is used to display the amount of time remaining to the start of the race. These are carried through the grid and personnel must adhere to their significance.

Ten minutes before the start of the race, all personnel, except drivers, team members and officials, must leave the starting grid. Boards are shown at five minutes, three minutes, one minute and 30 seconds before the start of the race. At the one-minute board, engines are started and all technicians and team staff are required to leave the grid. During this period a series of lights is used to signal stages of the start countdown. There are five banks of lights, each with five lights. Ten minutes prior to the race, the bottom two sets of red lights (ten in all) flash on and off twice. Five minutes prior to the start, the first two (vertical) red lights are extinguished. At this point, all cars must have their wheels fitted – if not, they must start from either the pit lane or the back of the grid. The next two go out with three minutes to go and another two with one minute to go. The penultimate set of red lights is turned off with 30 seconds to go.

When the count reaches zero, a green flag is displayed and the final set of red lights goes out, to be replaced by a set of five green lights across the top of the board – this signals that the cars on the starting grid can advance on their single formation lap. Generally cars are not allowed to overtake on the formation lap but drivers who are temporarily delayed are allowed to overtake to regain their grid position in the formation so long as they do not put the other cars in danger (this is new for 2000). Cars may be forced to the back of the grid if they overtake for any other reason. Cars return to their grid position and wait for the start.

When all cars are stationary on the grid, a series of red lights (two vertical at a time) comes on, one light after the other, until they are all switched on – there is approximately a one-second delay between each set of red lights being turned on. There is then a pre-set delay of up to three seconds, at which point all the red lights are extinguished together and the race can commence. Again flashing lights can be used to indicate an aborted start at any point during the sequence.

If rain should come after the five-minute mark then the race director has it within his power to allow teams to change their tyres if they wish. In this case abort lights are shown and the race start countdown begins again from the 15-minute mark.

Stopping the Race

The race may be stopped as a result of accidents or adverse weather conditions. If at any time during the final red-light sequence the race needs to be aborted, the lights freeze in their current state.

If the race has to be stopped once underway it is done by the waving of red flags. Cars return to their original grid positions and the race is re-started. If the race is stopped before two laps are completed, cars return to their original grid positions and the race is restarted. A new time will be given for the race start and this is normally as soon as feasibly possible after the original race was stopped. Cars that might have had to start from the pit lane now have an opportunity to join the starting grid. In the case of an accident, drivers have the opportunity to use their spare car. If the race is stopped with more than 75 per cent completed, the race is deemed to have been run and positions at the point of the race being stopped are the finishing positions.

Race Distance

Generally a Grand Prix race must not be shorter than 160 miles. The number of laps that a race comprises is the smallest number of laps that will exceed this distance. There is also a two-hour time limit on a race. Should this time limit be exceeded (perhaps due to bad weather conditions), the chequered flag will be shown to the leader at the end of the lap in which the two-hour mark is passed – even if the scheduled race distance has not been completed.

Pit Lane

There is a maximum speed assigned to all pit lanes that must not be exceeded. The maximum speed varies from circuit to circuit and is between 50 and 75 mph (80 and 120 kph). Cars starting from the pit lane can only join the race after the cars on the starting grid have all passed the exit from the pit lane. Cars in the pit lane are not able to take part in the formation lap.

Penalties

Minor violations of rules – such as pit lane speeding, 'jump' starts and dangerous driving (to name three) – may be penalised by a Stop-Go penalty. The driver is required to return to his paddock and wait for a ten-second count.

Drivers and teams who do not adhere to the rules face other penalties. For example, a driver who drives an extra lap, say in a practice session, is likely to get a fine. This is typically US$5,000-10,000. A driver who is found to have driven recklessly or created a crash that was avoidable might receive a suspended race ban that would be invoked if he repeated the feat in the time frame specified.

Over and Understeer

Two terms are often used regularly by drivers and commentators: oversteer and understeer. In a perfect world the car will be set up perfectly to ensure it takes the correct racing line around a curve or through a corner. If, when trying to drive the racing line, a driver finds himself going towards the corner and therefore having to compensate, the car is suffering from oversteer. If, on the other hand, the car goes towards the outside edge of the corner and again the driver has to compensate to maintain the racing line, the car is suffering from understeer.

Oversteer is when there is a lack of grip at the rear of the car. This can result in the driver losing the back of the car and spinning off. Tyre wear also increases. It is normally cured by increasing the amount of rear wing on the car, i.e. making it more perpendicular to create drag and therefore downforce. Oversteer can also be corrected by making the suspension softer and reducing the ride height of the car.

Understeer is a lack of grip at the front of the car which means that it turns too slowly and out towards the outside edge of the corner. It is caused when there is too little front wing or the front suspension is too stiff, or a combination of both. It can therefore be cured by increasing the front wing and softening the suspension.

Cars can suffer understeer during a race even if they are set up correctly. This happens when they are following behind a car 'on its gearbox'. The lead car has airflow over its front and rear wings to maintain downforce. However, the front of the following car is in a 'hole' because the front car is deflecting the air over it – therefore the front of the following car has reduced stability. Unless a car intends to brake late and try an overtaking manoeuvre at a corner, it will normally 'backoff' to ensure stability through the corner. ■

Flags and Signals

There are ten flags that can be shown and these are illustrated on the inside back cover of this annual. A flag's significance may be changed depending on whether it is held stationary or waved.

Red Flag: This is only shown at the start/finish line and is used to indicate that the race has been stopped.

White Flag: When held stationary it indicates the presence of a slower vehicle on the track. When waved it indicates that the driver may be seriously obstructed by a slower vehicle ahead of him on the track.

Black Flag: Shown with white number to indicate the driver to whom it applies. The driver indicated must stop at the pit within one lap and report to the clerk of the course. (This will normally be at the driver's pit paddock where a Stop-Go penalty might be indicated or disqualification.)

Black and White (Diagonal) Flag: Used only once per driver as a warning for unsportsmanlike behaviour.

Black with Red Spot Flag: Shown with white number to indicate the driver to whom it applies. The driver indicated has a mechanical failure and must stop at his pit.

Blue Flag: This flag is used to indicate that a faster car is following. When held stationary the driver concerned must give way, when waved the driver must give way urgently. During a race, failure to give way when the blue flag is waved may result in a penalty. A blue flag is also used at the exit from the pit lane to indicate to the driver exiting that traffic is approaching on the track.

Yellow and Red Striped Flag: When held stationary it indicates that there is oil or water on the track, when waved there is a slippery surface immediately ahead.

Yellow Flag: This flag indicates a hazard ahead and there should be no overtaking. When held stationary it indicates that there is a hazard on the track and drivers should drive well within their limits. When waved, cars must slow down and be prepared to change direction or follow an unusual line. When double waved, cars must slow down and be prepared to stop as the track is partially or wholly blocked.

Green Flag: This is used to signify the end of a danger area that will have been marked by a yellow flag. Effectively it is an all-clear. Also used to signify the start of the warm-up lap.

Chequered Flag: Signifies the end of the race.

GP Results '99

GP	Winner	Pole
Australian	E.Irvine (Ferrari)	M.Hakkinen (McLaren)
Brazilian	M.Hakkinen (McLaren)	M.Hakkinen (McLaren)
San Marino	M.Schumacher (Ferrari)	M.Hakkinen (McLaren)
Monaco	M.Schumacher (Ferrari)	M.Hakkinen (McLaren)
Spanish	M.Hakkinen (McLaren)	M.Hakkinen (McLaren)
Canadian	M.Hakkinen (McLaren)	M.Schumcaher (Ferrari)
French	H-H.Frentzen (Jordan)	R.Barrichello (Stewart)
British	D.Coulthard (McLaren)	M.Hakkinen (McLaren)
Austrian	E.Irvine (Ferarri)	M.Hakkinen (McLaren)
German	E.Irvine (Ferrari)	M.Hakkinen (McLaren)
Hungarian	M.Hakkinen (McLaren)	M.Hakkinen (McLaren)
Belgian	D.Coulthard (McLaren)	M.Hakkinen (McLaren)
Italian	H-H.Frentzen (Jordan)	M.Hakkinen (McLaren)
European	J.Herbert (Stewart)	H-H.Frentzen (Jordan)
Malaysian	E.Irvine (Ferrari)	M.Schumacher (Ferrari)
Japanese	M.Hakkinen (McLaren)	M.Schumacher (Ferrari)

Summary

Driver	Team	Wins	Poles	F.Laps
M.Hakkinen (Fin)	McLaren	5	11	6
E.Irvine (GB)	Ferrari	4	–	1
M.Schumacher (Ger)	Ferrari	2	3	5
H-H.Frentzen (Ger)	Jordan	2	1	–
D.Coulthard (GB)	McLaren	2	–	3
J.Herbert (GB)	Stewart	1	–	–
R.Barrichello (Bra)	Stewart	–	1	–
R.Schumacher (Ger)	Williams	–	–	1

Key to Results and Tables

r = retired, dq = disqualified, dnq = did not qualify, dnf = did not finish
dns = did not start, fl = fastest lap. † (in results) = fastest lap.

GP No: 631   Date: 7 March 1999
Track: 3.274 miles   Distance: 58 laps, 191.110 miles †
Conditions: Warm with cloud   Fastest Lap: M. Schumacher – 1:32.112
Lap Record: H-H.Frentzen – 1:30.585, Lap 36 at 130.935 mph, 9 Mar 1997

Pos	Driver	Car	Laps	Time/Reason	Fastest	mph
1	Irvine	Ferrari	57	1:35:01.659	1:33.560	118.590
2	Frentzen	Jordan	57	1:35:02.686	1:33.378	118.569
3	Schumacher,R.	Williams	57	1:35:08.671	1:33.407	118.445
4	Fisichella	Benetton	57	1:35:35.077	1:33.657	117.889
5	Barrichello	Stewart	57	1:35:56.357	1:32.894	117.463
6	de la Rosa	Arrows	57	1:36:25.976	1:35.220	116.862
7	Takagi	Arrows	57	1:36:27.947	1:35.877	116.822
8	Schumacher,M.	Ferrari	56	1 lap down	1:32.112	116.207
r	Zonta	BAR	48	overheating	1:34.756	115.162
r	Badoer	Minardi	42	gearbox	1:37.073	113.933
r	Wurz	Benetton	28	suspension	1:36.068	111.439
r	Diniz	Sauber	27	gearbox	1:34.748	112.220
r	Gene	Minardi	25	spin	1;37.454	111.370
r	Trulli	Prost	25	accident	1:34.980	111.347
r	Panis	Prost	23	wheel nut	1:35.910	115.471
r	Hakkinen	McLaren	21	throttle	1:33.309	108.865
r	Zanardi	Williams	20	accident	1:37.146	115.970
r	Coulthard	McLaren	13	gear stuck	1:33.603	125.045
r	Villeneuve	BAR	13	rear wing	1:34.771	122.363
r	Hill	Jordan	0	accident	–	–
r	Alesi	Sauber	0	transmission	–	–
r	Herbert	Stewart	–	dns	–	–

Starting Grid and Qualifying Times

1	Hakkinen (Fin)	1:30.462	2 Coulthard (GB)	1:30.946
3	Schumacher,M. (Ger)	1:31.781	4 Barrichello (Bra)	1:32.148
5	Frentzen (Ger)	1:32.276	6 Irvine (GB)	1:32.289
7	Fisichella (Ita)	1:32.540	8 Schumacher,R. (Ger)	1:32.691
9	Hill (GB)	1:32.695	10 Wurz (Aut)	1:32.789
11	Villeneuve (Can)	1:32.888	12 Trulli (Ita)	1:32.971
13	Herbert (GB)	1:32.991	14 Diniz (Bra)	1:33.374
15	Zanardi (Ita)	1:33.549	16 Alesi (Fra)	1:33.910
17	Takagi (Jap)	1:34.182	18 de la Rosa (Esp)	1:34.244
19	Zonta (Bra)	1:34.412	20 Panis (Fra)	1:35.068
21	Badoer (Ita)	1:35.316	22 Gene (Esp)	1:37.013

† *Race restarted and distance reduced by one lap – 57 laps, 187.185 miles*

Round 2: Brazil – Interlagos

GP No: 632   Date: 11 April 1999
Track: 2.667 miles   Distance: 72 laps, 192.024 miles
Conditions: Hot, clear sky   Fastest Lap: Mika Hakkinen – 1:18.448
Lap Record: J.Villeneuve – 1:18.397, Lap 28 at 122.471 mph, 30 Mar 1997

Pos	Driver	Car	Laps	Time/Reason	Fastest	mph
1	Hakkinen	McLaren	72	1:38:03.765	1:18.448	119.921
2	Schumacher,M.	Ferrari	72	1:38:08.710	1:18.616	119.818
3	Frentzen	Jordan	71	1 lap down	1:19.009	118.459
4	Schumacher,R.	Williams	71	1 lap down	1:19.395	117.865
5	Irvine	Ferrari	71	1 lap down	1:18.816	117.984
6	Panis	Prost	71	1 lap down	1:19.386	116.845
7	Wurz	Benetton	70	2 laps down	1:20.145	116.386
8	Takagi	Arrows	69	3 laps down	1:21.598	114.798
9	Gene	Minardi	69	3 laps down	1:21.731	113.772
r	de la Rosa	Arrows	52	hydraulics	1:21.698	115.132
r	Villeneuve	BAR	49	hydraulics	1:20.727	115.021
r	Zanardi	Williams	43	differential	1:21.473	111.790
r	Barrichello	Stewart	42	engine	1:19.477	112.375
r	Diniz	Sauber	42	accident	1:20.833	116.738
r	Fisichella	Benetton	38	clutch	1:20.484	117.631
r	Sarrazin	Minardi	31	accident	1:21.225	115.776
r	Alesi	Sauber	27	gearbox	1:18.897	115.952
r	Coulthard	McLaren	22	gearbox	1:19.310	102.452
r	Trulli	Prost	21	gearbox	1:20.969	110.696
r	Herbert	Stewart	15	hydraulics	1:20.324	116.897
r	Hill	Jordan	10	steering	1:21.140	111.938

Starting Grid and Qualifying Times

1 Hakkinen (Fin)	1:16.568	2 Coulthard (GB)	1:16.715
3 Barrichello (Bra)	1:17.305	4 Schumacher,M. (Ger)	1:17.578
5 Fisichella (Ita)	1:17.810	6 Irvine (GB)	1:17.843
7 Hill (GB)	1:17.884	8 Frentzen (Ger)	1:17.902
9 Wurz (Aut)	1:18.334	10 Herbert (GB)	1:18.374
11 Schumacher,R. (Ger)	1:18.506	12 Panis (Fra)	1:18.636
13 Trulli (Ita)	1:18.684	14 Alesi (Fra)	1:18.716
15 Diniz (Bra)	1:19.194	16 Zanardi (Ita)	1:19.462
17 de la Rosa (Esp)	1:19.979	18 Sarrazin (Fra)	1:20.016
19 Takagi (Jap)	1:20.096	20 Gene (Esp)	1:20.710
21 Villeneuve (Can)	Time ignored		

Zonta – qualifying accident. Injured and unable to participate

GP No: 633   Date: 2 May 1999
Track: 3.063 miles   Distance: 62 laps, 189.906 miles
Conditions: Hot and sunny   Fastest Lap: M.Schumacher – 1:28.547
Lap Record: H-H.Frentzen – 1:25.531 at 128.942 mph, 27 April 1997

Pos	Driver	Car	Laps	Time/Reason	Fastest	mph
1	Schumacher,M.	Ferrari	62	1:33:44.792	1:28.547	121.466
2	Coulthard	McLaren	62	1:33:49.057	1:29.199	121.374
3	Barrichello	Stewart	61	1:33:46.721	1:30.564	119.464
4	Hill	Jordan	61	1:33:47.629	1:30.140	119.445
5	Fisichella	Benetton	61	1:34:27.002	1:30.977	118.615
6	Alesi	Sauber	61	1:34:33.056	1:30.442	118.489
7	Salo	BAR	59	electrics	1:31.007	117.604
8	Badoer	Minardi	59	3 laps down	1:32.851	115.409
9	Gene	Minardi	59	3 laps down	1:33.175	114.944
10	Herbert	Stewart	58	engine	1:31.238	118.846
11	Zanardi	Williams	58	spin	1:30.254	118.683
r	Diniz	Sauber	49	spin	1:30.908	112.642
r	Panis	Prost	48	engine	1:30.081	116.082
r	Irvine	Ferrari	46	engine	1:29.726	120.722
r	Frentzen	Jordan	46	spin	1:30.229	119.887
r	Takagi	Arrows	29	hydraulics	1:31.587	115.017
r	Schumacher,R.	Williams	28	engine	1:30.737	119.845
r	Hakkinen	McLaren	17	accident	1:29.145	122.522
r	de la Rosa	Arrows	5	suspension	1:33.328	113.602
r	Wurz	Benetton	5	accident	1:33.337	113.431
r	Trulli	Prost	0	accident	–	–
r	Villeneuve	BAR	0	gearbox	–	–

Starting Grid and Qualifying Times

1	Hakkinen (Fin)	1:26.362	2	Coulthard (GB)	1:26.384
3	Schumacher,M. (Ger)	1:26.538	4	Irvine (GB)	1:26.993
5	Villeneuve (Can)	1:27.313	6	Barrichello (Bra)	1:27.409
7	Frentzen (Ger)	1:27.613	8	Hill (GB)	1:27.708
9	Schumacher,R. (Ger)	1:27.770	10	Zanardi (Ita)	1:28.142
11	Panis (Fra)	1:28.205	12	Herbert (GB)	1:28.246
13	Alesi (Fra)	1:28.253	14	Trulli (Ita)	1:28.403
15	Diniz (Bra)	1:28.599	16	Fisichella (Ita)	1:28.750
17	Wurz (Aut)	1:28.765	18	de la Rosa (Esp)	1:29.293
19	Salo (Fin)	1:29.451	20	Takagi (Jap)	1:29.656
21	Gene (Esp)	1:30.035	22	Badoer (Ita)	1:30.945

Round 4: Monaco – Monte Carlo

GP No: 634   Date: 16 May 1999
Track: 2.082 miles   Distance: 78 laps, 163.176 miles
Conditions: Hot and sunny   Fastest Lap: Mika Hakkinen – 1:22.259
Lap Record: M.Schumacher – 1:21.076 at 91.821 mph, 15 May 1994

Pos	Driver	Car	Laps	Time/Reason	Fastest	mph
1	Schumacher,M.	Ferrari	78	1:49:31.812	1:22.288	89.393
2	Irvine	Ferrari	78	1:50:02.288	1:22.572	88.980
3	Hakkinen	McLaren	78	1:50:09.295	1:22.259	88.887
4	Frentzen	Jordan	78	1:50:25.821	1:22.471	88.665
5	Fisichella	Benetton	77	1:49:32.705	1:23.473	88.235
6	Wurz	Benetton	77	1:49:47.799	1:23.236	88.033
7	Trulli	Prost	77	1:50:05.845	1:23.646	87.792
8	Zanardi	Williams	76	1:49:49.514	1:23.294	86.867
9	Barrichello	Stewart	71	suspension	1:23.583	88.276
r	Schumacher,R.	Williams	54	accident	1:22.837	86.174
r	Alesi	Sauber	50	accident	1:23.417	86.374
r	Diniz	Sauber	49	accident	1:22.637	87.498
r	Panis	Prost	40	engine	1:24.480	86.088
r	Coulthard	McLaren	36	oil leak	1:22.883	88.491
r	Salo	BAR	36	brakes	1:24.787	86.602
r	Takagi	Arrows	36	engine	1:26.482	85.215
r	Villeneuve	BAR	32	oil leak	1:23.537	87.855
r	Herbert	Stewart	32	suspension	1:24.919	86.739
r	de la Rosa	Arrows	30	gearbox	1:26.914	83.942
r	Gene	Minardi	24	accident	1:26.864	83.938
r	Badoer	Minardi	10	gearbox	1:28.691	82.403
r	Hill	Jordan	3	accident	1:28.848	80.128

Starting Grid and Qualifying Times

1	Hakkinen (Fin)	1:20.547	2	Schumacher,M. (Ger)	1:20.611
3	Coulthard (GB)	1:20.956	4	Irvine (GB)	1:21.011
5	Barrichello (Bra)	1:21.530	6	Frentzen (Ger)	1:21.556
7	Trulli (Ita)	1:21.769	8	Villeneuve (Can)	1:21.827
9	Fisichella (Ita)	1:21.938	10	Wurz (Aut)	1:21.968
11	Zanardi (Ita)	1:22.152	12	Salo (Fin)	1:22.241
13	Herbert (GB)	1:22.248	14	Alesi (Fra)	1:22.354
15	Diniz (Bra)	1:22.659	16	Schumacher,R. (Ger)	1:22.719
17	Hill (GB)	1:22.832	18	Panis (Fra)	1:22.916
19	Takagi (Jap)	1:23.290	20	Badoer (Ita)	1:23.765
21	de la Rosa (Esp)	1:24.260	22	Gene (Esp)	1:24.914

Round 5: Spain – Barcelona

GP No: 635   Date: 30 May 1999
Track: 2.937 miles   Distance: 65 laps, 190.97 miles
Conditions: Hot and sunny   Fastest Lap: M.Schumacher – 1:24.982
Lap Record: G.Fisichella – 1:22.242 at 128.604 mph, 24 May 1997

Pos	Driver	Car	Laps	Time/Reason	Fastest	mph
1	Hakkinen	McLaren	65	1:34:13.665	1:25.209	121.545
2	Coulthard	McLaren	65	1:34:19.903	1:25.487	121.412
3	Schumacher,M.	Ferrari	65	1:34:24.510	1:24.982	121.313
4	Irvine	Ferrari	65	1:34:43.847	1:25.343	120.90
5	Schumacher,R.	Williams	65	1:35:40.873	1:26.520	119.699
6	Trulli	Prost	64	1:34:24.028	1:26.505	119.456
7	Hill	Jordan	64	1:34:25.044	1:26.348	119.434
dq	Barrichello †	Stewart	64	–	1:26.006	
8	Salo	BAR	64	1:35:21.065	1:27.004	118.265
9	Fisichella	Benetton	64	1:35:22.704	1:27.098	118.231
10	Wurz	Benetton	64	1:35:29.548	1:27.029	118.090
11	de la Rosa	Arrows	63	1:34:41.268	1:27.409	117.232
12	Takagi	Arrows	62	1:34:38.929	1:29.184	115.417
r	Badoer	Minardi	50	spin	1:29.632	115.204
r	Villeneuve	BAR	40	gearbox	1:26.675	120.164
r	Diniz	Sauber	40	gearbox	1:26.315	119.611
r	Herbert	Stewart	40	transmission	1:27.442	118.442
r	Frentzen	Jordan	35	differential	1:26.894	119.533
r	Alesi	Sauber	27	electrics	1:26.542	119.419
r	Zanardi	Williams	24	gearbox	1:27.248	118.965
r	Panis	Prost	24	oil pressure	1:27.175	112.633
r	Gene	Minardi	0	gearbox	–	–

† *Disqualified for plank fastening infringement.*

Starting Grid and Qualifying Times

1	Hakkinen (Fin)	1:22.088	2	Irvine (GB)	1:22.219
3	Coulthard (GB)	1:22.244	4	Schumacher,M. (Ger)	1:22.277
5	Alesi (Fra)	1:22.388	6	Villeneuve (Can)	1:22.703
7	Barrichello (Bra)	1:22.920	8	Frentzen (Ger)	1:22.938
9	Trulli (Ita)	1:23.194	10	Schumacher,R. (Ger)	1:23.303
11	Hill (GB)	1:23.317	12	Diniz (Bra)	1:23.331
13	Fisichella (Ita)	1:23.333	14	Herbert (GB)	1:23.505
15	Panis (Fra)	1:23.559	16	Salo (Fin)	1:23.683
17	Zanardi (Ita)	1:23.703	18	Wurz (Aut)	1:23.824
19	de la Rosa (Esp)	1:24.619	20	Takagi (Jap)	1:25.280
21	Gene (Esp)	1:25.672	22	Badoer (Ita)	1:25.833

Round 6: Canada – Montreal

GP No: 636   Date: 13 June 1999
Track: 2.747 miles   Distance: 69 laps, 189.543 miles
Conditions: Hot and sunny   Fastest Lap: Eddie Irvine – 1:20.382
Lap Record: M.Schumacher – 1:19.379 at 124.591 mph, 7 June 1998

Pos	Driver	Car	Laps	Time/Reason	Fastest	mph
1	Hakkinen	McLaren	69	1:41:35.727	1:21.047	111.943
2	Fisichella	Benetton	69	1:41:36.509	1:21.345	111.929
3	Irvine	Ferrari	69	1:41:37.524	1:20.382	111.910
4	Schumacher,R.	Williams	69	1:41:38.119	1:22.002	111.899
5	Herbert	Stewart	69	1:41:38.532	1:22.078	111.892
6	Diniz	Sauber	69	1:41:39.438	1:21.864	111.875
7	Coulthard	McLaren	69	1:41:40.731	1:20.961	111.851
8	Gene	Minardi	68	1 lap down	1:22.888	110.245
9	Panis	Prost	68	1 lap down	1:22.100	110.231
10	Badoer	Minardi	67	2 laps down	1:23.394	108.657
11	Frentzen	Jordan	65	brakes	1:21.284	112.957
r	Zanardi	Williams	50	gearbox	1:23.442	109.732
r	Takagi	Arrows	41	transmission	1:22.792	108.882
r	Villeneuve	BAR	34	accident	1:22.283	110.530
r	Schumacher,M.	Ferrari	29	accident	1:20.709	111.186
r	de la Rosa	Arrows	22	transmission	1:23.280	105.961
r	Hill	Jordan	14	accident	1:23.953	100.102
r	Barrichello	Stewart	14	accident	1:23.785	93.678
r	Zonta	BAR	2	accident	2:03.038	87.966
r	Alesi	Sauber	0	accident	–	–
r	Trulli	Prost	0	accident	–	–
r	Wurz	Benetton	0	accident	–	–

Starting Grid and Qualifying Times

1	Schumacher,M. (Ger)	1:19.298	2	Hakkinen (Fin)	1:19.327
3	Irvine (GB)	1:19.440	4	Coulthard (GB)	1:19.729
5	Barrichello (Bra)	1:19.930	6	Frentzen (Ger)	1:20.158
7	Fisichella (Ita)	1:20.378	8	Alesi (Fra)	1:20.459
9	Trulli (Ita)	1:20.557	10	Herbert (GB)	1:20.829
11	Wurz (Aut)	1:21.000	12	Zanardi (Ita)	1:21.076
13	Schumacher,R. (Ger)	1:21.081	14	Hill (GB)	1:21.094
15	Panis (Fra)	1:21.252	16	Villeneuve (Can)	1:21.302
17	Zonta (Bra)	1:21.467	18	Diniz (Bra)	1:21.571
19	Takagi (Jap)	1:21.693	20	de la Rosa (Esp)	1:22.613
21	Badoer (Ita)	1:22.808	22	Gene (Esp)	1:23.387

GP No: 637   Date: 27 June 1999
Track: 2.641 miles   Distance: 72 laps, 190.152 miles
Conditions: Torrential rain   Fastest Lap: D.Coulthard – 1:19.227
Lap Record: N.Mansell – 1:17.070 at 123.355 mph, 5 July 1992

Pos	Driver	Car	Laps	Time/Reason	Fastest	mph
1	Frentzen	Jordan	72	1:58:24.343	1:20.994	96.303
2	Hakkinen	McLaren	72	1:58:35.435	1:19.758	96.141
3	Barrichello	Stewart	72	1:59:07.775	1:20.878	95.706
4	Schumacher,R.	Williams	72	1:59:09.818	1:20.313	95.679
5	Schumacher,M.	Ferrari	72	1:59:12.224	1:21.014	95.646
6	Irvine	Ferrari	72	1:59:13.244	1:20.328	95.633
7	Trulli	Prost	72	1:59:22.114	1:21.330	95.514
8	Panis	Prost	72	1:59:22.874	1:21.403	95.504
9	Zonta	BAR	72	1:59:53.107	1:20.881	95.103
10	Badoer	Minardi	71	1 lap down	1:22.900	94.409
dq	Takagi †	Arrows	71	used illegal tyres	–	–
11	de la Rosa	Arrows	71	1 lap down	1:22.535	93.835
r	Fisichella	Benetton	42	spin	1:21.423	92.507
r	Hill	Jordan	31	misfire	1:22.021	87.866
r	Zanardi	Williams	26	engine	1:21.983	104.457
r	Villeneuve	BAR	25	spin	1:21.461	108.210
r	Wurz	Benetton	25	spin	1:21.409	106.954
r	Gene	Minardi	25	spin	1:22.844	105.555
r	Alesi	Sauber	24	spin	1:20.848	111.478
r	Coulthard	McLaren	9	alternator	1:19.227	117.384
r	Diniz	Sauber	5	drive shaft	1:22.629	112.287
r	Herbert	Stewart	4	gearbox	1:25.608	102.296

† Takagi used team-mate's tyres by mistake.

Starting Grid and Qualifying Times

1	Barrichello (Bra)	1:38.441	2	Alesi (Fra)	1:38.881
3	Panis (Fra)	1:40.400	4	Coulthard (GB)	1:40.403
5	Frentzen (Ger)	1:40.690	6	Schumacher,M. (Ger)	1:41.127
7	Fisichella (Ita)	1:41.825	8	Trulli (Ita)	1:42.096
9	Herbert (GB)	1:42.199	10	Zonta (Bra)	1:42.228
11	Diniz (Bra)	1:42.942	12	Villeneuve (Can)	1:43.748
13	Wurz (Aut)	1:44.319	14	Hakkinen (Fin)	1:44.368
15	Zanardi (Ita)	1:44.912	16	Schumacher,R. (Ger)	1:45.189
17	Irvine (GB)	1:45.218	18	Hill (GB)	1:45.334
19	Gene (Esp)	1:46.324	20	Badoer (Ita)	1:46.784
21	de la Rosa (Esp)	1:48.215	22	Takagi (Jap)	1:48.322

GP No: 638   Date: 11 July 1999
Track: 3.194 miles   Distance: 60 laps, 191.640 miles
Conditions: Hot and sunny   Fastest Lap: Mika Hakkinen – 1:28.309
Lap Record: M.Schumacher – 1:24.475 at 136.115 mph, 13 July 1997

Pos	Driver	Car	Laps	Time/Reason	Fastest	mph
1	Coulthard	McLaren	60	1:32:30.144	1:28.846	124.256
2	Irvine	Ferrari	60	1:32:31.973	1:28.782	124.215
3	Schumacher,R.	Williams	60	1:32:57.555	1:29.414	123.645
4	Frentzen	Jordan	60	1:32:57.933	1:29.330	123.637
5	Hill	Jordan	60	1:33:08.750	1:29.252	123.397
6	Diniz	Sauber	60	1:33:23.787	1:29.819	123.066
7	Fisichella	Benetton	60	1:33:24.758	1:30.296	123.045
8	Barrichello	Stewart	60	1:33:38.734	1:29.493	122.739
9	Trulli	Prost	60	1:33:42.189	1:30.964	122.664
10	Wurz	Benetton	60	1:33:42.267	1:30.625	122.662
11	Zanardi	Williams	60	1:33:47.268	1:30.522	122.552
12	Herbert	Stewart	60	1:33:47.853	1:30.103	122.540
13	Panis	Prost	60	1:33:50.636	1:30.793	122.479
14	Alesi	Sauber	59	1 lap down	1:30.334	121.253
15	Gene	Minardi	58	2 laps down	1:31.612	119.861
16	Takagi	Arrows	58	2 laps down	1:32.442	119.149
r	Zonta	BAR	41	suspension	1:30.611	120.227
r	Hakkinen	McLaren	35	wheel hub	1:28.309	118.325
r	Villeneuve	BAR	29	gearbox	1:31.342	121.891
r	Badoer	Minardi	6	gearbox	1:32.409	108.882
r	de la Rosa	Arrows	0	gearbox	–	–
dns	Schumacher,M.	Ferrari	–	accident	–	–

Starting Grid and Qualifying Times

1	Hakkinen (Fin)	1:24.804	2 Schumacher,M. (Ger)	1:25.223
3	Coulthard (GB)	1:25.594	4 Irvine (GB)	1:25.677
5	Frentzen (Ger)	1:25.991	6 Hill (GB)	1:26.099
7	Barrichello (Bra)	1:26.194	8 Schumacher,R. (Ger)	1:26.438
9	Villeneuve (Can)	1:26.719	10 Alesi (Fra)	1:26.761
11	Herbert (GB)	1:26.873	12 Diniz (Bra)	1:27.196
13	Zanardi (Ita)	1:27.223	14 Trulli (Ita)	1:27.227
15	Panis (Fra)	1:27.543	16 Zonta (Bra)	1:27.699
17	Fisichella (Ita)	1:27.857	18 Wurz (Aut)	1:28.010
19	Takagi (Jap)	1:28.037	20 de la Rosa (Esp)	1:28.148
21	Badoer (Ita)	1:28.695	22 Gene (Esp)	1:28.772

Round 9: Austria – A1-Ring

GP No: 639
Track: 2.684 miles
Conditions: Cloudy but warm
Lap Record: J.Villeneuve – 1:11.814 at 134.657 mph, 21 September 1997

Date: 25 July 1999
Distance: 71 laps, 190.564 miles
Fastest Lap: Mika Hakkinen – 1:12.107

Pos	Driver	Car	Laps	Time/Reason	Fastest	mph
1	Irvine	Ferrari	71	1:28:12.438	1:12.787	129.610
2	Coulthard	McLaren	71	1:28:12.751	1:12.855	129.602
3	Hakkinen	McLaren	71	1:28:34.720	1:12.107	129.066
4	Frentzen	Jordan	71	1:29.05.241	1:13.176	128.329
5	Wurz	Benetton	71	1:29:18.796	1:13.654	128.005
6	Diniz	Sauber	71	1:29.23.371	1:13.093	127.896
7	Trulli	Prost	70	1 lap down	1:14.112	127.397
8	Hill	Jordan	70	1 lap down	1:13.960	127.369
9	Salo	Ferrari	70	1 lap down	1:13.481	127.224
10	Panis	Prost	70	1 lap down	1:13.465	127.121
11	Gene	Minardi	70	1 lap down	1:14.517	126.053
12	Fisichella	Benetton	68	engine	1:13.579	127.530
13	Badoer	Minardi	68	3 laps down	1:14.622	123.069
14	Herbert	Stewart	67	4 laps down	1:12.641	120.753
15	Zonta	BAR	63	clutch	1:14.063	126.818
r	Barrichello	Stewart	55	engine	1:13.278	128.322
r	Alesi	Sauber	49	out of fuel	1:13.228	127.810
r	de la Rosa	Arrows	38	brakes	1:14.914	124.609
r	Zanardi	Williams	35	out of fuel	1:14.381	126.246
r	Villeneuve	BAR	34	drive shaft	1:13.977	126.310
r	Takagi	Arrows	25	engine	1:15.361	125.243
r	Schumacher,R.	Williams	8	spin	1:16.173	123.091

Starting Grid and Qualifying Times

1	Hakkinen (Fin)	1:10.954	2	Coulthard (GB)	1:11.153
3	Irvine (GB)	1:11.973	4	Frentzen (Ger)	1:12.266
5	Barrichello (Bra)	1:12.342	6	Herbert (GB)	1:12.488
7	Salo (Fin)	1:12.514	8	Schumacher,R. (Ger)	1:12.515
9	Villeneuve (Can)	1:12.833	10	Wurz (Aut)	1:12.850
11	Hill (GB)	1:12.901	12	Fisichella (Ita)	1:12.924
13	Trulli (Ita)	1:12.999	14	Zanardi (Ita)	1:13.101
15	Zonta (Bra)	1:13.172	16	Diniz (Bra)	1:13.223
17	Alesi (Fra)	1:13.226	18	Panis (Fra)	1:13.457
19	Badoer (Ita)	1:13.606	20	Takagi (Jap)	1:13.641
21	de la Rosa (Esp)	1:14.139	22	Gene (Esp)	1:14.363

GP No: 640   Date: 1 August 1999
Track: 4.239 miles   Distance: 45 laps, 190.755 miles
Conditions: Hot and sunny   Fastest Lap: D.Coulthard – 1:45.270
Lap Record: David Coulthard – 1:45.270 at 144.985 mph, lap 43, 1 Aug 1999

Pos	Driver	Car	Laps	Time/Reason	Fastest	mph
1	Irvine	Ferrari	45	1:21:58.594	1:47.687	139.636
2	Salo	Ferrari	45	1:21.59.601	1:47.945	139.608
3	Frentzen	Jordan	45	1:22:03.789	1:47.619	139.489
4	Schumacher,R.	Williams	45	1:22:11.403	1:48.083	139.274
5	Coulthard	McLaren	45	1:22:15.417	1:45.270	139.160
6	Panis	Prost	45	1:22.28.473	1:46.823	138.794
7	Wurz	Benetton	45	1:22:31.927	1:48.455	138.697
8	Alesi	Sauber	45	1:23:09.885	1:48.334	137.642
9	Gene	Minardi	45	1:23:46.912	1:49.894	136.628
10	Badoer	Minardi	44	1 lap down	1:49.942	136.103
11	Herbert	Stewart	40	gearbox	1:48.408	138.622
r	de la Rosa	Arrows	37	accident	1:50.534	136.198
r	Hakkinen	McLaren	25	accident	1:47.433	139.154
r	Zanardi	Williams	21	differential	1:49.835	136.161
r	Zonta	BAR	20	engine	1:49.179	135.568
r	Takagi	Arrows	15	engine	1:50.286	135.811
r	Hill	Jordan	13	brakes	1:48.925	135.997
r	Trulli	Prost	10	engine	1:49.285	137.350
r	Fisichella	Benetton	7	suspension	1:47.785	132.070
r	Barrichello	Stewart	6	hydraulics	1:47.788	130.820
r	Villeneuve	BAR	0	accident	–	–
r	Diniz	Sauber	0	accident	–	–

Starting Grid and Qualifying Times

1	Hakkinen (Fin)	1:42.950	2	Frentzen (Ger)	1:43.000
3	Coulthard (GB)	1:43.288	4	Salo (Fin)	1:43.577
5	Irvine (GB)	1:43.769	6	Barrichello (Bra)	1:43.938
7	Panis (Fra)	1:43.979	8	Hill (GB)	1:44.001
9	Trulli (Ita)	1:44.209	10	Fisichella (Ita)	1:44.338
11	Schumacher,R. (Ger)	1:44.468	12	Villeneuve (Can)	1:44.508
13	Wurz (Aut)	1:44.522	14	Zanardi (Ita)	1:45.034
15	Gene (Esp)	1:45.331	16	Diniz (Bra)	1:45.335
17	Herbert (GB)	1:45.454	18	Zonta (Bra)	1:45.460
19	Badoer (Ita)	1:45.917	20	de la Rosa (Esp)	1:45.935
21	Alesi (Fra)	1:45.962	22	Takagi (Jap)	1:46.209

GP No: 641   Date: 15 August 1999
Track: 2.465 miles   Distance: 77 laps, 190.043 miles
Conditions: Sunny   Fastest Lap: David Coulthard – 1:20.699
Lap Record: N.Mansell – 1:18.308 at 113.349 mph, 16 August 1992

Pos	Driver	Car	Laps	Time/Reason	Fastest	mph
1	Hakkinen	McLaren	77	1:46:23.536	1:20.710	107.201
2	Coulthard	McLaren	77	1:46:33.242	1:20.699	107.039
3	Irvine	Ferrari	77	1:46:50.784	1:21.010	106.746
4	Frentzen	Jordan	77	1:46:55.351	1:20.991	106.670
5	Barrichello	Stewart	77	1:47.07.344	1:21.707	106.471
6	Hill	Jordan	77	1:47.19.262	1:21.180	106.274
7	Wurz	Benetton	77	1:47.24.548	1:21.539	106.187
8	Trulli	Prost	76	1 lap down	1:21.936	105.467
9	Schumacher,R.	Williams	76	1 lap down	1:21.745	105.318
10	Panis	Prost	76	1 lap down	1:22.587	105.100
11	Herbert	Stewart	76	1 lap down	1:22.455	104.723
12	Salo	Ferrari	75	2 laps down	1:22.681	104.332
13	Zonta	BAR	75	2 laps down	1:21.343	104.315
14	Badoer	Minardi	75	2 laps down	1:23.456	103.985
15	de la Rosa	Arrows	75	2 laps down	1:23.520	103.855
16	Alesi	Sauber	74	out of fuel	1:20.830	105.708
17	Gene	Minardi	74	3 laps down	1:24.807	102.503
r	Villeneuve	BAR	60	clutch	1:21.975	104.419
r	Fisichella	Benetton	52	fuel pressure	1:21.469	106.350
r	Takagi	Arrows	26	drive shaft	1:25.483	100.960
r	Diniz	Sauber	19	spin	1:22.452	105.667
r	Zanardi	Williams	10	differential	1:24.297	100.297

Starting Grid and Qualifying Times

1	Hakkinen (Fin)	1:18.156	2	Irvine (GB)	1:18.263
3	Coulthard (GB)	1:18.384	4	Fisichella (Ita)	1:18.515
5	Frentzen (Ger)	1:18.664	6	Hill (GB)	1:18.667
7	Wurz (Aut)	1:18.733	8	Barrichello (Bra)	1:19.095
9	Villeneuve (Can)	1:19.127	10	Herbert (GB)	1:19.389
11	Alesi (Fra)	1:19.390	12	Diniz (Bra)	1:19.782
13	Trulli (Ita)	1:19.788	14	Panis (Fra)	1:19.841
15	Zanardi (Ita)	1:19.924	16	Schumacher,R. (Ger)	1:19.945
17	Zonta (Bra)	1:20.060	18	Salo (Fin)	1:20.369
19	Badoer (Ita)	1:20.961	20	de la Rosa (Esp)	1:21.328
21	Takagi (Jap)	1:21.675	22	Gene (Esp)	1:21.867

GP No: 642   Date: 29 August 1999
Track: 4.330 miles   Distance: 44 laps, 190.520 miles
Conditions: Sunny and warm   Fastest Lap: Mika Hakkinen – 1:53.955
Lap Record: J.Villeneuve – 1:52.692 at 138.321 mph, 24 August 1997

Pos	Driver	Car	Laps	Time/Reason	Fastest	mph
1	Coulthard	McLaren	44	1:25:43.057	1:54.088	133.343
2	Hakkinen	McLaren	44	1:25:53.526	1:53.955	133.072
3	Frentzen	Jordan	44	1:26:16.490	1:55.412	132.482
4	Irvine	Ferrari	44	1:26:28.005	1:55.582	132.188
5	Schumacher,R.	Williams	44	1:26:31.124	1:55.964	132.108
6	Hill	Jordan	44	1:26:37.973	1:54.954	131.935
7	Salo	Ferrari	44	1:26:39.306	1:55.299	131.900
8	Zanardi	Williams	44	1:26:50.079	1:55.786	131.628
9	Alesi	Sauber	44	1:26:56.905	1:56.016	131.455
10	Barrichello	Stewart	44	1:27:03.799	1:56.131	131.282
11	Fisichella	Benetton	44	1:27:15.252	1:57.037	130.995
12	Trulli	Prost	44	1:27:19.211	1:56.367	130.896
13	Panis	Prost	44	1:27:24.600	1:56.681	130.761
14	Wurz	Benetton	44	1:27:40.802	1:57.526	130.359
15	Villeneuve	BAR	43	1 lap down	1:57.619	130.144
16	Gene	Minardi	43	1 lap down	1:56.789	129.394
r	de la Rosa	Arrows	35	transmission	1:58.480	127.751
r	Badoer	Minardi	33	suspension	1:57.929	128.849
r	Zonta	BAR	33	gearbox	1:58.918	123.137
r	Herbert	Stewart	27	brakes	1:57.094	130.179
r	Diniz	Sauber	19	accident	1:58.179	128.555
r	Takagi	Arrows	0	clutch	–	–

Starting Grid and Qualifying Times

1 Hakkinen (Fin)	1:50.329	2 Coulthard (GB)	1:50.484
3 Frentzen (Ger)	1:51.332	4 Hill (GB)	1:51.372
5 Schumacher,R. (Ger)	1:51.414	6 Irvine (GB)	1:51.895
7 Barrichello (Bra)	1:51.974	8 Zanardi (Ita)	1:52.014
9 Salo (Fin)	1:52.124	10 Herbert (GB)	1:52.164
11 Villeneuve (Can)	1:52.235	12 Trulli (Ita)	1:52.644
13 Fisichella (Ita)	1:52.782	14 Zonta (Bra)	1:52.840
15 Wurz (Aut)	1:52.847	16 Alesi (Fra)	1:52.921
17 Panis (Fra)	1:53.148	18 Diniz (Bra)	1:53.778
19 Takagi (Jap)	1:54.099	20 Badoer (Ita)	1:54.197
21 Gene (Esp)	1:54.557	22 de la Rosa (Esp)	1:54.579

GP No: 643 Date: 12 September 1999
Track: 3.585 miles Distance: 53 laps, 189.857 miles
Conditions: Sunny and hot Fastest Lap: R.Schumacher – 1:25.579
Lap Record: N.Mansell – 1:18.308 at 113.349 mph, 13 Sept 1997

Pos	Driver	Car	Laps	Time/Reason	Fastest	mph
1	Frentzen	Jordan	53	1:17:02.923	1:25.917	147.848
2	Schumacher,R.	Williams	53	1:17:06.195	1:25.579	147.743
3	Salo	Ferrari	53	1:17:14.855	1:25.630	147.468
4	Barrichello	Stewart	53	1:17:20.553	1:25.825	147.286
5	Coulthard	McLaren	53	1:17:21.085	1:25.832	147.270
6	Irvine	Ferrari	53	1:17:30.325	1:26.387	146.978
7	Zanardi	Williams	53	1:17:30.970	1:26.047	146.956
8	Villeneuve	BAR	53	1:17:44.720	1:26.338	146.523
9	Alesi	Sauber	53	1:17:45.121	1:25.911	146.511
10	Hill	Jordan	53	1:17:59.182	1:26.342	146.071
11	Panis	Prost	52	1 lap down	1:25.953	146.078
r	Herbert	Stewart	40	clutch	1:26.253	145.574
r	Takagi	Arrows	35	spin	1:29.216	148.555
r	de la Rosa	Arrows	35	acc. damage	1:28.516	133.463
r	Hakkinen	McLaren	29	spin	1:26.060	148.119
r	Trulli	Prost	29	gearbox	1:26.493	143.499
r	Zonta	BAR	25	wheel bearing	1:26.945	142.636
r	Badoer	Minardi	23	accident	1:28.914	142.493
r	Wurz	Benetton	11	electronics	1:28.338	139.971
r	Diniz	Sauber	1	spin	1:39.370	123.992
r	Fisichella	Benetton	1	accident	1:40.305	122.804
r	Gene	Minardi	0	accident	–	–

Starting Grid and Qualifying Times

1	Hakkinen (Fin)	1:22.432	2	Frentzen (Ger)	1:22.926
3	Coulthard (GB)	1:23.177	4	Zanardi (Ita)	1:23.432
5	Schumacher,R. (Ger)	1:23.636	6	Salo (Fin)	1:23.657
7	Barrichello (Bra)	1:23.739	8	Irvine (GB)	1:23.765
9	Hill (GB)	1:23.979	10	Panis (Fra)	1:24.016
11	Villeneuve (Can)	1:24.188	12	Trulli (Ita)	1:24.293
13	Alesi (Fra)	1:24.591	14	Wurz (Aut)	1:24.593
15	Herbert (GB)	1:24.594	16	Diniz (Bra)	1:24.596
17	Fisichella (Ita)	1:24.862	18	Zonta (Bra)	1:25.114
19	Badoer (Ita)	1:25.348	20	Gene (Esp)	1:25.695
21	de la Rosa (Esp)	1:26.383	22	Takagi (Jap)	1:26.509

Round 14: European – Nurburgring

GP No: 644　　　　　　　　　　　Date: 26 September 1999
Track: 2.831 miles　　　　　　　　Distance: 66 laps, 186.840 miles
Conditions: Cool, some rain　　　　Fastest Lap: Mika Hakkinen – 1:21.282
Lap Record: H-H.Frentzen – 1:18.805 at 129.309 mph, 28 Sept 1997

Pos	Driver	Car	Laps	Time/Reason	Fastest	mph
1	Herbert	Stewart	66	1:41:54.314	1:23.010	110.004
2	Trulli	Prost	66	1:42.16.933	1:23.742	109.598
3	Barrichello	Stewart	66	1:42:17.180	1:22.960	109.577
4	Schumacher,R.	Williams	66	1:42:33.822	1:22.237	109.297
5	Hakkinen	McLaren	66	1:42:57.264	1:21.282	108.883
6	Gene	Minardi	66	1:42:59.468	1:23.657	108.844
7	Irvine	Ferrari	66	1:43:00.997	1:22.332	108.817
8	Zonta	BAR	65	1 lap down	1:23.067	108.079
9	Panis	Prost	65	1 lap down	1:23.905	107.917
10	Villeneuve	BAR	61	clutch	1:22.564	108.012
r	Badoer	Minardi	53	gearbox	1:23.745	106.925
r	de la Rosa	Arrows	52	gearbox	1:24.857	103.171
r	Fisichella	Benetton	48	spun-out	1:22.244	107.971
r	Salo	Ferrari	44	spun-out	1:23.404	102.764
r	Takagi	Arrows	42	accident	1:24.848	102.835
r	Coulthard	McLaren	37	spun-out	1:21.835	109.936
r	Alesi	Sauber	35	transmission	1:23.097	108.095
r	Frentzen	Jordan	32	electronics	1:22.082	110.082
r	Zanardi	Williams	10	accident	1:24.300	91.939
r	Hill	Jordan	0	electrics	no time	
r	Wurz	Benetton	0	accident	no time	
r	Diniz	Sauber	0	accident	no time	

Starting Grid and Qualifying Times

1	Frentzen (Ger)	1:19.910	2	Coulthard (GB)	1:20.176
3	Hakkinen (Fin)	1:20.376	4	Schumacher,R. (Ger)	1:20.444
5	Panis (Fra)	1:20.638	6	Fisichella (Ita)	1:20.781
7	Hill (GB)	1:20.818	8	Villeneuve (Can)	1:20.825
9	Irvine (GB)	1:20.842	10	Trulli (Ita)	1:20.965
11	Wurz (Aut)	1:21.144	12	Salo (Fin)	1:21.314
13	Diniz (Bra)	1:21.345	14	Herbert (GB)	1:21.379
15	Barrichello (Bra)	1:21.490	16	Alesi (Fra)	1:21.634
17	Zonta (Bra)	1:22.267	18	Zanardi (Ita)	1:22.284
19	Badoer (Ita)	1:22.631	20	Gene (Esp)	1:22.760
21	Takagi (Jap)	1:23.401	22	de la Rosa (Esp)	1:23.698

GP No: 645   Date: 17 October 1999
Track: 3.443 miles   Distance: 56 laps, 192.865 miles
Conditions: Humid, overcast   Fastest Lap: M.Schumacher – 1:40.267
Lap Record: M.Schumacher – 1:40.267 on 17 October 1999.

Pos	Driver	Car	Laps	Time/Reason	Fastest	mph
1	Irvine	Ferrari	56	1:36:38.494	1:41.254	119.412
2	Schumacher,M.	Ferrari	56	1:36:39.534	1:40.267	
3	Hakkinen	McLaren	56	1:36:48.237	1:41.103	119.526
4	Herbert	Stewart	56	1:36:56.032	1:41.383	119.366
5	Barrichello	Stewart	56	1:37:10.790	1:40.810	119.064
6	Frentzen	Jordan	56	1:37:13.378	1:40.631	119.011
7	Alesi	Sauber	56	1:37:32.902	1:41.328	118.614
8	Wurz	Benetton	56	1:37:39.428	1:41.950	118.482
9	Gene	Minardi	55	1 lap down	1:42.490	116.953
10	Zanardi	Williams	55	1 lap down	1:42.056	116.425
11	Fisichella	Benetton	52	4 laps down	1:40.960	109.363
r	Villeneuve	BAR	48	hydraulics	1:41.769	117.815
r	Diniz	Sauber	44	spun-out	1:41.639	117.905
r	de la Rosa	Arrows	30	engine	1:43.885	115.617
r	Badoer	Minardi	15	overheating	1:46.367	107.289
r	Coulthard	McLaren	14	fuel pressure	1:42.940	118.811
r	Schumacher,R.	Williams	7	spun-out	1:46.418	114.821
r	Takagi	Arrows	7	drive shaft	1:46.441	94.110
r	Zonta	BAR	6	water leak	1:46.444	111.952
r	Panis	Prost	5	engine	1:46.874	111.872
r	Hill	Jordan	0	accident	–	–
dns	Trulli	Prost		engine on formation lap		

Starting Grid and Qualifying Times

1	Schumacher,M. (Ger)	1:39.688	2	Irvine (GB)	1:40.635
3	Coulthard (GB)	1:40.806	4	Hakkinen (Fin)	1:40.866
5	Herbert (GB)	1:40.937	6	Barrichello (Bra)	1:41.351
7	Wurz (Aut)	1:41.444	8	Schumacher,R. (Ger)	1:41.558
9	Hill (GB)	1:42.050	10	Villeneuve (Can)	1:42.087
11	Fisichella (Ita)	1:42.110	12	Panis (Fra)	1:42.208
13	Zonta (Bra)	1:42.310	14	Frentzen (Ger)	1:42.380
15	Alesi (Fra)	1:42.522	16	Zanardi (Ita)	1:42.885
17	Diniz (Bra)	1:42.933	18	Trulli (Ita)	1:42.948
19	Gene (Esp)	1:43.563	20	de la Rosa (Esp)	1:43.579
21	Badoer (Ita)	1:44.321	22	Takagi (Jap)	1:44.637

Round 16: Japan – Suzuka

GP No: 646   Date: 31 October 1999
Track: 3.642 miles   Distance: 53 laps, 192.987 miles
Conditions: Warm and sunny   Fastest Lap: M.Schumacher – 1:41.319
Lap Record: H-H.Frentzen – 1:38.942 at 130.662 mph, 12 Oct 1997

Pos	Driver	Car	Laps	Time/Reason	Fastest	mph
1	Hakkinen	McLaren	53	1:31:18.785	1:41.577	126.813
2	Schumacher,M.	Ferrari	53	1:31:23.800	1:41.319	126.697
3	Irvine	Ferrari	53	1:32:54.473	1:43.297	124.587
4	Frentzen	Jordan	53	1:32:57.420	1:42.972	124.571
5	Schumacher,R.	Williams	53	1:32:58.279	1:42.567	124.551
6	Alesi	Sauber	52	1 lap down	1:43.669	124.140
7	Herbert	Stewart	52	1 lap down	1:43.706	124.089
8	Barrichello	Stewart	52	1 lap down	1:43.496	124.069
9	Villeneuve	BAR	52	1 lap down	1:43.898	123.801
10	Wurz	Benetton	52	1 lap down	1:43.963	123.347
11	Diniz	Sauber	52	1 lap down	1:44.112	123.127
12	Zonta	BAR	52	1 lap down	1:44.869	122.150
13	de la Rosa	Arrows	51	2 laps down	1:45.556	121.566
14	Fisichella	Benetton	47	engine	1:44.379	122.463
r	Takagi	Arrows	43	gearbox	1:46.150	120.395
r	Badoer	Minardi	43	engine	1:45.377	119.647
r	Coulthard	McLaren	39	hydraulics	1:42.106	122.992
r	Gene	Minardi	31	gearbox	1:45.359	121.968
r	Hill	Jordan	21	retired	1:43.939	120.576
r	Panis	Prost	19	gearbox	1:43.188	122.649
r	Trulli	Prost	3	engine	1:44.304	120.584
r	Zanardi	Williams	0	electrics	no time	

Starting Grid and Qualifying Times

1	Schumacher,M. (Ger)	1:37.470	2	Hakkinen (Fin)	1:37.820
3	Coulthard (GB)	1:38.239	4	Frentzen (Ger)	1:38.696
5	Irvine (GB)	1:38.975	6	Panis (Fra)	1:39.623
7	Trulli (Ita)	1:39.644	8	Herbert (GB)	1:39.706
9	Schumacher,R. (Ger)	1:39.717	10	Alesi (Fra)	1:39.721
11	Villeneuve (Can)	1:39.732	12	Hill (GB)	1:40.140
13	Barrichello (Bra)	1:40.140	14	Fisichella (Ita)	1:40.261
15	Wurz (Aut)	1:40.303	16	Zanardi (Ita)	1:40.403
17	Diniz (Bra)	1:40.740	18	Zonta (Bra)	1:40.861
19	Takagi (Jap)	1:41.067	20	Gene (Esp)	1:41.529
21	de la Rosa (Esp)	1:41.708	22	Badoer (Ita)	1:42.515

FIA DRIVERS' CHAMPIONSHIP 1999

Pos	Driver	Team	Points
1	Mika Hakkinen (Fin)	McLaren-Mercedes	76
2	Eddie Irvine (GB)	Ferrari	74
3	Heinz-Harald Frentzen (Ger)	Jordan Mugen-Honda	54
4	David Coulthard (GB)	McLaren-Mercedes	48
5	Michael Schumacher (Ger)	Ferrari	44
6	Ralf Schumacher (Ger)	Williams-Supertec	35
7	Rubens Barrichello (Bra)	Stewart-Ford	21
8	Johnny Herbert (GB)	Stewart-Ford	15
9	Giancarlo Fisichella (Ita)	Benetton-Playlife	13
10	Mika Salo (Fin)	BAR-Supertec/Ferrari	10
11	Damon Hill (GB)	Jordan Mugen-Honda	7
	Jarno Trulli (Ita)	Prost-Peugeot	7
13	Pedro Diniz (Bra)	Sauber-Petronas	3
	Alexander Wurz (Aut)	Benetton-Playlife	3
15	Jean Alesi (Fra)	Sauber-Petronas	2
	Olivier Panis (Fra)	Prost-Peugeot	2
17	Pedro de la Rosa (Esp)	Arrows	1
	Marc Gene (Esp)	Minardi-Ford	1

Drivers who failed to score a point:

	Luca Badoer (Ita)	Minardi-Ford
	Stephane Sarrazin (Fra)	Minardi-Ford
	Toransuke Takagi (Jap)	Arrows
	Jacques Villeneuve (Can)	BAR-Supertec
	Alessandro Zanardi (Ita)	Williams-Supertec
	Ricardo Zonta (Bra)	BAR-Supertec

CONSTRUCTORS' CHAMPIONSHIP

Pos	Team	Drivers	Points
1	Ferrari	M.Schumacher, Irvine, Salo	128
2	McLaren-Mercedes	Hakkinen, Coulthard	124
3	Jordan Mugen-Honda	Hill, Frentzen	61
4	Stewart-Ford	Barrichello, Herbert	36
5	Williams-Supertec	R.Schumacher, Zanardi	35
6	Benetton-Playlife	Fisichella, Wurz	16
7	Prost-Peugeot	Panis, Trulli	9
8	Sauber-Petronas	Alesi, Diniz	5
9	Arrows	Takagi, de la Rosa	1
	Minardi-Ford	Badoer, Gene, Salo	1

Driver	Team	As	Br	Sm	Mo	Sp	Ca	Fr	GB	At	Ge	Hu	Be	Ita	Eu	Ma	Jp	Pts
Alesi	Sauber	r	6	r	r	r	10	r	14	r	8	16	9	9	r	7	6	2
Badoer	Minardi	–	8	r	r	r	r	10	r	13	10	14	r	r	r	r	r	0
Barrichello	Stewart	5	3	9	r	dq	3	8	r	r	r	2f	5	4	3	5	8	21
Coulthard	McLaren	r	2	r	2	2	7	rf	1	2	5f	15	1	5	r	r	r	48
de la Rosa	Arrows	6	r	r	r	11	r	11	r	r	r	r	r	r	r	13	r	1
Diniz	Sauber	r	r	r	r	6	6	r	6	6	4	r	11	r	r	11	r	3
Fisichella	Benetton	4	5	5	5	9	2	r	7	12	3	4	r	6	5f	11	14	13
Frentzen	Jordan	2	3	4	4	r	11	2	4	7	r	3	3	1	6	6	4	54
Gene	Minardi	r	9	9	r	8	8	r	15	11	9	17	16	r	r	9	r	1
Hakkinen	McLaren	r	1f	3f	3f	1	1	2	rf	3f	r	1	2f	5f	r	3	1	76
Herbert	Stewart	r	10	r	7	7	5	5	12	8	11	11	6	1	1	4	7	15
Hill	Jordan	r	4	r	r	r	r	r	5	r	11	r	10	r	r	r	r	7
Irvine	Ferrari	1	5	2	1	4	3f	r	2	1	1	6	4	6	7	1	3	74
Panis	Prost	r	6	r	r	r	9	8	13	10	6	10	r	7	9	r	r	2
Salo	BAR	–	7	r	8	r	–	–	r	9	2	12	13	3	r	–	–	10
Sarrazin	Minardi	–	–	–	–	–	–	–	–	–	–	–	7	–	r	–	–	0
Schumacher, M.	Ferrari	8f	2	1f	1	3f	5	4	dns	r	r	r	r	r	2f	2f	2	44
Schumacher, R.	Williams	3	4	r	5	4	4	r	r	4	r	9	5	4	4	5	r	35
Takagi	Arrows	7	8	r	12	r	dq	16	r	r	r	r	r	8	2	r	r	0
Trulli	Prost	r	r	7	6	r	r	9	7	7	8	8	12	2	r	r	r	7
Villeneuve	BAR	r	r	r	r	6	10	10	5	r	7	r	15	10	r	dns	9	0
Wurz	Benetton	r	7	6	10	10	r	r	11	5	r	7	14	7	8	8	10	3
Zanardi	Williams	r	11	8	8	r	r	11	r	15	13	8	7	8	r	10	r	0
Zonta	BAR	r	dns	–	–	–	9	15	r	9	r	13	8	r	r	12	12	0

DRIVERS – GRID POSITIONS – RACE BY RACE '99

Driver	Team	As	Br	Sm	Mo	Sp	Ca	Fr	GB	At	Ge	Hu	Be	Ita	Eu	Ma	Jp	Pts
Alesi	Sauber	16	14	13	14	5	8	2	10	17	21	11	16	13	16	15	10	2
Badoer	Minardi	21	–	22	20	7	21	20	21	19	19	18	20	7	19	21	22	0
Barrichello	Stewart	4	3	6	5	7	5	1	7	5	6	9	7	7	15	6	13	21
Coulthard	McLaren	2	2	2	3	3	4	4	3	2	3	3	2	3	2	3	3	48
de la Rosa	Arrows	18	17	18	21	19	20	21	20	12	20	20	22	21	22	20	21	1
Diniz	Sauber	14	15	15	15	13	18	11	17	16	16	12	18	16	13	17	14	3
Fisichella	Benetton	7	5	16	9	13	7	7	17	12	10	12	4	17	6	11	14	13
Frentzen	Jordan	5	8	7	6	8	6	5	5	4	2	5	3	2	1	4	4	54
Gene	Minardi	22	20	21	22	21	22	19	22	22	15	22	21	20	20	19	20	1
Hakkinen	McLaren	1	10	1	1	1	1	14	1	1	17	1	1	1	3	2	1	76
Herbert	Stewart	13	10	12	13	14	10	9	11	6	17	10	10	15	14	5	8	15
Hill	Jordan	9	7	8	17	11	14	18	6	11	8	6	4	9	7	9	12	7
Irvine	Ferrari	6	6	4	4	2	3	17	4	3	5	2	6	8	8	5	5	74
Panis	Prost	20	12	11	18	15	15	3	15	18	7	14	17	10	9	12	6	2
Salo	BAR/Ferrari	–	–	19	12	16	–	–	–	7	4	18	9	6	12	–	–	10
Sarrazin	Minardi	–	18	–	–	–	–	–	–	–	–	–	–	–	–	–	–	0
Schumacher, M.	Ferrari	3	4	3	2	4	1	6	2	–	–	–	–	–	–	1	1	44
Schumacher, R.	Williams	8	11	9	16	10	19	20	8	8	11	15	5	5	8	9	9	35
Takagi	Arrows	17	13	14	19	20	9	16	8	13	9	13	12	12	10	22	19	0
Trulli	Prost	12	13	17	7	9	8	12	14	9	12	9	11	8	18	7	11	7
Villeneuve	BAR	11	21	5	8	6	16	12	9	10	13	7	11	8	11	10	11	0
Wurz	Benetton	10	9	17	10	18	11	13	18	10	13	7	15	14	7	15	15	3
Zanardi	Williams	15	16	10	11	17	12	15	13	14	14	15	8	4	18	16	16	0
Zonta	BAR	19	–	–	–	17	10	16	15	18	17	14	18	17	13	18	–	0

DRIVERS – POINTS TALLY – RACE BY RACE '99

Driver	Team	As	Br	Sm	Mo	Sp	Ca	Fr	GB	At	Ge	Hu	Be	Ita	Eu	Ma	Jp	Pts
Alesi	Sauber	0	1	0	0	0	0	0	0	0	0	0	0	0	0	0	1	2
Badoer	Minardi	0	–	0	0	0	0	0	0	0	0	0	0	0	0	0	0	0
Barrichello	Stewart	2	0	4	0	3	0	4	0	0	1	0	0	3	4	0	0	21
Coulthard	McLaren	0	0	6	2	6	0	0	10	6	2	6	10	0	0	0	0	48
de la Rosa	Arrows	1	0	0	0	0	0	0	0	0	0	0	0	0	0	0	0	1
Diniz	Sauber	0	0	0	0	0	3	0	0	0	0	0	0	0	0	0	0	3
Fisichella	Benetton	3	0	2	0	0	6	1	0	0	0	0	0	0	0	1	0	13
Frentzen	Jordan	6	4	3	3	0	3	10	2	2	4	0	4	10	0	0	3	54
Gene	Minardi	0	0	0	0	0	0	0	0	0	0	0	0	0	1	0	0	1
Hakkinen	McLaren	0	10	0	4	10	10	6	0	4	0	10	6	0	2	4	10	76
Herbert	Stewart	0	0	0	2	0	0	0	0	0	0	0	0	0	10	3	0	15
Hill	Jordan	0	0	3	0	0	0	2	0	0	0	0	0	0	2	0	0	7
Irvine	Ferrari	10	2	0	6	3	4	0	6	10	10	4	3	2	0	10	4	74
Panis	Prost	0	0	0	0	0	0	2	0	0	0	0	0	0	0	0	0	2
Salo	BAR/Ferrari	–	0	0	0	0	0	0	0	0	6	0	0	4	0	0	0	10
Sarrazin	Minardi	–	0	0	0	0	0	0	0	0	0	0	0	0	0	0	0	0
Schumacher,M.	Ferrari	0	6	10	10	4	0	2	0	0	0	0	0	0	0	6	6	44
Schumacher,R.	Williams	4	3	0	0	0	3	3	4	3	3	3	3	6	0	0	0	35
Takagi	Arrows	0	0	0	0	0	0	0	0	0	0	0	0	0	0	0	0	0
Trulli	Prost	0	0	1	0	0	0	0	0	0	0	0	0	0	6	0	0	7
Villeneuve	BAR	0	0	0	0	0	0	0	0	0	0	0	0	0	0	0	0	0
Wurz	Benetton	0	0	0	0	2	0	0	0	0	0	0	0	0	0	0	1	3
Zanardi	Williams	0	0	0	0	0	0	0	0	0	0	0	0	0	0	0	0	0
Zonta	BAR	0	0	0	0	0	0	0	0	0	0	0	0	0	0	0	–	0

DRIVERS – LAPS COMPLETED – RACE BY RACE '99

Driver	Team	As	Br	Sm	Mo	Sp	Ca	Fr	GB	At	Ge	Hu	Be	Ita	Eu	Ma	Jp	Total
Alesi	Sauber	0	27	61	50	27	0	24	59	49	45	74	44	53	35	56	52	656
Badoer	Minardi	42	–	59	10	50	67	71	6	68	44	75	33	23	53	15	43	659
Barrichello	Stewart	57	42	61	71	0	14	72	60	55	6	77	44	53	66	56	52	786
Coulthard	McLaren	13	22	52	36	65	9	60	71	0	45	77	44	53	37	62	39	716
de la Rosa	Arrows	57	52	5	30	63	22	71	0	38	37	71	35	35	52	30	51	653
Diniz	Sauber	27	42	49	49	40	69	5	60	71	0	19	19	1	0	44	52	547
Fisichella	Benetton	57	38	61	77	64	65	42	60	68	7	52	44	1	48	52	47	787
Frentzen	Jordan	57	71	46	78	35	72	72	60	71	45	77	44	53	32	56	53	915
Gene	Minardi	25	69	59	24	0	68	25	58	70	45	77	43	0	66	55	31	712
Hakkinen	McLaren	21	72	17	78	65	69	72	35	71	25	77	44	29	66	56	53	850
Herbert	Stewart	0	15	58	32	40	69	4	60	67	40	76	27	40	66	56	52	702
Hill	Jordan	0	10	61	3	64	14	31	60	71	13	77	44	53	0	0	21	521
Irvine	Ferrari	57	71	46	78	65	69	72	60	71	45	77	44	53	66	56	53	983
Panis	Prost	23	71	48	40	24	68	72	60	70	45	76	44	52	65	5	19	782
Salo	BAR/Ferrari	–	–	59	36	64	–	72	–	70	45	75	44	53	44	–	–	490
Sarrazin	Minardi	–	31															31
Schumacher,M.	Ferrari	56	72	78	65	69	29	72								56	53	543
Schumacher,R.	Williams	57	71	28	54	65	69	72	60	8	45	76	44	53	66	7	53	828
Takagi	Arrows	57	69	29	36	62	41	–	58	25	15	26	0	35	42	7	43	545
Trulli	Prost	25	21	0	77	64	0	72	60	70	10	76	44	29	66	–	3	617
Villeneuve	BAR	13	49	0	32	40	34	25	29	34	0	60	43	53	61	48	52	573
Wurz	Benetton	28	70	5	77	64	0	25	60	71	45	77	44	11	0	56	52	685
Zanardi	Williams	20	43	58	76	24	50	26	60	35	21	10	44	53	10	55	0	585
Zonta	BAR	48	0	–	–	–	2	72	41	20	75	75	33	25	65	6	52	502

CONSTRUCTORS' POINTS WON – RACE BY RACE '99

Team	As	Br	Sm	Mo	Sp	Ca	Fr	GB	At	Ge	Hu	Be	It	Eu	Ma	Jp	Tot
Arrows	1	0	0	0	0	0	0	0	0	0	0	0	0	0	0	0	1
BAR	0	0	0	0	0	0	0	0	0	0	0	0	0	0	0	0	0
Benetton	3	2	2	0	1	6	0	0	1	0	0	1	0	0	0	0	16
Ferrari	10	8	10	16	7	4	3	6	10	16	4	3	5	0	16	10	128
Jordan	6	4	3	3	0	0	10	3	6	4	4	4	10	0	3	1	61
McLaren	0	10	6	4	16	10	6	10	10	0	16	16	4	0	4	12	124
Minardi	0	0	0	0	0	0	0	0	0	0	0	0	0	1	0	0	1
Prost	0	1	0	0	0	0	1	0	0	1	0	0	0	6	0	0	9
Sauber	0	0	1	1	0	1	0	0	0	0	0	0	0	2	0	0	5
Stewart	2	0	4	0	0	2	4	0	0	0	2	0	3	14	5	0	36
Williams	4	3	0	0	2	3	3	4	0	3	0	2	6	3	0	2	35

CONSTRUCTORS' TOTAL LAPS – RACE BY RACE '99

Team	As	Br	Sm	Mo	Sp	Ca	Fr	GB	At	Ge	Hu	Be	It	Eu	Ma	Jp	Total
Arrows	114	121	34	66	125	63	71	58	63	52	101	35	70	94	37	94	1198
BAR	61	49	59	68	104	36	97	70	97	20	135	76	78	126	54	104	1234
Benetton	85	108	66	154	128	69	67	120	139	52	129	88	12	48	108	99	1472
Ferrari	113	143	108	156	130	98	144	60	141	90	152	88	106	110	112	106	1857
Jordan	57	81	107	81	99	79	103	120	141	58	154	88	106	32	56	74	1436
McLaren	34	94	79	114	130	138	81	95	142	70	154	88	82	103	70	92	1566
Minardi	67	100	118	34	50	135	96	64	138	89	149	76	23	119	70	74	1402
Prost	48	92	48	117	88	68	144	120	140	55	152	88	81	131	5	22	1399
Sauber	27	69	110	99	67	69	29	120	120	45	93	63	54	35	100	104	1203
Stewart	57	57	119	103	40	83	76	120	122	46	153	71	93	132	112	104	1488
Williams	77	114	86	130	89	119	98	120	43	66	86	88	106	76	62	53	1413

Winning Margins

Biggest win margin: 30.476s – Monaco Grand Prix
Narrowest win margin: 0.313s – Austrian Grand Prix

GP	Ist Place	2nd Place	Margin
Australian	Irvine (Ferrari)	Frentzen (Jordan)	1.027s
Brazilian	Hakkinen (McLaren)	Schumacher (Ferrari)	4.945s
San Marino	Schumacher (Ferrari)	Coulthard (McLaren)	4.265s
Monaco	Schumacher (Ferrari)	Irvine (Ferrari)	30.476s
Spanish	Hakkinen (McLaren)	Coulthard (McLaren)	6.238s
Canadian	Hakkinen (McLaren)	Fisichella (Benetton)	0.782s
French	Frentzen (Jordan)	Hakkinen (McLaren)	11.092s
British	Coulthard (McLaren)	Irvine (Ferrari)	1.829s
Austrian	Irvine (Ferrari)	Coulthard (McLaren)	0.313s
German	Irvine (Ferrari)	Salo (Ferrari)	1.007s
Hungarian	Hakkinen (McLaren)	Coulthard (McLaren)	9.706s
Belgian	Coulthard (McLaren)	Hakkinen (McLaren)	10.469s
Italian	Frenzten (Jordan)	Schumacher (Williams)	3.272s
European	Herbert (Stewart)	Trulli (Prost)	22.619s
Malaysian	Irvine (Ferrari)	Schumacher (Ferrari)	1.040s
Japanese	Hakkinen (McLaren)	Schumacher (Ferrari)	5.015s

Team Match-ups

Team	Driver	Driver	Race	Qualify
Arrows	Takagi	de la Rosa	2-5	8-8
BAR	Villeneuve	Zonta	3-4	11-2
	Villeneuve	Salo	0-2	3-0
Benetton	Fisichella	Wurz	7-6	13-3
Ferrari	M.Schumacher	Irvine	6-4	9-1
	Salo	Irvine	1-5	2-4
Jordan	Hill	Frentzen	2-13	2-14
McLaren	Hakkinen	Coulthard	9-6	13-3
Minardi	Badoer	Gene	3-7	9-6
	Sarrazin	Gene	0-1	1-0
Prost	Panis	Trulli	4-8	8-8
Sauber	Alesi	Diniz	7-3	12-4
Stewart	Barrichello	Herbert	8-6	13-3
Williams	R.Schumacher	Zanardi	12-3	11-5

FASTEST LAPS BY RACE 1999

Grand Prix	Fin	Driver	Team	Laps	Time	Grid
1 Australian	8	Schumacher,M.	Ferrari	56	1:32.112	3
2 Brazilian	1	Hakkinen	McLaren	72	1:18.448	1
3 San Marino	1	Schumacher,M.	Ferrari	62	1:28.547	3
4 Monaco	3	Hakkinen	McLaren	78	1:22.259	1
5 Spanish	3	Schumacher,M.	Ferrari	65	1:24.982	4
6 Canadian	3	Irvine	Ferrari	69	1:20.382	3
7 French	r	Coulthard	McLaren	9	1:19.227	4
8 British	r	Hakkinen	McLaren	35	1:28.309	1
9 Austrian	3	Hakkinen	McLaren	71	1:12.107	1
10 German	5	Coulthard	McLaren	45	1:45.270	3
11 Hungarian	2	Coulthard	McLaren	77	1:20.699	3
12 Belgian	2	Hakkinen	McLaren	44	1:53.955	1
13 Italian	2	Schumacher,R.	Williams	53	1:25.579	5
14 European	5	Hakkinen	McLaren	66	1:21.282	3
15 Malaysian	2	Schumacher,M.	Ferrari	56	1:40.267	1
16 Japanese	2	Schumacher,M.	Ferrari	53	1:41.319	1

DRIVER LAP LEADERS 1999

	Driver	Team	Miles Led	Laps Led
1	M.Hakkinen	McLaren-Mercedes	1168.85	383
2	M.Schumacher	Ferrari	453.62	176
3	D.Coulthard	McLaren-Mercedes	485.94	145
4	E.Irvine	Ferrari	443.06	133
5	R.Barrichello	Stewart-Ford	177.72	67
6	H-H.Frentzen	Jordan-Mugen Honda	198.23	64
7	J.Herbert	Stewart-Ford	47.85	17
8	R.Schumacher	Williams-Supertec	22.37	8
9	G.Fisichella	Benetton-Playlife	11.19	4
10	M.Salo	Ferrari	8.08	2
11	D.Hill	Jordan-Mugen Honda	3.19	1

TEAM LAP LEADERS 1999

	Team	Driver(s)	Miles Led	Laps Led
1	McLaren	Hakkinen, Coulthard	1654.79	528
2	Ferrari	Schumacher, Irvine, Salo	904.76	311
3	Stewart	Barrichello, Herbert	225.57	84

Team	Driver(s)		Miles Led	Laps Led
4	Jordan	Hill, Frentzen	201.42	65
5	Williams	R.Schumacher	22.37	8
6	Benetton	Fisichella	11.19	4

1999-2000 DRIVERS' ALL-TIME RECORDS

Driver	No	WC	1	2	3	4	5	6	P	F	TP	B
Alesi, J.	167	0	1	16	15	11	14	9	2	4	236	1
Badoer, L.	49	0	0	0	0	0	0	0	0	0	0	7
Barrichello, R.	112	0	0	2	4	9	9	4	2	0	77	2
Coulthard, D.	90	0	6	18	6	4	6	5	8	11	221	1
de la Rosa, P.	16	0	0	0	0	0	1	0	0	1	6	
Diniz, P.	82	0	0	0	0	0	2	6	0	0	10	5
Fisichella, G.	57	0	0	4	1	4	3	3	1	1	49	2
Frentzen, H-H.	97	0	3	3	9	11	8	9	2	6	142	1
Gene, M.	16	0	0	0	0	0	0	1	0	0	1	6
Hakkinen, M.	128	2	14	7	15	8	9	6	21	13	294	1
Heidfeld, N.	0	0	0	0	0	0	0	0	0	0	0	0
Herbert, J.	143	0	3	1	3	11	6	5	0	0	98	1
Hill, D.	115	1	22	15	5	7	2	5	20	19	360	1
Irvine, E.	96	0	4	6	14	8	6	5	0	1	173	1
Panis, O.	90	0	1	3	1	3	4	7	0	0	56	1
Salo, M.	76	0	0	1	1	1	5	2	0	0	25	2
Sarrazin, S.	1	0	0	0	0	0	0	0	0	0	0	–
Schumacher, M.	126	2	35	22	14	6	5	4	23	39	570	1
Schumacher, R.	49	0	0	2	4	5	8	3	0	1	62	2
Takagi, T.	32	0	0	0	0	0	0	0	0	0	0	7
Trulli, J.	44	0	0	1	0	1	0	2	0	0	11	2
Villeneuve, J.	65	1	11	5	5	3	4	3	13	9	180	1
Wurz, A.	35	0	0	0	1	5	2	1	0	1	24	3
Zanardi, A.	41	0	0	0	0	0	0	1	0	0	1	6
Zonta, R.	12	0	0	0	0	0	0	0	0	0	0	8

*No=Number of Grands Prix; WC=Number of World Championship titles;
1, 2, etc.=Number of times finished in this position; P=Number of Poles;
F=Number of Fastest Laps; TP=Total number of World Championship
Points won to date; B=Best position achieved – this is included primarily
for those drivers who have not had a top six finish.*

1999 DRIVERS BY COMPLETION %

	St	Cm	Rt	Fs	Hp	Pd	Pts	Psn	Comp
Irvine	16	15	1	0	1	9	74	2/24	93.75
Frentzen	16	13	3	0	1	6	54	3/24	81.25
Schumacher,M.	11	8	2	1	1	6	44	5/24	80.00
Salo	9	7	2	0	2	2	10	10/24	77.78
Schumacher,R.	16	12	4	0	2	3	35	6/24	75.00
Hakkinen	16	11	5	0	1	10	76	1/24	68.75
Panis	16	11	5	0	6	0	2	15/24	68.75
Barrichello	16	11	4	0	3	3	21	7/24	68.75
Fisichella	16	10	6	0	2	1	13	9/24	62.50
Wurz	16	10	6	0	5	0	3	13/24	62.50
Gene	16	10	6	0	6	0	1	17/24	62.50
Herbert	15	9	5	1	1	1	15	8/24	60.00
Coulthard	16	9	7	0	1	6	48	4/24	56.25
Trulli	15	8	7	1	2	1	7	11/24	53.33
Alesi	16	8	8	0	6	0	2	15/24	50.00
Hill	16	7	9	0	4	0	7	11/24	43.75
Badoer	15	6	9	0	8	0	0	–	40.00
Zonta	13	5	7	1	8	0	0	–	38.46
Zanardi	16	6	10	0	7	0	0	–	37.50
de la Rosa	16	5	11	0	6	0	1	17/24	31.25
Takagi	16	5	10	0	7	0	0	–	31.25
Diniz	16	4	12	0	6	0	3	13/24	25.00
Villeneuve	16	4	12	0	8	0	0	–	25.00
Sarrazin	1	0	1	0	–	0	0	–	0.00

*St=Number of starts; Cm=Races completed; Rt=Races retired in;
Fs=Races failed to start for (ie, outside 107% rule or dns); Hp=Highest
position achieved in a race; Pd=Number of Podium finishes;
Pts=Drivers' World Championship points; Psn=Position in DWC table;
Comp%=Race completion percentage.*

1999 TEAMS BY COMPLETION %

	St	Cm	Rt	Fq	Hp	Pd	Pts	Psn	Comp%
Ferrari	31	28	4	0	1	17	128	1/11	90.32
Stewart	31	20	11	0	1	4	36	4/11	64.52
Benetton	32	20	12	0	2	1	16	6/11	62.50
Jordan	32	20	12	0	1	6	61	3/11	62.50
McLaren	32	20	12	0	1	16	124	2/11	62.50
Prost	31	19	12	1	2	1	9	7/11	61.29

	St	Cm	Rt	Fq	Hp	Pd	Pts	Psn	Comp%
Williams	32	18	14	0	2	3	35	5/11	56.25
Minardi	32	16	16	0	6	0	1	9/11	50.00
Sauber	32	12	20	0	6	0	5	8/11	37.50
BAR	31	11	20	0	7	0	0	–	35.48
Arrows	32	10	21	0	6	0	1	9/11	31.25

St=Number of starts; Cm=Races completed; Rt=Races retired in; Fq=Races failed to qualify for (ie, outside 107% rule); Hp=Highest position achieved in a race; Pd=number of podium finishes; Pts=Constructors' World Championship points; Psn=Position in CWC table; Comp%=Race completion percentage.

6-YEAR DRIVER POINTS RECORDS

Driver	1994	1995	1996	1997	1998	1999
Alesi, J.	24	42	47	36	9	2
Badoer, L.	–	0	0	–	–	0
Barrichello, R.	19	11	14	6	4	21
Coulthard, D.	14	49	18	36	56	48
de la Rosa, P.	–	–	–	–	–	1
Diniz, P.	–	0	0	2	3	3
Fisichella, G.	–	–	0	20	16	13
Frentzen, H-H.	7	15	7	42	17	54
Gene, M.	–	–	–	–	–	1
Hakkinen, M.	26	17	31	27	100	76
Heidfeld, N.	–	–	–	–	–	–
Herbert, J.	–	45	4	15	1	15
Hill, D.	91	69	97	7	20	7
Irvine, E.	6	10	11	24	47	74
Panis, O.	9	16	13	16	0	2
Salo, M.	–	5	5	2	3	10
Sarrazin, S.	–	–	–	–	–	0
Schumacher, M.	92	102	59	78	86	44
Schumacher, R.	–	–	–	13	14	35
Takagi, T.	–	–	–	–	0	0
Trulli, J.	–	–	–	3	1	7
Villeneuve, J.	–	–	78	81	21	0
Wurz, A.	–	–	–	4	17	3
Zanardi, A.	0	–	–	–	–	–
Zonta, R.	–	–	–	–	–	0

– indicates driver did not participate. List is of drivers who competed in 1999 season or who will compete in 2000 season.

DRIVERS' WORLD CHAMPIONSHIP
WINNERS 1950-1999

R=Races; W=Wins; P=Poles; F=Fastest laps

Year	Driver	Age	Ctry	Car	R	W	P	F
1950	Giuseppe Farina	44	Ita	Alfa Romeo	7	3	2	3
1951	Juan-Manuel Fangio	40	Arg	Alfa Romeo	8	3	4	5
1952	Alberto Ascari	34	Ita	Ferrari	8	6	5	5
1953	Alberto Ascari	35	Ita	Ferrari	9	5	6	4
1954	Juan-Manuel Fangio	43	Arg	Merc/Maserati	9	6	5	3
1955	Juan-Manuel Fangio	44	Arg	Mercedes	7	4	3	3
1956	Juan-Manuel Fangio	45	Arg	Lancia/Ferrari	8	3	5	3
1957	Juan-Manuel Fangio	46	Arg	Maserati	8	4	4	2
1958	Mike Hawthorn	29	GB	Ferrari	11	1	4	5
1959	Jack Brabham	33	Aus	Cooper	9	2	1	1
1960	Jack Brabham	34	Aus	Cooper	10	5	3	3
1961	Phil Hill	34	USA	Ferrari	8	2	5	2
1962	Graham Hill	33	GB	BRM	9	4	1	3
1963	Jim Clark	27	GB	Lotus	10	7	7	6
1964	John Surtees	30	GB	Ferrari	10	2	2	2
1965	Jim Clark	29	GB	Lotus	10	6	6	6
1966	Jack Brabham	40	Aus	Brabham	9	4	3	1
1967	Denis Hulme	31	NZ	Brabham	11	2	0	2
1968	Graham Hill	39	GB	Lotus	12	3	2	0
1969	Jackie Stewart	30	GB	Matra	11	6	2	5
1970	Jochen Rindt	28	Aut	Lotus	13	5	3	1
1971	Jackie Stewart	32	GB	Tyrrell	11	6	6	3
1972	Emerson Fittipaldi	26	Bra	Lotus	12	5	3	1
1973	Jackie Stewart	34	Bra	Tyrrell	15	5	3	1
1974	Emerson Fittipaldi	28	Bra	McLaren	15	3	2	0
1975	Niki Lauda	26	Aut	Ferrari	14	5	9	2
1976	James Hunt	29	GB	McLaren	16	6	8	2
1977	Niki Lauda	28	Aut	Ferrari	17	3	2	3
1978	Mario Andretti	38	USA	Lotus	16	6	8	3
1979	Jody Scheckter	29	USA	Ferrari	15	3	1	1
1980	Alan Jones	34	Aus	Williams	14	5	3	5
1981	Nelson Piquet	29	Bra	Brabham	15	3	4	1
1982	Keke Rosberg	34	Fin	Williams	16	1	1	0
1983	Nelson Piquet	31	Bra	Brabham	15	3	1	4
1984	Niki Lauda	35	Aut	McLaren	16	5	0	5
1985	Alain Prost	30	Fra	McLaren	16	5	2	5

Year	Driver	Age	Ctry	Car	R	W	P	F
1986	Alain Prost	31	Fra	McLaren	16	4	1	2
1987	Nelson Piquet	35	Bra	Williams	16	3	4	4
1988	Ayrton Senna	28	Bra	McLaren	16	8	13	3
1989	Alain Prost	34	Fra	McLaren	16	4	2	5
1990	Ayrton Senna	30	Bra	McLaren	16	6	10	2
1991	Ayrton Senna	31	Bra	McLaren	16	7	8	2
1992	Nigel Mansell	39	GB	Williams	16	9	14	8
1993	Alain Prost	38	Fra	Williams	16	7	13	6
1994	Michael Schumacher	25	Ger	Benetton	16	8	6	8
1995	Michael Schumacher	26	Ger	Benetton	17	9	4	8
1996	Damon Hill	36	GB	Williams	16	8	9	5
1997	Jacques Villeneuve	26	Can	Williams	17	7	11	3
1998	Mika Hakkinen	30	Fin	McLaren	16	9	10	7
1999	Mika Hakkinen	31	Fin	McLaren	16	5	11	6

DRIVERS' WORLD CHAMPIONSHIP
WINS BY NUMBER 1950-99

Titles	Driver	Country	Year
5	Juan-Manuel Fangio	Argentina	1951, 1954, 1955, 1956, 1957
4	Alain Prost	France	1985, 1986, 1989, 1993
3	Jack Brabham	Australia	1959, 1960, 1966
3	Jackie Stewart	Great Britain	1969, 1971, 1973
3	Niki Lauda	Austria	1975, 1977, 1984
3	Nelson Piquet	Brazil	1981, 1983, 1987
3	Ayrton Senna	Brazil	1988, 1990, 1991
2	Alberto Ascari	Italy	1952, 1953
2	Graham Hill	Great Britain	1962, 1968
2	Jim Clark	Great Britain	1963, 1965
2	Emerson Fittipaldi	Brazil	1972, 1974
2	Michael Schumacher	Germany	1994, 1995
2	Mika Hakkinen	Finland	1998, 1999
1	Giuseppe Farina	Italy	1950
1	Mike Hawthorn	Great Britain	1958
1	Phil Hill	USA	1961
1	John Surtees	Great Britain	1964
1	Denis Hulme	New Zealand	1967
1	Jochen Rindt	Austria	1970
1	James Hunt	Great Britain	1976

Titles	Driver	Country	Year
1	Mario Andretti	USA	1978
1	Jody Scheckter	USA	1979
1	Alan Jones	Australia	1980
1	Keke Rosberg	Finland	1982
1	Nigel Mansell	Great Britain	1992
1	Damon Hill	Great Britain	1996
1	Jacques Villeneuve	Canada	1997

DRIVERS WITH 100 WORLD CHAMPIONSHIP POINTS OR MORE

Driver	Points	GPs	Driver	Points	
Prost	768.5	199	Arnoux	181	149
Senna	610	161	Ickx	181	116
Schumacher, M.	570	126	Andretti, Mario	180	128
Piquet	481.5	204	Surtees	180	111
Mansell	480	187	Villeneuve, J.	180	65
Lauda	420.5	171	Hunt	179	92
Berger	385	210	Irvine	173	96
Hill, D.	360	115	Watson	169	152
Stewart, Jackie	359	99	Rosberg	159.5	114
Reutemann	298	146	Frentzen	142	97
Hakkinen	294	128	Depailler	139	95
Fittipaldi, E.	281	144	Gurney	133	86
Patrese	281	256	Boutsen	132	163
Hill, G.	270	176	de Angelis	122	108
Clark	255	72	Farina	115.33	33
Brabham, J.	253	126	Hawthorn	112.64	45
Hulme	248	112	Ascari	107.64	31
Scheckter, J.	246	112	Rindt	107	60
Fangio	244.5	51	Tambay	103	114
Alesi	236	167	Ginther	102	52
Laffite	228	176	Villeneuve, G.	101	67
Coulthard	221	90	Pironi	101	70
Regazzoni	209	132			
Peterson	206	123	*Current drivers bubbling under:*		
Jones	199	116	Herbert	98	143
McLaren	188.5	100	*NB: Points are points scored*		
Moss	185.64	66	*towards drivers world*		
Alboreto	185.5	194	*championship totals only.*		

DRIVERS WITH FIVE OR MORE GRAND PRIX WINS

Wins	Driver
51	Alain Prost (France)
41	Ayrton Senna (Brazil)
35	Michael Schumacher (Germany)
31	Nigel Mansell (Great Britain)
27	Jackie Stewart (Great Britain),
25	Jim Clark (Great Britain), Niki Lauda (Austria)
24	Juan-Manuel Fangio (Italy)
23	Nelson Piquet (Brazil)
22	Damon Hill (Great Britain)
16	Stirling Moss (Great Britain)
14	Jack Brabham (Australia), Emerson Fittipaldi (Brazil), Graham Hill (Great Britain), Mika Hakkinen (Finland)
13	Alberto Ascari (Italy)
12	Mario Andretti (USA), Alan Jones (Australia), Carlos Reutemann (Argentina)
11	Jacques Villeneuve (Canada)
10	James Hunt (Great Britain), Ronnie Peterson (Switzerland), Jody Scheckter (USA), Gerhard Berger (Austria)
8	Denis Hulme (New Zealand), Jacky Ickx (Belgium)
7	Rene Arnoux (France)
6	Tony Brooks (Great Britain), Jacques Laffite (France), Riccardo Patrese (Italy), Jochen Rindt (Austria), John Surtees (Great Britain), Gilles Villeneuve (Canada), David Coulthard (Great Britain)
5	Michele Alboreto (Italy), Giuseppe Farina (Italy), Clay Regazzoni (Switzerland), Keke Rosberg (Finland), John Watson (Great Britain)

DRIVERS WITH FIVE OR MORE POLE POSITIONS

Poles	Driver
65	Ayrton Senna (Brazil)
33	Jim Clark (Great Britain), Alain Prost (France)
32	Nigel Mansell (Great Britain)
29	Juan-Manuel Fangio (Italy)
24	Niki Lauda (Austria), Nelson Piquet (Brazil)

23	Michael Schumacher (Germany)
21	Mika Hakkinen (Finland)
20	Damon Hill (Great Britain)
18	Mario Andretti (USA), Rene Arnoux (France)
17	Jackie Stewart (Great Britain)
16	Stirling Moss (Great Britain)
14	Giuseppe Farina (Italy), James Hunt (Great Britain), Ronnie Peterson (Switzerland)
13	Jack Brabham (Australia), Graham Hill (Great Britain), Jacky Ickx (Belgium), Jacques Villeneuve (Canada)
12	Gerhard Berger (Austria)
10	Jochen Rindt (Austria)
8	Riccardo Patrese (Italy), John Surtees (Great Britain), David Coulthard (Great Britain)
7	Jacques Laffite (France)
6	Emerson Fittipaldi (Brazil), Phil Hill (USA), Jean-Pierre Labouille (France), Alan Jones (Australia), Carlos Reutemann (Argentina)
5	Chris Amon (New Zealand), Giuseppe Farina (Italy), Clay Regazzoni (Switzerland), Keke Rosberg (Finland), Patrick Tambay (France)

DRIVERS WITH FIVE OR MORE FASTEST LAPS

No	Driver
41	Alain Prost (France)
39	Michael Schumacher (Germany)
30	Nigel Mansell (Great Britain)
28	Jim Clark (Great Britain)
24	Niki Lauda (Austria)
23	Juan-Manuel Fangio (Italy), Nelson Piquet (Brazil)
21	Gerhard Berger (Austria)
19	Stirling Moss (Great Britain), Ayrton Senna (Brazil), Damon Hill (Great Britain)
15	Clay Regazzoni (Switzerland), Jackie Stewart (Great Britain)
14	Jacky Ickx (Belgium)
13	Alan Jones (Australia), Riccardo Patrese (Italy), Mika Hakkinen (Finland)
12	Rene Arnoux (France), Alberto Ascari (Italy), Jack Brabham (Great Brirain)
11	John Surtees (Great Britain), David Coulthard (Great Britain)

10	Mario Andretti (USA), Graham Hill (Great Britain)
9	Denis Hulme (New Zealand), Ronnie Peterson (USA), Jacques Villeneuve (Canada)
8	James Hunt (Great Britain), Gilles Villeneuve (Canada)
6	Giuseppe Farina (Italy), Emerson Fittipaldi (Brazil), Dan Gurney (USA), Mike Hawthorn (Great Britain), Phil Hill (USA), Jacques Laffite (France), Carlos Reutermann (Argentina), Heinz-Harald Frentzen (Germany)
5	Michele Alboreto (Italy), Jose Gonzalez (Argentina), Nino Farina (Italy), Carlos Pace (Brazil), Didier Pironi (France), John Watson (Great Britain), Jody Scheckter (USA), John Watson (Great Britain)

DRIVERS WITH MORE THAN FIVE POLE POSITIONS IN A SEASON

Poles	Races	Driver	Year(s)
14	16	Mansell	1992
13	16/16	Senna	1988 and 1989
	16	Prost	1993
11	16	Hakkinen	1999
10	16	Senna	1990
	17	Villeneuve, J.	1997
9	15/14	Lauda	1974 and 1975
	15	Peterson	1973
	16	Piquet	1984
	16	Hill, Damon	1996
	16	Hakkinen	1998
8	16/16	Senna	1986 and 1991
	16	Hunt	1976
	16	Andretti	1978
	16	Mansell	1987
7	10	Clark	1963
	17	Andretti	1977
	16	Senna	1985
	17	Hill, Damon	1995
6	9/10/11	Clark	1962, 1965 and 1967
	9	Ascari	1953
	11	Stewart	1971
	17	Hunt	1977
	16	Schumacher, M.	1994

DRIVERS WITH THREE OR MORE SUCCESSIVE GRAND PRIX WINS

Wins	Driver	Year	Grand Prix
9	Ascari	1952/53	Bel, Fra, GB, Ger, Hol, Ita/ Arg, Hol, Bel
5	Brabham	1960	Hol, Bel, Fra, GB, Por
	Clark	1965	Bel, Fra, GB, Hol, Ger
	Mansell	1992	SA, Mex, Bra, Esp, San
4	Senna	1988	GB, Ger, Hon, Bel
		1991	USA, Bra, San, Mon
	Fangio	1953/54	Ita/Arg, Bel, Fra
	Clark	1963	Bel, Hol, Fra, GB
	Brabham	1966	Fra, GB, Hol, Ger
	Rindt	1970	Hol, Fra, GB, Ger
	Prost	1993	Can, Fra, GB, Ger
	M. Schumacher	1994	Bra, Pac, San, Mon
3	Fangio	1954	Ger, Sui, Ita
		1957	Arg, Mon, Fra
	Stewart	1969	Hol, Fra, GB
		1971	Fra, GB, Ger
	Lauda	1975	Mon, Bel, Swe
		1975/76	USA/Bra, SA
	Jones	1979	Ger, Aut, Hol
		1980/81	Can, USAE/USAW
	Prost	1984/85	Eur, Por/Bra
		1990	Mex, Fra, GB
	Mansell	1991	Fra, GB, Ger
		1992	Fra, GB, Ger
	Moss	1957/58	Pes, Ita/Arg
	Clark	1967/68	USA, Mex/SA
	Senna	1989	San, Mon, Mex
	D. Hill	1993	Hun, Bel, Ita
		1994	Bel, Ita, Por
		1996	Aus, Bra, Arg
	M. Schumacher	1995	Eur, Pac, Jap
		1998	Can, Fra, GB

DRIVERS WHO HAVE CONTESTED 100 GRANDS PRIX OR MORE

No	Driver
256	Riccardo Patrese (Ita)
210	Gerhard Berger (Aut)
208	Andrea de Cesaris (Ita)
204	Nelson Piquet (Bra)
199	Alain Prost (Fra)
194	Michele Alboreto (Ita)
187	Nigel Mansell (GB)
176	Graham Hill (GB), Jacques Laffite (Fra)
171	Niki Lauda (Aut)
167	Jean Alesi (Fra)
163	Thierry Boutsen (Bel)
161	Ayrton Senna (Bra)
158	Martin Brundle (GB)
152	John Watson (GB)
149	Rene Arnoux (Fra)
146	Carlos Reutemann (Arg), Derek Warwick (GB)
144	Emerson Fittipaldi (Bra)
143	Johnny Herbert (GB)
134	Jean-Pierre Jarier (Fra)
132	Eddie Cheever (USA), Clay Regazzoni (Swi)
128	Mario Andretti (USA), Mika Hakkinen (Fin)
126	Jack Brabham (Aus), Michael Schumacher (Ger)
123	Ronnie Peterson (USA)
118	Pierluigi Martini (Ita)
116	Jacky Ickx (Bel), Alan Jones (Aus)
115	Damon Hill (GB)
114	Patrick Tambay (Fra), Keke Roseberg (Fin)
112	Denis Hulme (NZ), Jody Scheckter (USA), Rubens Barrichello (Bra)
111	John Surtees (GB)
109	Philippe Alliot (Fra)
108	Elio de Angelis (Ita)
105	Jochen Mass (Ger)
104	Joakim Bonnier † (Swi)
100	Bruce McLaren (NZ)

† including shared drives.

DRIVERS TO HAVE WON THEIR FIRST GRAND PRIX

Drivers	Year	Grand Prix	Car	Grid
Baghelti	1961	French	Ferrari	12
Farina †	1950	British	Alfa Romeo	1
Parsons	1950	Indianapolis	Kurtis Kraft	5

† Farina also took pole and fastest lap – the only driver to do so in his first Grand Prix start!

DRIVERS TO HAVE COME SECOND IN THEIR FIRST GRAND PRIX

Drivers	Year	Grand Prix	Car	Grid
Amick,G.	1958	Indianapolis 500	Epperly	25
Ascari	1950	Monaco	Ferrari	7
Fagioli	1950	British	Alfa Romeo	2
Holland	1950	Indianapolis 500	Deidt	10
Kling	1954	French	Mercedes	2
Nazaruk	1951	Indianapolis 500	Kurtis Kraft	7
Parkes	1966	French	Ferrari	3
Serafini	1950	Italian	Ferrari	6
Villeneuve,J.	1996	Australian	Williams-Renault	1

DRIVERS TO WIN THEIR NATIONAL GRAND PRIX

Wins	Driver	Nat	Year(s)
6	Prost	French	1981, 1983, 1988, 1989, 1990, 1993
5	Clark	British	1962, 1963, 1964, 1965, 1967
4	Fangio	Argentine	1954, 1955, 1956, 1957
	Mansell	British	1986, 1987, 1991, 1992
2	Ascari	Italian	1951, 1952
	Moss	British	1955, 1957
	Stewart	British	1969, 1971
	Fittipaldi, E.	Brazilian	1973, 1974
	Piquet	Brazilian	1983, 1986
	Senna	Brazilian	1991, 1993
1	Farina	Italian	1950
	Collins	British	1958
	Scarfiotti	Italian	1966
	Pace	Brazilian	1975
	Scheckter	S. African	1975
	Andretti	American	1977
	Hunt	British	1977
	Villeneuve, G.	Canadian	1978
	Jabouille	French	1979
	Watson	British	1981
	Arnoux	French	1982

Wins	Driver	Nat	Year(s)
	Lauda	Austrian	1984
	Hill, Damon	British	1994
	Herbert	British	1995
	Schumacher, M.	German	1995
	Coulthard	British	1999

GRANDS PRIX WITH DRIVER FATALITIES

Year	GP	Venue	Driver	Car	During
1954	Germany	Nurburgring	O. Marimon	Maserati	P
1955	Indianapolis	Indianapolis	B. Vukovich		R
1958	France	Reims	L. Musso	Ferrari	R
1958	Germany	Nurburgring	P. Collins	Ferrari	R
1958	Morocco	Casablanca	S. Lewis-Evans	Vanwall	R
1959	Indianapolis	Indianapolis	J. Unser		R
			B. Cortner		R
1960	Belgium	Spa-Fran.	C. Bristow	Cooper	R
			A. Stacey	Lotus	R
1961	Italy	Monza	Von Trips	Ferrari	R
1964	Germany	Nurburgring	C. de Beaufort	Porsche	P
1966	Germany	Nurburgring	J. Taylor	Brabham	R
1967	Monaco	Monaco	L. Bandini	Ferrari	†R
1968	France	Rouen	J. Schlesser	Honda	R
1969	Germany	Nurburgring	G. Mitter		P
1970	Holland	Zandvoort	P. Courage	De Tomaso	R
1970	Italy	Monza	J. Rindt	Lotus	P
1973	Holland	Zandvoort	R. Williamson	March	R
1973	USA	Watkins Glen	F. Cevert	Tyrrell	P
1974	USA	Watkins Glen	H. Koinigg	Surtees	R
1975	Austria	Osterreichring	M. Donohue	M-Penske	P
1977	South Africa	Kyalami	T. Pryce	Shadow	R
1978	Italy	Monza	R. Peterson	Lotus	*R
1982	Belgium	Zolder	G. Villeneuve	Ferrari	P
1982	Canada	Montreal	R. Paletti	Osella Ford	R
1994	San Marino	Imola	R. Ratzenberger	Simtek	P
			A. Senna	Williams	R

P=Practice, R=Race
† Died three days after race from burns.
* Died the next day from injuries received during start of race.

CONSTRUCTORS' CUP WINNERS

Year	Team	Year	Team	Year	Team
1958	Vanwall	1973	Lotus	1988	McLaren
1959	Cooper	1974	McLaren	1989	McLaren
1960	Cooper	1975	Ferrari	1990	McLaren
1961	Ferrari	1976	Ferrari	1991	McLaren
1962	BRM	1977	Ferrari	1992	Williams
1963	Lotus	1978	Lotus	1993	Williams
1964	Ferrari	1979	Ferrari	1994	Williams
1965	Lotus	1980	Williams	1995	Benetton
1966	Brabham	1981	Williams	1996	Williams
1967	Brabham	1982	Ferrari	1997	Williams
1968	Lotus	1983	Ferrari	1998	McLaren
1969	Matra	1984	McLaren	1999	Ferrari
1970	Lotus	1985	McLaren		
1971	Tyrrell	1986	Williams		
1972	Lotus	1987	Williams		

CONSTRUCTORS' CUP WINS BY CONSTRUCTOR

Titles	Car	Year(s)
9	Williams	1980, 1981, 1986, 1987, 1992, 1993, 1994, 1996, 1997
	Ferrari	1961, 1964, 1975, 1976, 1977, 1979, 1982, 1983, 1999
8	McLaren	1974, 1984, 1985, 1988, 1989, 1990, 1991, 1998
7	Lotus	1963, 1965, 1968, 1970, 1972, 1973, 1978
2	Cooper	1959, 1960
2	Brabham	1966, 1967
1	Vanwall	1958
1	BRM	1962
1	Matra	1969
1	Tyrrell	1971
1	Benetton	1995

GRAND PRIX WINS PER CAR TYPE

Wins	Car Type	Wins	Car Type	Wins	Car Type
125	Ferrari	9	Maserati,	2	Epperly,
123	McLaren		Matra,		Honda
103	Williams		Mercedes,	1	Eagle,
79	Lotus		Vanwall,		Hesketh,
35	Brabham		Ligier		Penske,
27	Benetton		(Prost)		Porsche,
23	Tyrrell	5	Kurtis Kraft		Shadow,
17	BRM	3	March,		Stewart
16	Cooper		Jordan,		
15	Renault		Watson,		
10	Alfa Romeo		Wolf		

GRANDS PRIX PARTICIPATED PER CAR TYPE

GP	Car Type	GP	Car Type	GP	Car Type
619	Ferrari	113	Sauber	35	Honda
492	McLaren	110	Alfa Romeo	34	Theodore
491	Lotus	104	Shadow	33	Porsche
430	Tyrrell	103	Fittipaldi	28	Vanwall
403	Williams	98	Ensign	25	Eagle
394	Brabham	89	ATS	22	Pacific
375	Prost (Ligier)		(Germany)	20	Rial
337	Arrows	78	Dallara	19	Lola Haas
283	Benetton	71	Maserati	17	Onyx, Forti
237	Minardi	62	Matra	16	Simtek, BAR
227	March	54	Zakspeed	15	Parnelli
197	BRM	52	Hesketh	12	Mercedes
146	Jordan	49	Stewart	11	Forti
149	Lola	48	AGS,	10	Merzario
132	Osella		Larousse	4	Lancia
129	Cooper	47	Wolf		
123	Renault	40	Gordini,		
118	Surtees		Penske		

GRAND PRIX POLE POSITIONS PER CAR TYPE

Poles	Car Type	Poles	Car Type
127	Ferrari	9	Ligier (Prost)
108	Williams	8	Mercedes
107	Lotus	7	Vanwall
103	McLaren	6	Kurtis Kraft
39	Brabham	5	March
31	Renault	4	Matra
16	Benetton	3	Shadow
14	Tyrrell	2	Lancia, Jordan, Watson
12	Alfa Romeo	1	Arrows, Ewing, Honda,
11	BRM, Cooper		Lesovsky, Lola, Porsche,
10	Maserati		Wolf, Stevens, Stewart

GRAND PRIX FASTEST LAPS PER CAR TYPE

Laps	Car Type	Laps	Car Type
136	Ferrari	7	March
111	Williams	6	Kurtis Kraft, Vanwall
90	McLaren	4	Surtees
71	Lotus	2	Eagle, Honda,
42	Brabham		Shadow, Wolf,
38	Benetton		Jordan
20	Tyrrell	1	Lancia, Lesovsky,
18	Renault, Maserati		Watson
15	BRM		
14	Alfa Romeo, Cooper		
12	Matra		
9	Ligier (Prost), Mercedes		

WORLD CHAMPIONSHIP LAST RACE DECIDERS

Year	GP	Circuit	Drivers
1950	Italian	Monza	Farina (30), Fangio (27), Fagioli (24)
1951	Spanish	Pedralbes	Fangio (31), Ascari (25)
1956	Italian	Monza	Fangio (30), Collins (25)*
1958	Morocco	Casablanca	Hawthorn (42), Moss (41)
1959	USA	Sebring	Brabham (31), Brooks (27), Moss (25.5)
1962	S. African	E. London	G. Hill (42), Clark (30)
1964	Mexican	Mexico City	Surtees (40), G. Hill (39), Clark (32)
1967	Mexican	Mexico City	Hulme (51), Brabham (46)
1968	Mexican	Mexico City	G. Hill (48), Stewart (36), Hulme (33)
1974	USA	Watkins Glen	E. Fittipaldi (55), Regazzoni (52), Scheckter (45)
1976	Japanese	Mount Fuji	Hunt (69), Lauda (68)
1981	USA	Las Vegas	Piquet (50), Reutemann (49), Laffite (46)
1982	USA	Las Vegas	Rosberg (44), Watson (39)†
1983	S. African	Kyalami	Piquet (59), Prost (57), Arnoux (49)
1984	Portuguese	Estoril	Lauda (72), Prost (71.5)
1986	Australian	Adelaide	Prost (72), Mansell (70), Piquet (69)
1994	Australian	Adelaide	M. Schumacher (92), D. Hill (91)
1996	Japanese	Suzuka	D. Hill (97), J. Villeneuve (78)
1997	European	Jerez	J. Villeneuve (81), M. Schumacher (78)
1998	Japanese	Suzuka	M. Hakkinen (90), M. Schumacher (86)
1999	Japanese	Suzuka	M.Hakkinen (66), E.Irvine (70)

Finished third in Championship after Moss.   † Finished joint second with Pironi. Numbers in brackets are final points total.

Drivers 2000

Introduction

These pages contain an A-Z of drivers who have been named as teams'
major drivers for the 2000 Grand Prix season plus all the drivers who
featured in the 1999 Grand Prix season. While every attempt has been
made to ensure that this list is as accurate as possible, new drivers may
have come to light after this book went to press. Each entry lists a brief
resumé of each driver's F1 career to date and then provides a summary of
Grand Prix details. This is followed by a list of each of the Grand Prix
races he has competed in. The Grand Prix record shows the race and the
position number achieved, or r for retired. Next to the Points heading is
shown the year, position in Drivers' Championship and points scored.

Team and Driver Number Allocation 2000

No.	Driver	Team-Car
1	Mika Hakkinen (Fin)	McLaren Mercedes MP4-15
2	David Coulthard (GB)	McLaren Mercedes MP4-15
3	Michael Schumacher (Ger)	Ferrari F320
4	Rubens Barrichello (Bra)	Ferrari F320
5	Heinz-Harald Frentzen (Ger)	Jordan Mugen-Honda EJ10
6	Jarno Trulli (Ita)	Jordan Mugen-Honda EJ10
7	Eddie Irvine (GB)	Jaguar Racing
8	Johnny Herbert (GB)	Jaguar Racing
9	Ralf Schumacher (Ger)	Williams BMW FW22
10		Williams BMW FW22
11	Giancarlo Fisichella (Ita)	Benetton Playlife B200
12	Alexander Wurz (Aut)	Benetton Playlife B200
14	Jean Alesi (Fra)	Prost Peugeot AP03
15	Nick Heidfeld Ger)	Prost Peugeot AP03
16	Pedro Diniz (Bra)	Sauber Petronas C19
17	Mika Salo (Fin)	Sauber Petronas C19
18	Pedro de la Rosa (Esp)	Arrows Supertec A21
19		Arrows Supertec A21
20	Marc Gene (Esp)	Minardi M02
21		Minardi M02
22	Jacques Villeneuve (Can)	BAR Honda 002
23	Ricardo Zonta (Bra)	BAR Honda 002

ALESI, Jean   France

1999: Sauber Petronas   *2000: Prost Peugeot*

By the time of the Hungarian Grand Prix Jean Alesi was already talking about his departure from the Swiss based Sauber team, and within a matter of days after the race his move to his native France and the Prost team was signed, sealed and delivered. The 1999 season was not the happiest for Jean – in the ten races up to the Hungaroring he had managed just three finishes, and scored just one championship point.

Unable to get the set-up right for the opening race in Australia, Jean started 16th on the grid and his troubles were completed when his car suffered a transmission failure at the restart of the race. In Brazil Alesi reported the car to be handling better but could not move beyond the seventh row of the grid. His second dnf of the fledgling season came after 27 laps when his gearbox gave up the ghost – this after he had stalled the car during his pit stop.

His first finish and first point of the season came at Imola. It celebrated the team's 100th Grand Prix and was achieved from 13th on the grid. A three-stop strategy paid off for the Frenchman who used the pit lane to move up through the placings. Despite a detour across the grass, he took advantage of a couple of retirements to take the chequered flag in sixth position.

After the lift of a points finish, indeed a finish, Jean's world collapsed again as he went two races without a completion. At Monaco he complained of a lack of grip and slapped a barrier at Casino after his wheels started to lock whenever he changed down through the gears and he retired after a check-up in the pits. The Spanish Grand Prix brought his best grid position thus far and his fifth place came after he had held pole for some time during the qualifying session. During the race he ran as high as third before an electrical problem forced him out after 27 laps.

Eighth on the grid was another respectable starting point for Jean in Montreal, coming in the weekend of his 35th birthday at the venue of his only win in Formula One. However, there were no racing presents on hand from the gods when he was bumped out of the race by Jarno Trulli at the very first corner. In France for his home Grand Prix, everything started to look rosy and he took advantage of the weather conditions to set an early pace, and to earn a starting place on the front row of the grid. During the race the rain poured down to provide conditions that normally see Alesi at his best – not this time though as he spun out on his 25th lap.

At Silverstone Jean was hampered by the restart. Having qualified 10th he made up five positions at the first start but, after the accident to Michael Schumacher, he couldn't repeat the feat at the restart. Throttle problems troubled him throughout the race and, despite a long third pit stop, the problem couldn't be resolved. The Frenchman soldiered on to finish 14th, one lap down.

The Austrian Grand Prix rather typified the season for Jean once again. Having lined up a terrible 17th, he failed to hear his radio requesting him to pit and on a subsequent lap he ran out of even fumes, having completed 49 laps. In Germany, car problems meant lack of practice time and after a fraught qualifying session, Jean found himself with the ignominy of starting from the very last row of the grid, not for any technical violations but simply on merit of times. With 11 retirements during the race, Jean went through the motions to finish in eighth place.

If he was hoping for better fortunes in Hungary, they were short lived. Having at least qualified in a mid-grid 11th place he ran home to finish 16th from 17 finishers. It didn't help that he twice was within a sniff of running out of fuel and suffered a Stop-Go penalty for pit-lane speeding. After the race Jean's disillusionment with his position at the team came to the fore and, in a typically frank press conference, he announced he would be leaving the team at the end of the season. The question of where to was answered within a matter of days when Prost announced they had secured his signature for the 2000 season.

Perhaps that announcement spurred him on a little as he managed two ninth place finishes in the next two events in Belgium and Italy, from positions down the grid, but only managed 35 laps at the European Grand Prix when his gearbox gave up on him. Jean qualified a disappointing 15th in the Petronas home race but managed to get past much of the middle order and was up to an incredible fifth place when he made the first of his two pit stops. After that he ran seventh where he remained to the end. He bowed out for Sauber in Japan, securing only his second point of the season.

His two points represented his worst ever record in a season of F1, worse even than his rookie year in 1989 when he scored eight points. It was a curious end to a two-year relationship with the Swiss team, coming as it did on the back of a first year which seemed so positive for both parties, and came at the end of a decade of F1 driving for the Frenchman. In retrospect he had never quite the cavalier attitude in his two years with Sauber, something that was so characteristic of his years with Ferrari and Benetton. Perhaps the move will be the catalyst for him to recapture his form. Time though is not on his side and this is perhaps his final team and the homecoming is more than appropriate.

Born: 11/6/64, Avignon, France.

Grand Prix 1999 Record

Grand Prix	Grid	Qual Time	Fin	Laps	Race Time	Reason
Australian	16	1:33.910	r	0		transmission
Brazilian	14	1:18.716	r	27		gearbox
San Marino	13	1:28.253	6	61	1:34:33.056	
Monaco	14	1:22.354	r	50		accident
Spanish	5	1:22.388	r	27		electrics
Canadian	8	1:20.459	r	0		accident
French	2	1:38.881	r	24		spin
British	10	1:26.761	14	59	1 lap down	
Austrian	17	1:13.226	-	49		out of fuel
German	21	1:45.962	8	45	1:23:09.885	
Hungarian	11	1:19.390	16	74		out of fuel
Belgian	16	1:52.921	9	44	1:26:56.905	
Italian	13	1:24.591	9	53	1:17:45.121	
European	16	1:21.634	r	35		transmission
Malaysian	15	1:42.522	7	56	1:37:32.902	
Japanese	10	1:39.721	6	52	1 lap down	

1999 Position Summary

Started:	16	Finished:	8
Pole Positions:	0	Fastest Laps:	0
Points:	2		
1st:	0	2nd:	0
3rd:	0	4th:	0
5th:	0	6th:	2

Grand Prix Career Record

Started:	167	(1989-1999)
Completed:	98	58.68%
Retired:	69	41.32%
Points:	236	1989-8/9, 1990-9/13, 1991-7/21, 1992-7/18, 1993-6/16, 1994-5/24, 1995-5/42, 1996-4/47, 1997-3/36, 1998-11/9, 1999-15/2
Point Finishes:	66	39.52%
Pole Positions:	2	1994 (Ita), 1997 (Ita)
Fastest Laps:	4	1991 (USA), 1995 (Mon), 1996 (Arg, Mon)
1st:	1	1995 (Can)
2nd:	16	1990 (USA, Mon), 1993 (Ita), 1994 (GB), 1995 (Arg, San, GB, Eur), 1996 (Bra, Esp, Ger, Ita), 1997 (Can, GB, Ita, Lux)
3rd:	15	1991 (Mon, Ger, Por), 1992 (Esp, Can), 1993 (Mon), 1994 (Bra, Can, Jap), 1996 (Arg, Can, Fra, Hun), 1997 (Esp), 1998 (Bel)

4th:	11	1989 (Fra, Esp), 1991 (Fra, Esp), 1992 (Bra, Aus), 1993 (Por, Aus), 1994 (Esp), 1996 (Bel, Por)
5th:	14	1989 (Ita), 1991 (Hun), 1992 (Ger, Jap), 1994 (Mon), 1995 (Bra, Fra, Por, Pac), 1997 (San, Fra, Jap), 1998 (Arg, Ita)
6th:	9	1990 (San), 1991 (Bra), 1994 (Aus), 1996 (San), 1997 (Bra, Ger), 1998 (San), 1999 (San, Jap)

Year	Team	No.	Grand Prix
1989	Tyrrell-Ford	8	Fra 4, GB r, Ger 10, Hun 9, Ita 5, Esp 4, Jap r, Aus r
1990	Tyrrell-Ford	15	US 2, Bra 7, San 6, Mon 2, Can r, Mex 7, Fra r, GB 8, Ger 11, Hun r, Bel 8, Ita r, Por 8, Esp r, Aus 8
1991	Ferrari	16	US 12, Bra 6, San r, Mon 3, Can r, Mex r, Fra 4, GB r, Ger 3, Hun 5, Bel r, Ita r, Por 3, Esp 4, Jap r, Aus r
1992	Ferrari	16	SA r, Mex r, Bra 4, Esp 3, San r, Mon r, Can 3, Fra r, GB r, Ger 5, Hun r, Bel r, Ita r, Por r, Jap 5, Aus 4
1993	Ferrari	16	SA r, Bra 8, Eur r, San r, Esp r, Mon 3, Can r, Fra r, GB 9, Ger 7, Hun r, Bel r, Ita 2, Por 4, Jap r, Aus 4
1994	Ferrari	14	Bra 3, Mon 5, Esp 4, Can 3, Fra r, GB 2, Ger r, Hun r, Bel r, Ita r, Por r, Eur 10, Jap 3, Aus 6
1995	Ferrari	17	Bra 5, Arg 2, San 2, Esp r, Mon r, Can 1, Fra 5, GB 2, Ger r, Hun r, Bel r, Ita r, Por 5, Eur 2, Pac 5, Jap r, Aus r
1996	Benetton-Renault	16	Aus r, Bra 2, Arg 3, Eur r, San 6, Mon r, Esp 2, Can 3, Fra 3, GB r, Ger 2, Hun 3, Bel 4, Ita 2, Por 4, Jap r
1997	Benetton-Renault	17	Aus r, Bra 6, Arg 7, San 5, Mon r, Esp 3, Can 2, Fra 5, GB 2, Ger 6, Hun 11, Bel 8, Ita 2, Aut r, Lux 2, Jap 5, Eur 13
1998	Sauber-Petronas	16	Aus r, Bra 9, Arg 5, San 6, Esp 10, Mon 12, Can r, Fra 7, GB r, Aut r, Ger 10, Hun 7, Bel 3, Ita 5, Lux 10, Jap 7
1999	Sauber-Petronas	16	Aus r, Bra r, SM 6, Mon r, Esp r, Can r, Fra r, GB 14, Aut r, Ger 8, Hun 16, Bel 9, Ita 9, Eur r, Mal 7, Jap 6

1999: Minardi Ford   *2000: –*

After three years in the F1 wilderness, Luca Badoer returned to Formula 1 racing by joining the Minardi team for the second time. His last season behind a Grand Prix wheel was in 1996 when he was a member of the Forti Ford team that lasted just six races before succumbing to financial pressures. He completed his time after that as a Minardi test driver and more recently as a Ferrari test driver.

Running in the re-designed but uncompetitive Minardi, Luca Badoer was at least a reasonably consistent finisher, although he often crossed the finishing line one to three laps down on the leaders and never looked like improving on his best ever race finish of seventh. Not surprisingly his qualifying runs were invariably way off the pace and although he was always reasonably within the 107% margin, it was never enough to lift him off the back two rows of the grid. Indeed his highest starting position was 19th, although he did record this on a number of occasions.

He started his fourth stint behind the wheel in Australia for his 36th career Grand Prix and, although he did rise as high as 11th during the race, his gearbox failed after 42 laps of the race. Luca was missing for the Brazilian race after breaking a bone in his right hand in an accident when completing his 'day-job' as test driver for Ferrari. It needed surgery.

The San Marino outing provided him with his best finish of the year coming home eighth despite having started in the very last grid position, a good effort considering he was still not totally recovered from his injury. The gearbox problems of Melbourne started to surface during the final laps but he held on for his first finish of the season albeit three laps down. While the gearbox was kept functioning at Imola, it didn't stand the torture of Monaco and failed after 10 laps.

In Spain he spun and stalled the car on lap 51, having started at the back of the grid and having not made much impression on a fairly processional race. Canada and France brought two successive tenth place finishes, one and two laps down respectively, with the former including a Stop-Go penalty for ignoring the blue flags. The British Grand Prix brought a third gearbox failure of the season although there might have been extenuating circumstances after he tangled with Takagi at the second start and had to pit to try and sort out the damage thereafter. However, despite a vain attempt, he didn't manage to re-take to the track.

A succession of low order finishes came in Austria (13th) after digging his nose into the back of Hill's Jordan, Germany (his third 10th of the season) – 14th and two laps down. There then followed four non-finishes at the Belgian, Italian, European and Malaysian Grands Prix, two of which were through mechanical problems and the latter to overheating after debris had found its way into his cooling ducts. The retirement at the Nurburgring came at a point when Luca was running an amazingly high fourth and left him in tears when his chances of a first podium finish disappeared. In Japan for the final race the story was very much the same, starting at the back of the grid and retiring on lap 44 with engine problems.

Luca was clear about the low point of his season – that came when the Ferrari test driver was passed over by Ferrari as the replacement of Michael Schumacher, following the German's accident at Silverstone.
Born: 25/1/71, Montebelluna, Treviso, Italy.

Grand Prix 1999 Record

Grand Prix	Grid	Qual Time	Fin	Laps	Race Time	Reason
Australian	21	1:35.316	r	42		gearbox
San Marino	22	1:30.945	8	59	3 laps down	
Monaco	20	1:23.765	r	10		gearbox
Spanish	22	1:25.833	r	50		spin
Canadian	21	1:22.808	10	67	2 laps down	
French	20	1:46.784	10	71	1 lap down	
British	21	1:28.695	r	6		gearbox
Austrian	19	1:13.606	13	68	3 laps down	
German	19	1:45.917	10	44	1 lap down	
Hungarian	19	1:20.961	14	75	2 laps down	
Belgian	20	1:54.197	r	33		suspension
Italian	19	1:25.348	r	23		accident
European	19	1:22.631	r	53		gearbox
Malaysian	21	1:44.321	r	15		overheating
Japanese	22	1:42.515	r	43		engine

1999 Position Summary

Started:	15	Finished:	6
Pole Positions:	0	Fastest Laps:	0
Points:	0		
1st:	0	2nd:	0
3rd:	0	4th:	0
5th:	0	6th:	0

Grand Prix Record

Started:	49	(1993-1999)
Completed:	23	46.94%
Retired:	26	53.06%
Pole Positions:	0	
Fastest Laps:	0	
1st - 6th:	0	

Best Finish: 7th 1993 (San), 1995 (Can)

Year	Team	No.	Grand Prix
1993	Lola-Ferrari	12	SA r, Bra 12, San 7, Esp r, Can 15, Fra r, GB r, Ger r, Hun r, Bel 13, Ita 10, Por 14
1995	Minardi-Ford	16	Bra r, Arg r, San 14, Esp r, Mon r, Can 7, Fra 13, GB 10, Ger r, Hun 8, Bel r, Ita r, Por 14, Eur 11, Pac 15, Jap 9, (Aus dns)
1996	Forti-Ford	6	(Aus dnq), Bra 11, Arg r, (Eur dnq), San 10, Mon r, (Esp dnq), Can r, Fra r, (GB dnq)
1999	Minardi-Ford	15	Aus r, San 8, Mon r, Esp r, Can 10, Fra 10, GB r, Aut 13, Ger 10, Hun 14, Bel r, Ita r, Eur r, Mal r, Jap r

BARRICHELLO, Rubens   Brazil

1999: Stewart Ford   *2000: Ferrari*

Consistency was something that Rubens Barrichello added to his locker in 1999. Something that undoubtedly drew the attentions of the bosses in Marinello, where he will be based as a Ferrari driver for season 2000 at least. Of course he was aided by a more reliable and more dynamic car thanks to the efforts of his Stewart team and Ford during the close season. This was more than evident just by looking at his grid positions where he was invariably occupying a place within the first four rows and even brought the team their first ever pole position, the second of the Brazilian's career.

After some great early testing, Barrichello arrived in Melbourne for the first race and raced to fourth on the grid, making the most of the Stewart team's new CR1 engine. Ironically an engine fire on the grid meant that the start had to be aborted, which saw Rubens move swiftly into the T-car and then start from the pit lane. From the start he set off on a charge through the back markers and had reclaimed his starting position by the time he pitted just after lap 22. He then received a 10-second Stop-Go penalty when he passed his 2000 team-mate Michael Schumacher before the start line after the Safety Car had peeled away. During that time he set the second fastest lap of the race, but pit stops left him in fifth place for the finish. Two points from a last place start has to be considered an excellent drive, in fact a brilliant drive!

The engine problems experienced on the grid in Australia reappeared in Brazil where another good starting position – third – was lost when the engine failed on lap 43. During his home race he had run as high as second. The third row of the grid was the setting for the start of Rubens' race in San Marino. He gained a place at the start and moved into third by

78

the halfway point by way of single stopping in the race. The start worked and the Brazilian had his first podium of the season. A slightly better qualifying run left him still on the third row in Monaco, but on the inside of the track in fifth position. The race provided the worst placing of the season when he was classified ninth, after going off at Piscine on the penultimate lap.

In Spain the Brazilian dropped to the fourth row of the grid for the first time. From seventh he had a poor start and struggled to make any headway against those in front of him from there on, finishing eighth when it was found the fastening of the plank on the underside of his car was illegal and he was excluded from the race. Canada provided the first official dnf of the season when accident damage put him out after just 14 laps completed. A coming together with Jarno Trulli had left his helmet damaged, which was repaired via a pit stop, but the damage to his steering was too great to allow him to continue.

Everything went right in France. A quick early lap in the qualifying session set a time that eventually proved to be good enough to take that maiden Stewart pole position. Rubens made a great start and kept the lead but then started to look nervy as he was pursued by Coulthard, and he surrendered his lead to the Scot after just six laps. Michael Schumacher initially pushed him back to third where he ultimately stayed to secure his second third place in five races.

There would have been high hopes for the Stewart's home Grand Prix but they weren't quite fulfilled. Understeer was the problem during qualifying and the Brazilian had to settle for seventh on the grid. Looking for a good start he made a poor one and dropped back a place and, despite running in the points at one period, had to settle for a final eighth placing. The Austrian and German races provided consecutive non-finishes. Again, Rubens was more than on the pace in the qualifying sessions, securing his almost habitual place on the third row, but his engine failed on lap 56 while he was running fourth and at Hockenheim a hydraulics failure ended his interest after just six laps.

Things got back on track in Hungary. Qualifying provided him with his worst start position to that point in the season but a terrific start moved him from eighth and, by utilising a one-stop strategy and a first long stint, he was a comfortable third by the time of his first pit stop on lap 40. He dropped to eighth again at his stop but produced two points when those in front of him took their second stops to leave the Brazilian in fifth place.

Despite a late surge in qualifying at the Belgian meeting, to secure seventh, Rubens was never really in the hunt with a strangely uncompetitive car. Lack of grip hampered him much of the way and he came home in his worst position of the season – 10th. He also qualified seventh in Italy and with his car handling much better he managed to get past Coulthard, Salo and Zanardi to finish fourth, holding off a charging Coulthard in the final stages.

At the Nurburgring, Rubens had a great race in different conditions to take the bottom step of the podium – this after a great race that had seen him struggle up from a season's worst 15th place on the grid. Prior to this he had never been outside the top eight – the team's one stop strategy working perfectly.

By now the word about his move to Ferrari for the 2000 season was out on the street and it must have been a big boost for him and he secured two more points in Malaysia with a fifth place finish. His final race in tartan at Suzuka was a low key affair with his car off the pace, qualifying 13th and finishing outside the points in eighth place.

His trawl of 21 points was his best total since coming into Formula One and one of the most interesting facets of the season will be how he integrates with Michael Schumacher. Rubens' contract does not call for him to act as a number two for the team and he will therefore in theory be at liberty to race the German. He has of course been number one at Stewart for the previous three years and invariably the dominant driver. As the 2000 season got underway he still waits to record his first Grand Prix victory. He has come close on a couple of occasions but has looked nervy and seemingly wilted under the pressure. Given the car, he could put that record straight – indeed should – but it is the internal battles he may face that could provide the most intrigue!

Born: 23/5/72, Sao Paulo, Brazil.

Grand Prix 1999 Record

Grand Prix	Grid	Qual Time	Fin	Laps	Race Time	Reason
Australian	4	1:32.148	5	57	1:35:56.357	
Brazilian	3	1:17.305	r	42		engine
San Marino	6	1:27.409	3	61	1:33:46.721	
Monaco	5	1:21.530	9	71		suspension
Spanish	7	1:22.920	dq (8)	–		illegal board fastening
Canadian	5	1:19.930	r	14		accident damage
French	1	1:38.441	3	72	1:59:07.775	
British	7	1:26.194	8	60	1:33:38.734	
Austrian	5	1:12.342	r	55		engine
German	6	1:43.938	r	6		hydraulics
Hungarian	8	1:19.095	5	77	1:47.07.344	
Belgian	7	1:51.974	10	44	1:27:03.799	
Italian	7	1:23.739	4	53	1:17:20.553	
European	15	1:21.490	3	66	1:42:17.180	
Malaysian	6	1:41.351	5	56	1:37:10.790	
Japanese	13	1:40.140	8	52	1 lap down	

1999 Position Summary

Started:	16	Finished:	11	
Pole Positions:	1	Fastest Laps:	0	
Points:	21			
1st:	0	2nd:	0	
3rd:	3	4th:	1	
5th:	3	6th:	0	

Grand Prix Career Record

Started:	112	(1993-1999)
Completed:	54	48.21%
Retired:	26	53.06%
Points:	77	1993-17/2, 1994-6/19, 1995-11/11, 1996-8/14,
		1997-13/6, 1998-12/4, 1999-7/21
Point Finishes:	28	25.00%
Pole Positions:	2	1994 (Bel), 1999 (Fra)
Fastest Laps:	0	
1st:	0	
2nd:	2	1995 (Can), 1997 (Mon)
3rd:	4	1994 (Aus), 1999 (San, Fra, Eur)
4th:	9	1994 (Bra, GB, Ita, Por, Aus), 1995 (Eur),
		1996 (Arg, GB), 1999 (Ita)
5th:	9	1993 (Jap), 1996 (Eur, San, Ita), 1998 (Spa, Can),
		1999 (Aus, Hun, Mal)
6th:	4	1995 (Fra, Bel), 1996 (Ger, Hun)

Year	Team	No.	Grand Prix
1993	Jordan-Hart	16	SA r, Bra r, Eur 10, San r, Esp 12, Mon 9, Can r, Fra 7, GB 10, Ger r, Hun r, Bel r, Ita r, Por 13, Jap 5, Aus 11
1994	Jordan-Hart	15	Bra 4, Pac 3, Mon r, Esp r, Can 7, Fra r, GB 4, Ger r, Hun r, Bel r, Ita 4, Por 4, Eur 12, Jap r, Aus 4
1995	Jordan-Peugeot	17	Bra r, Arg r, San r, Esp 7, Mon r, Can 2, Fra 6, GB 11, Ger r, Hun 7, Bel 6, Ita r, Por 11, Eur 4, Pac r, Jap r, Aus r
1996	Jordan-Peugeot	16	Aus r, Bra r, Arg 4, Eur 5, San 5, Mon r, Esp r, Can r, Fra 9, GB 4, Ger 6, Hun 6, Bel r, Ita 5, Por r, Jap 9
1997	Stewart-Ford	17	Aus r, Bra r, Arg r, San r, Mon 2, Esp r, Can r, Fra r, GB r, Ger r, Hun r, Bel r, Ita 13, Aut 14, Lux r, Jap r, Eur r

1998	Stewart-Ford	15	Aus r, Bra r, Arg 10, San r, Esp 5, Mon r, Can 5, Fra 10, GB r, Aut r, Ger r, Hun r, (Bel dns), Ita 10, Lux 11, Jap r
1999	Stewart-Ford	16	Aus 5, Bra r, San 3, Mon 9, Esp dq, Can r, Fra 3, GB 8, Aut r, Ger r, Hun 5, Bel 10, Ita 4, Eur 3, Mal 5, Jap 8

COULTHARD, David   Great Britain

1999: McLaren Mercedes   *2000: McLaren Mercedes*

In a season where David Coulthard was under pressure (mainly from the media it seemed) to deliver some championship-winning performances, things got off to a bad start. Just one finish in the first four races and only 12 points from the first seven outings provided an air of gloom for his supporters. The Scot always portrayed a positive front, even though it took a serious battering when he ran into the back of team-mate Mika Hakkinen at the start of the Austrian Grand Prix. Despite that, it was invariably mechanical and reliability problems with the car that produced retirements, rather than driving errors by the Scot.

In qualifying David was never off the first two rows but could not shake a pole position mainly because of the electrifying qualifying runs of his team-mate Mika Hakkinen. Three second places on the front row in the opening three races were viewed positively as they provided for all McLaren front rows.

The gearbox was the bane of DC's life for the first two races of the season. For the opener in Melbourne the car got stuck in sixth gear during the 14th lap while in Brazil he lost fifth gear after 22 laps, before the gearbox itself called it a day. Interlagos hadn't started well though – he burned out his clutch on the grid and stalled the car, rejoining the race three laps down.

A second place in San Marino mirrored his grid position, which might have been pole but for two-hundredths of a second. David took over the lead when Hakkinen struck out on lap 17, but fractions of a second in the pit lane cost him the lead as Michael Schumacher got out in front on lap 35. An unexpected trip off at Rivazza cost the Scot crucial time, and with it the chance of regaining first place when Schuey had his second pit stop.

Gearbox gremlins reappeared in Monaco. Having qualified third he lost a place at the start to Irvine and by the 30th lap he was experiencing the problems that caused him to retire on lap 37. But he bounced back well in Spain, improving on his starting position by one place to make it a McLaren one-two, this time out-starting Irvine's Ferrari for a great get-away which he maintained despite some late pressure from Michael.

DC managed his third finish of the season in Canada, but came in one position out of the points. Having qualified a disappointing fourth, the Scot found himself in a constant tussle with Eddie Irvine, and led for one lap when others around him pitted. The emergency of the safety car closed the gaps up but at the restart he tangled with Irvine and lost time when this caused a pit stop. He then had to return for a 10-second Stop-Go penalty after he misread the pit-lane lights. In combination, it all proved too expensive for him to salvage even a point from the race. An alternator failure as early as the 10th lap put him out of the French Grand Prix where he had, for the first time in the season, out-qualified team-mate Hakkinen, with an impressive fourth in the rain that created such a grid upset for the race.

Coulthard went into the British Grand Prix in seventh place in the Drivers' Championship, but emerged in fifth position following his first F1 victory at Silverstone. Starting on the second row, the Scot managed his pit stops to perfection, ultimately taking the lead through them on lap 27. When the final round of stops balanced out he retained first place and finished almost two seconds ahead of the pursuing Irvine.

The roles were reversed in Austria as Coulthard again out-finished his team-mate but this time battled home second to Irvine's Ferrari. It was achieved in a red-faced fashion though as the Scot ran into the back of his team-mate's car on the second corner of the first lap, forcing Hakkinen off and to the back of the field. It was, he said, his worst nightmare, taking his team-mate out and allowing a Ferrari to win. But such is F1 racing. The incident though allowed Coulthard the lead which he held until lap 39 when he came in for fuel and tyres. Irvine pushed and got out in front after Coulthard pitted five laps later and, despite a charge, DC couldn't get close enough to chance taking the lead.

Tyre problems saw Coulthard skip between his and the spare car during qualifying in Germany and as such third place was not a bad starting position for the Hungarian meeting. A clash with Salo saw him pit to replace a damaged wing and his second Stop-Go penalty of the season, this time for chicane-cutting, saw him lose more ground. He battled to fifth place though for two points. In Hungary he repeated his starting position but was slow getting away and dropped places. But pit management helped him regain those lost positions, ultimately getting into second spot and six points after Irvine ran on to the grass late on.

He was back in second place as part of another McLaren front row at Spa and he made a brilliant start to get ahead of Hakkinen by the first corner. The two did touch as they rounded La Source and David must have had memories of Austria. However they stayed on the circuit in a race that the Scot really had to win to maintain any thoughts of a Drivers'

Championship. And so he did, driving a near perfect race in the lead from that point.

The Italian race was a repeat of the German meeting as far as David was concerned. Third on the grid, having a bad start and then making ground to finish fifth. However, with Hakkinen and Irvine not having the best outings, the Scot found himself still only 12 points adrift in the championship points stake. For the European GP, David out-qualified his team-mate for only the second time of the season but lost his advantage at the start as Hakkinen got ahead of him. The wet caused him a number of problems and he ultimately slid off the road on lap 38.

DC arrived in Malaysia knowing that he had to win to keep his slim chances of the championship alive – even then he would need the correct amount of attrition around him. Sitting in third place on the grid behind Irvine but ahead of Hakkinen, it didn't look good, especially as the returning Schumacher backed him up in the opening sectors of the race. The Scot did manage to get past the German on lap five but on his 15th lap he lost fuel pressure and was out of the race and the Drivers' Championship battle.

With Hakkinen shooting for the title, DC's instructions in Japan for the final race of the season were to help with that and fight out the last battle of the season in an effort to ease his McLaren team ahead of Ferrari for the Constructors' Cup. He went some way towards achieving the first but the second went out of the door with his hydraulic system that stopped working on lap 40. There was more controversy after the race when Michael Schumacher accused him of holding him up, just two weeks after he had done the same to DC at Sepang. DC brushed it all off in his own inimitable style and it is clear who would win any psychological war between these two.

DC's war for the 2000 season though may be with his own belief. He has played the perfect team player when called upon and in team manager Ron Dennis he has someone who believes that both drivers should race. Given improved reliability for 2000, his first target must be to start pushing Hakkinen in qualifying and competing on pole position for an equal number of races. If David can do this then the World Championship will be a more realistic target than it has been in the past couple of years.

Born: 27/3/71, Twynholm, Scotland.

Grand Prix 1999 Record

Grand Prix	Grid	Qual Time	Fin	Laps	Race Time	Reason
Australian	2	1:30.946	r	13		gear stuck
Brazilian	2	1:16.715	r	22		gearbox
San Marino	2	1:26.384	2	62	1:33:49.057	
Monaco	3	1:20.956	r	36		oil leak

Spanish	3	1:22.244	2	65	1:34:19.903	
Canadian	4	1:19.729	7	69	1:41:40.731	
French	4	1:40.403	r	9		alternator
British	3	1:25.594	1	60	1:32:30.144	
Austrian	2	1:11.153	2	71	1:28:12.751	
German	3	1:43.288	5	45	1:22:15.417	
Hungarian	3	1:18.384	2	77	1:46:33.242	
Belgian	2	1:50.484	1	44	1:25:43.057	
Italian	3	1:23.177	5	53	1:17:21.085	
European	2	1:20.176	r	37		spun-out
Malaysian	3	1:40.806	r	14		fuel pressure
Japanese	3	1:38.239	r	39		hydraulics

1999 Position Summary

Started:	16	Finished:	9
Pole Positions:	0	Fastest Laps:	3
Points:	48		
1st:	2	2nd:	4
3rd:	0	4th:	0
5th:	2	6th:	0

Grand Prix Career Record

Started:	90	(1994-1999)
Completed:	54	60.00%
Retired:	36	40.00%
Points:	221	1994-8/14, 1995-3/49, 1996-7/18, 1997-3/36, 1998-3/56, 1999-4/48
Point Finishes:	45	50.00%
Pole Positions:	8	1995 (Arg, Ita, Por, Eur, Pac), 1998 (Arg, San, Can)
Fastest Laps:	11	1994 (Ger, Por), 1995 (Bel, Por), 1997 (Can), 1998 (Fra, Aut, Ger), 1999 (Fra, Ger, Hun)
1st:	6	1995 (Por), 1997 (Aus, Ita), 1998 (San), 1999 (GB, Bel)
2nd:	18	1994 (Por), 1995 (Bra, Ger, Hun, Pac), 1996 (Mon), 1997 (Aut, Eur), 1998 (Aus, Bra, Esp, Aut, Ger, Hun), 1999 (San, Esp, Aut, Hun)
3rd:	6	1995 (Fra, GB, Eur), 1996 (Eur), 1998 (Lux, Jap)
4th:	4	1994 (Bel), 1995 (San), 1996 (Can), 1997 (GB)
5th:	6	1994 (Can, GB), 1996 (GB, Ger), 1999 (Ger, Ita)
6th:	5	1994 (Ita), 1996 (Fra), 1997 (Esp), 1998 (Arg, Fra)

Year	Team	No.	Grand Prix
1994	Williams-Renault	8	Esp r, Can 5, GB 5, Ger r, Hun r, Bel 4, Ita 6, Por 2
1995	Williams-Renault	17	Bra 2, Arg r, San 4, Esp r, Mon r, Can r, Fra 3, GB 3, Ger 2, Hun 2, Bel r, Ita r, Por 1, Eur 3, Pac 2, Jap r, Aus r
1996	McLaren-Mercedes	16	Aus r, Bra r, Arg 7, Eur 3, San r, Mon 2, Esp r, Can 4, Fra 6, GB 5, Ger 5, Hun r, Bel r, Ita r, Por 13, Jap 8
1997	McLaren-Mercedes	17	Aus 1, Bra 10, Arg r, San r, Mon r, Esp 6, Can 7, Fra 7, GB 4, Ger r, Hun r, Bel r, Ita 1, Aut 2, Lux r, Jap 10, Eur 2
1998	McLaren-Mercedes	16	Aus 2, Bra 2, Arg 6, San 1, Esp 2, Mon r, Can r, Fra 6, GB r, Aut 2, Ger 2, Hun 2, Bel 7, Ita r, Lux 3, Jap 3
1999	McLaren-Mercedes	16	Aus r, Bra r, San 2, Mon r, Esp 2, Can 7, Fra r, GB 1, Aut 2, Ger 5, Hun 2, Bel 1, Ita 5, Eur r, Mal r, Jap r

de la ROSA, Pedro   Spain

1999: Arrows   *2000: Arrows*

After his first Formula 1 race, Pedro de la Rosa – a former Jordan test driver – must have been thinking that Grand Prix driving was a piece of cake. Positioned 18th on the grid in an uncompetitive car, there were no real surprises to this particular story line for the Australian Grand Prix. However, a good start saw him move up six places, and before the race had reached its halfway point, he was running sixth where he stayed to score his first championship point in his very first race. Not bad! The next three races were a little more true to the sort of form expected with three retirements – all down to mechanical problems. In Brazil the hydraulics went on lap 53 when he was running eighth and again out-performing his more experienced team-mate, Takagi. At Imola his race came to a more abrupt end when he was hit by the Benetton of Alexander Wurz and was forced to retire with a broken suspension after just five laps. In Monaco it was the gearbox that failed almost from the start and he was struggling in last place when it finally gave out after 30 laps of the street circuit. Monaco though had proved difficult for the fledgling driver who could not get beyond 21st place on the grid for the start of the race.

His second finish of the season came at his home Grand Prix in Spain, but despite his local knowledge of the circuit he could only muster an 11th place, but still ahead of Takagi. In Canada it was the transmission that ended hopes of a second consecutive finish, while he came home 11th for the second time in France, although being over one lap down. Ironically he acquired the spot having finished behind his team-mate who was excluded from the final placings.

His British Grand Prix didn't get beyond the starting grid where he remained in 20th place when the restart took place – his gearbox responsible for the second time in the season. In Austria faulty brakes sent him spinning into the gravel while he was running 15th and the German race brought his third consecutive dnf, this time when he spun off having just started his 38th lap. He achieved his fourth finish of the season at the Hungaroring, completing the race two laps down in 15th place. That was to be his final finish for the next four races. In Belgium and Italy retirements came after 35 laps in both with transmission and accident damage problems respectively while at the Nurburgring it was the gearbox that terminated his outing with 11 laps remaining.

Pedro described his qualifying performance at Sepang as the best of the season, although he still only managed a 20th place start and he retired with engine failure a little over half way through the race. The season finished on a more positive note in Japan where he finished in 13th place, two laps down.

Born: 24/02/71, Barcelona, Spain.

Grand Prix 1999 Record

Grand Prix	Grid	Qual Time	Fin	Laps	Race Time	Reason
Australian	18	1:34.244	6	57	1:36:25.976	
Brazilian	17	1:19.979	r	52		hydraulics
San Marino	18	1:29.293	r	5		suspension
Monaco	21	1:24.260	r	30		gearbox
Spanish	19	1:24.619	11	63	1:34:41.268	
Canadian	20	1:22.613	r	22		transmission
French	21	1:48.215	11	71	1 lap down	
British	20	1:28.148	r	0		gearbox
Austrian	21	1:14.139	r	38		brakes
German	20	1:45.935	r	37		accident
Hungarian	20	1:21.328	15	75	2 laps down	
Belgian	22	1:54.579	r	35		transmission
Italian	21	1:26.383	r	35		accident damage
European	22	1:23.698	r	52		gearbox
Malaysian	20	1:43.579	r	30		engine
Japanese	21	1:41.708	13	51	2 laps down	

1999 Position Summary

Started:	16	Finished:	5
Pole Positions:	0	Fastest Laps:	0
Points:	1		

1st:	0	2nd:	0
3rd:	0	4th:	0
5th:	0	6th:	1

Grand Prix Career Record

Started:	16	(1999)
Completed:	5	31.25%
Retired:	11	68.75%
Points:	1	1999-17/1
Point Finishes:	1	6.25%
Pole Positions:	0	
Fastest Laps:	0	
1st-5th:	0	
6th:	1	1999 (Esp)

Year	Team	No.	Grand Prix
1999	Arrows	16	Aus 6, Bra r, San r, Mon r, Esp 11, Can r, Fra 11, GB r, Aut r, Ger r, Hun 15, Bel r, Ita r, Eur r, Mal r, Jap 13

DINIZ, Pedro   Brazil

1999: Sauber Petronas   *2000: Sauber Petronas*

As Pedro arrived in Japan for the final race of the season he had managed just three finishes in the preceding 15 outings. Only Villeneuve in the BAR had a worse completion record out of all the regular starters. Pedro though at least achieved a point in each of those races by coming home sixth. Not the most enviable of records and one that fell when he completed the Japanese Grand Prix in 11th place and one lap down on those finishing in the points.

Qualifying, as in the past, always provided more problems and during that opening period he never once managed to get past the sixth row of the grid, with the seventh or eighth rows being familiar starting points. The first five races all brought dnfs for him and his Sauber. In Melbourne he improved on his 14th placed start to climb to ninth but retired after 27 laps when his gearbox gave up the ghost. Brazil, San Marino and Monaco all saw Diniz starting from 15th place. In Brazil, a relatively good performance saw him move up to sixth position before he tangled with a lapped Takagi to force him to retire after 42 laps. This drive was performed with 19 stitches in his knee after he sustained a biking accident in training on the lead-up to the race in Brazil.

A spin on oil on the track at Imola after 49 laps ended his outing there, although he was already trailing after having to pit to change his steering wheel. Another accident, this time at Monaco, put him out on lap 50, when he crashed out at Ste Devote after suffering brake problems. The roaring 40s continued to haunt him in Spain, with lap 41 being the point at which his gearbox failed after his second stop.

For the start of the Canadian Grand Prix Pedro's hopes can't have been that high. He was lined up in a season's worst 18th place and managed to sneak his way up to 12th during the start. By the midway point he was already occupying the sixth spot and, although he lost this position after the Safety Car came in, he regained it when Frentzen went off in front of him. His first finish and first point of an already long season.

The French Grand Prix saw Pedro produce his best qualifying position to date, albeit a lowly 11th, and he was running there when his drive shaft failed on lap six. Pedro bounced back from that setback with another sixth place finish, this time at the British meeting, helped mainly after Johnny Herbert was pulled in for a Stop-Go penalty. It was same again in Austria with the Brazilian running as high as fifth before settling for sixth and his third point of the season.

The dnfs reappeared at the German and Hungarian races. At Hockenheim another poor qualifying session saw him starting 16th but he was totally innocent when he became a victim of a tangle between Villeneuve and Gene to put him out at the very first corner. At the Hungaroring he bettered his qualifying position by starting 12th but spun out after 19 laps. An accident at the same stage of the Belgian race had the same result while a spin coming out of the chicane in the second lap at Monza, having run wide to avoid Wurz, ended his expectations of a finish there.

The Brazilian experienced what could have been a deadly accident at the Nurburgring when, going through the first corner, he was hit by Wurz, and flipped over to one side. Worryingly the car's roll bar collapsed and Pedro found his head hitting the ground. His helmet suffered damage and indicated just how lucky he had been. In the end all he carried into the penultimate race of the season in Malaysia was a stiff neck that didn't get any better when an early spin into the gravel during qualifying at Sepang restricted Pedro's efforts to his second worst performance of the season in 17th place. He got as high as ninth place before doing the same again on lap 45 and had to retire.

Whether the threat of possible legal action from his former team Arrows, had anything to do with a rotten season only Pedro will know. With a new partner for the 2000 season he will look to get back on the improvement track.

Born: 22/5/70, Sao Paulo, Brazil.

Grand Prix 1999 Record

Grand Prix	Grid	Qual Time	Fin	Laps	Race Time	Reason
Australian	14	1:33.374	r	27		gearbox
Brazilian	15	1:19.194	r	42		accident
San Marino	15	1:28.599	r	49		spin
Monaco	15	1:22.659	r	49		accident
Spanish	12	1:23.331	r	40		gearbox
Canadian	18	1:21.571	6	69	1:41:39.438	
French	11	1:42.942	r	5		drive shaft
British	12	1:27.196	6	60	1:33:23.787	
Austrian	16	1:13.223	6	71	1:29.23.371	
German	16	1:45.335	r	0		accident
Hungarian	12	1:19.782	r	19		spin
Belgian	18	1:53.778	r	19		accident
Italian	16	1:24.596	r	1		spin
European	13	1:21.345	r	0		accident
Malaysian	17	1:42.933	r	44		spin
Japanese	17	1:40.740	11	52	1 lap down	

1999 Position Summary

Started:	16	Finished:	5
Pole Positions:	0	Fastest Laps:	0
Points:	3		
1st:	0	2nd:	0
3rd:	0	4th:	0
5th:	0	6th:	3

Grand Prix Career Record

Started:	82	(1995-99)
Completed:	31	37.25%
Retired:	51	62.20%
Points:	10	1996-15/2, 1997-16/2, 1998-13/3, 1999-13/3
Point Finishes:	8	9.76%
Pole Positions:	0	
Fastest Laps:	0	
1st-4th:	0	
5th:	2	1997 (Lux), 1998 (Lux)
6th:	6	1996 (Esp, Ita), 1998 (Mon), 1999 (Can, GB, Aut)

Year	Team	No.	Grand Prix
1995	Forti-Ford	17	Bra 10, Arg uc, San uc, Esp r, Mon 10, Can r, Fra r, GB r, Ger r, Hun r, Bel 13, Ita 9, Por 16, Eur 13, Pac 17, Jap r, Aus 7

1996	Ligier-Mugen H.	16	Aus 10, Bra 8, Arg r, Eur 10, San 7, Mon r, Esp 6, Can r, Fra r, GB r, Ger r, Hun r, Bel r, Ita 6, Por r, Jap r
1997	Arrows-Yamaha	17	Aus 10, Bra r, Arg r, San r, Mon r, Esp r, Can 8, Fra r, GB r, Ger r, Hun r, Bel 7, Ita r, Aut 13, Lux 5, Jap 12, Eur r
1998	Arrows	16	Aus r, Bra r, Arg r, San r, Esp r, Mon 6, Can 9, Fra 14, GB r, Aut r, Ger r, Hun 11, Bel 5, Ita r, Lux r, Jap r
1999	Sauber-Petronas	16	Aus r, Bra r, San r, Mon r, Esp r, Can 6, Fra r, GB 6, Aut 6, Ger r, Hun r, Bel r, Ita r, Eur r, Mal r, Jap 11

FISICHELLA, Giancarlo   Italy

1999: Benetton Playlife   *2000: Benetton Playlife*

If Giancarlo had a twin brother then you might be forgiven for thinking that his look-alike had taken over his role for the second half of the season. The ever-smiling Italian had the proverbial season of two halves. Consistent and competitive in the first half up to the British Grand Prix – uncompetitive and unreliable in the second part.

In qualifying Giancarlo struggled to maintain any sort of consistency with positions ranging from the third row right down to the tail-enders. What he did do though was to put in some regular points finishes and manage to equal his best ever finish by driving home to second place at the Canadian Grand Prix. A seventh place at Silverstone was the end of the good run of form though, and in the remaining eight races he managed just four finishes and the best of those was recording an eleventh place.

Points came in the opening race and, given that the Italian encountered yellow flags at several points in his qualifying runs, seventh wasn't a bad place to start from on the grid. In the Melbourne sun he made a place at the start and held that until a couple of players retired ahead of him to allow him to cross the finish line in fourth place. Brazil provided his best starting position for the first half of the year – fifth – but it also coincided with his first dnf when his clutch failed after 38 laps.

Understeer hampered GC's qualifying runs at Imola and 16th place on the grid produced an air of gloom for Benetton supporters. But it lifted in the race as Giancarlo weaved his way through the back markers and was up to tenth place before the race had run half its course. From there on he continued to move through the field and by lap 47 was just outside a points position. With just a handful of laps remaining he made the break into the points and finished a strong fifth – rather against the odds. Monaco was a race that mirrored San Marino but this time Giancarlo started ninth, made a good start and managed to finish fifth after drivers in front of him went off in the final laps. Three points finishes from four starts wasn't a bad way to start the season.

Spain proved to be one of the disappointments of the season, coming home tenth but elevated to ninth after Barrichello was excluded. However, there was a massive appearance in Canada where the Italian equalled his best ever finish with a second place. Having crashed during one qualifying run, Giancarlo had little time to improve on his seventh place on the grid. A strong run in the early stages saw him move up the placings and he was on the podium after attrition in front of him.

Back in Europe the French meeting saw his second dnf of the season which was made all the more galling because he spun on lap 43. The next four races provided disappointment. At Silverstone, he was held off by Pedro Diniz in the fight for the final championship point, while in Austria he dropped to a 12th place finish and three laps down after a crash needed a lengthy stop in the pit lane, after which he suffered a blown engine right at the end. Then followed two consecutive dnfs. In Germany his Benetton suspension gave out after just seven laps, following a moment with his team-mate Wurz which required him to pit for a new nose. In Hungary he achieved his best qualifying position for the season – fourth – but it was to no avail as his race came to an end after 52 laps when his engine failed while running in fifth place. He broke the bad run, albeit for just one race, when he started 13th on the grid in Belgium and opting for a one-stop drive, managed to move up to 12th and finished 11th.

In Monza it got even worse as the Italian's race was probably the worst of the season, making it a bad homecoming. Gianny complained that lack of grip was the reason for a season's worst equal 17th on the grid which was improved by a couple of places by the end of his first lap, only for him to spin off at the chicane while on his second circuit. There was a massive reversal in form for the European race even if luck deserted him. Having qualified sixth – his third best position on the grid for the season – Giancarlo drove probably his best race of the season and with the weather playing into his hands, staying on dries while others dabbled with wets, he found himself in the lead with 22 laps remaining. There he stayed until, five laps from a win, he spun out. His anger when exiting the car showed that the spin was down to his own mistake.

Brake problems during qualifying saw Giancarlo line-up 11th on the grid for the Malaysian Grand Prix. Having run into the back of Hill shortly after the start, damaging his suspension in the process, he stayed out to finish four laps down and was eventually classified 11th and the last of the finishers. Things failed to improve for the final race of the season in Suzuka where he qualified 13th and was classified 14th, despite having an engine failure six laps from home.

It was a good year for Giancarlo in that he became a father when his girlfriend Luna gave birth to daughter Carlotta last April. On the macadam the 13 championship points Giancarlo managed was his worst tally in his three years as an F1 driver, but it still represented the majority of the 16 points scored by his team. He remains a driver with potential but there are still question marks about his ability to hold up under pressure. Confidence is key here and things might start to develop further for him if and when he achieves that first all-important Grand Prix win.

Born: 14/1/73, Roma, Italy.

Grand Prix 1999 Record

Grand Prix	Grid	Qual Time	Fin	Laps	Race Time	Reason
Australian	7	1:32.540	4	57	1:35:35.077	
Brazilian	5	1:17.810	r	38		clutch
San Marino	16	1:28.750	5	61	1:34:27.002	
Monaco	9	1:21.938	5	77	1:49:32.705	
Spanish	13	1:23.333	9	64	1:35:22.704	
Canadian	7	1:20.378	2	69	1:41:36.509	
French	7	1:41.825	r	42		spin
British	17	1:27.857	7	60	1:33:24.758	
Austrian	12	1:12.924	12	68	3 laps down	engine
German	10	1:44.338	r	7		suspension
Hungarian	4	1:18.515	r	52		fuel pressure
Belgian	13	1:52.782	11	44	1:27:15.252	
Italian	17	1:24.862	r	1		accident
European	6	1:20.781	r	48		spun-out
Malaysian	11	1:42.110	11	52	4 laps down	
Japanese	14	1:40.261	14	47		engine

1999 Position Summary

Started:	16	Finished:	10
Pole Positions:	0	Fastest Laps:	0
Points:	13		
1st:	0	2nd:	1
3rd:	0	4th:	1
5th:	2	6th:	0

Grand Prix Career Record

Started:	57	(1996-1999)
Completed:	37	64.91%
Retired:	20	35.09%
Points:	49	1997-8/20, 1998-9/16, 1999-9/13
Point Finishes:	15	26.32%
Pole Positions:	1	1998 (Aut)

Fastest Laps:	1	1997 (Esp)
1st:	0	
2nd:	4	1997 (Bel), 1998 (Mon, Can), 1999 (Can)
3rd:	1	1997 (Can)
4th:	4	1997 (San, Ita, Aut), 1999 (Aus)
5th:	3	1998 (GB), 1999 (San, Mon)
6th:	3	1997 (Mon), 1998 (Bra, Lux)

Year	Team	No.	Grand Prix
1996	Minardi-Ford	8	Aus r, Eur 13, San r, Mon r, Esp r, Can 8, Fra r, GB 11
1997	Jordan-Peugeot	17	Aus r, Bra 8, Arg r, San 4, Mon 6, Esp 9, Can 3, Fra 9, GB 7, Ger 11, Hun r, Bel 2, Ita 4, Aut 4, Lux r, Jap 7, Eur 11
1998	Benetton-Playlife	16	Aus r, Bra 6, Arg 7, San r, Esp r, Mon 2, Can 2, Fra 9, GB 5, Aut r, Ger 7, Hun 8, Bel r, Ita 8, Lux 6, Jap 8
1999	Benetton-Playlife	16	Aus 4, Bra r, San 5, Mon 5, Esp 9, Can 2, Fra r, GB 7, Aut 12, Ger r, Hun r, Bel 11, Ita r, Eur r, Mal 11, Jap 14

FRENTZEN, Heinz-Harald   Germany

1999: Jordan Mugen-Honda   2000: Jordan Mugen-Honda
When he was driving for Sauber, Heinz-Harald was often regarded as the driver with the best potential. This was something that Sir Frank Williams was quick to see and took him to the Williams team where, it has to be said, the affable German always looked out of place. Having scored 42 points in his first season, he managed just 17 in 1998 and the rumours were rife of his departure. In came Eddie Jordan and the Buzzin Hornets' yellow proved to be an instant hit. Team-mate Damon Hill was having problems within the team so it was Frentzen who was gathering the majority of the points that kept him and the Jordan team in the race for the higher places in both championships. In short, HH was producing the form that had caught the eye during his three years with the Swiss team.

The season opener could only have been bettered by one place. In his first Jordan drive the German raced home second after he had spent much of the early part of the weekend getting to know the grassier areas of Victoria Park in central Melbourne. Despite the unexpected detours he qualified fifth and built his race from there. The podium was there again in Brazil, this time one step lower but achieved from eighth on the grid. It was a close thing though as Frentzen's car was running on fumes at the end. San Marino provided his first dnf of the season. Having qualified seventh he took a spin on his 47th lap while running fourth. The number four featured in HH's drive in Monaco to complete a set of two, three, four finishes with a neat pit stop moving him up two places from his starting position. Four races gone and 13 championship points recorded.

There were no more points to increase his tally in Spain where he equalled his worst grid position to date (eighth) but was forced out of the race when his differential went on his 36th lap. It was a second consecutive non-finish in Canada where a brake disc ended his effort in Montreal. But it was third time lucky in France where the German came back with a huge drive that saw him almost double his points tally. Starting fifth on the grid, Frentzen moved into fourth spot as the lights went out and, as Alesi and Hakkinen went out, up into second spot which was temporarily lost to Schuey Snr. The front eventually became his when Schumacher and Barrichello went out and left Heinz-Harald to record his and Jordan's second ever Grand Prix win and leave him just three points behind the then third-placed Eddie Irvine. The result was made all the more impressive when it was announced that HH had driven the race with a triple compound fracture in his right leg, which he had sustained during an accident in Montreal.

After that the points continued to flow at a steady pace. For Jordan's home Grand Prix Heinz-Harold stole one place at the start to put him in fourth position and, despite leading the race for a couple of laps, it was the position he eventually finished in after the pit stops had sorted themselves out. It was much the same again in Austria when this time his fourth place came from the second row of the grid, but only after a bad start by the German had been made up on the track.

The preparation for his home Grand Prix in Germany was not good with spins and all sorts of problems hampering his set-up preparations on the Friday. However, these were put behind him so that he started second on the grid, having been ousted by Mika Hakkinen by just 500ths of a second in the dying moments of the qualifying session. A hesitant start dropped him back but he regained position before the pit stops failed to work in his favour. He kept going for a podium finish on the third step. The points lifted him into third place in the Drivers' Championship behind Irvine and Hakkinen.

The Hungarian race provided HH with his fourth fourth place of the season. Having started fifth, he moved up and down the order after his two pit stops, finishing slightly ahead and with another three points. In Belgium he made even better progress by securing third on the grid and held his position to finish on the podium for the fifth time in the season. Clearly on an all-time high, he produced an even better performance in Italy where he secured his second win of the season from the front row of the grid. HH managed to hold his second place at the start and was trailing Hakkinen by some eight seconds when the Finn errored his way out of the race. With three races to go HH was just ten points behind the tied leadership and was clearly the form driver at that point.

From three, to two, to one. At the Nurburgring Heinz-Harold lined up in pole position – only the second of his career – for the European Grand Prix. He shot away at the start and was having a storming race until he suffered an electrical problem and had the frustration of his car grinding to a halt after 32 laps. Despite that, he arrived at Sepang for the penultimate race of the season, having dropped only a further two points behind the leader Hakkinen and knowing it was a make-or-break weekend as far as his Drivers' Championship bid was concerned. Qualifying was a catalogue of disasters, which saw him spin off, lose his headrest and then have to use the T-car that was set-up for Hill. He managed 14th place as his starting point, but it was never going to be good enough to challenge for the victory. As it was he finished sixth and was then elevated to fourth with the exclusion of Schumacher and Irvine.

The final race of the season in Japan again echoed the fours that dominated his season. A fourth place on the grid was mirrored in his finishing position and, with the other finishes and non-finishes going his way, his tally of 54 points was enough to give him third place in the Drivers' Championship and a platform from which to build and at least sustain in season 2000. When HH stops driving for points and starts driving for wins he will be a real championship contendor.

Born: 18/5/67, Mönchengladbach, Germany.

Grand Prix 1999 Record

Grand Prix	Grid	Qual Time	Fin	Laps	Race Time	Reason
Australian	5	1:32.276	2	57	1:35:02.686	
Brazilian	8	1:17.902	3	71	1:35:58.877	
San Marino	7	1:27.613	r	46		spin
Monaco	6	1:21.556	4	78	1:50:25.821	
Spanish	8	1:22.938	r	35		differential
Canadian	6	1:20.158	11	65		brakes
French	5	1:40.690	1	72	1:58:24.343	
British	5	1:25.991	4	60	1:32:57.933	
Austrian	4	1:12.266	4	71	1:29.05.241	
German	2	1:43.000	3	45	1:22:03.789	
Hungarian	5	1:18.664	4	77	1:46:55.351	
Belgian	3	1:51.332	3	44	1:26:16.490	
Italian	2	1:22.926	1	53	1:17:02.923	
European	1	1:19.910	r	32		electronics
Malaysian	14	1:42.380	6	56	1:37:13.378	
Japanese	4	1:38.696	4	53	1:32:57.420	

1999 Position Summary

Started:	16	Finished:	14
Pole Positions:	1	Fastest Laps:	0
Points:	54		
1st:	2	2nd:	1
3rd:	3	4th:	5
5th:	0	6th:	1

Grand Prix Career Record

Started:	97	(1994-1999)
Completed:	63	64.95%
Retired:	34	35.05%
Points:	142	1994-13/7, 1995-9/15, 1996-12/7, 1997-2/42, 1998-7/17, 1999-3/54
Point Finishes:	43	44.33%
Pole Positions:	2	1997 (Mon), 1999 (Eur)
Fastest Laps:	6	1997 (Aus, San, Hun, Lux, Jap, Eur)
1st:	3	1997 (San), 1999 (Fra, Ita)
2nd:	3	1997 (Fra, Jap), 1999 (Aus)
3rd:	9	1995 (Ita), 1997 (Bel, Ita, Aus, Lux), 1998 (Aus), 1999 (Bra, Ger, Bel)
4th:	11	1994 (Fra), 1995 (Bel), 1996 (Mon, Esp), 1997 (Can), 1998 (Bel), 1999 (Mon, GB, Aut, Hun, Jap)
5th:	8	1994 (Pac), 1995 (Arg, Hun), 1998 (Bra, San, Hun, Lux, Jap)
6th:	9	1994 (Eur, Jap), 1995 (San, Mon, GB, Por), 1996 (Jap), 1997 (Eur), 1999 (Mal)

Year	Team	No.	Grand Prix
1994	Sauber-Mercedes	15	Bra r, Pac 5, San 7, (Mon dnq), Esp r, Can r, Fra 4, GB 7, Ger r, Hun r, Bel r, Ita r, Por r, Eur 6, Jap 6, Aus 7
1995	Sauber-Ford	17	Bra r, Arg 5, San 6, Esp 8, Mon 6, Can r, Fra 10, GB 6, Ger r, Hun 5, Bel 4, Ita 3, Por 6, Eur r, Pac 7, Jap 8, Aus r
1996	Sauber-Ford	16	Aus 8, Bra r, Arg r, Eur r, San r, Mon 4, Esp 4, Can r, Fra r, GB 8, Ger 8, Hun r, Bel r, Ita r, Por 7, Jap 6
1997	Williams-Renault	17	Aus 8, Bra 9, Arg r, San 1, Mon r, Esp 8, Can 4, Fra 2, GB r, Ger r, Hun r, Bel 3, Ita 3, Aut 3, Lux 3, Jap 2, Eur 6

1998 Williams-Mecachrome
      16   Aus 3, Bra 5, Arg 9, San 5, Esp 8, Mon r,
            Can r, Fra 15, GB r, Aut r, Ger 9, Hun 5,
            Bel 4, Ita 7, Lux 5, Jap 5
1999 Jordan-Mugen-H. 16   Aus 2, Bra 3, San r, Mon 4, Esp r, Can 11,
            Fra 1, GB 4, Aut 4, Ger 3, Hun 4, Bel 3,
            Ita 1, Eur r, Mal 6, Jap 4

GENE, Marc   Spain

1999: Minardi Ford   *2000: Minardi*

To say Marc Gene was a surprise recruitment for the Minardi team is a bit of an understatement. He spent the 1998 season working in Barcelona as an accountant for Price Waterhouse Cooper, driving in his spare time. That spare time was put to good effect though as he won the open Iberian-based Fortuna by Nissa title. He also had experience as an F3 driver in Britain and sampled F3000 during 1997. However, the size of the jump up into F1 cannot be underestimated.

Officially Gene was outside the 107% qualifying time for his first F1 race in Melbourne, but was allowed to line up at the back of the grid on the basis of his practice times during the sessions on the Friday. His first race though lasted just 25 laps before he spun off and out. The Spaniard seemed to learn from his experiences Down Under and produced two highly creditable ninth places in his next two races. For Brazil he edged himself off the back row but only after Villeneuve had been kicked to the back of the grid. He had an incident-free race home to his first ever completion. He repeated the feat at Imola, this time after having an 'off' after a tussle with Takagi early on.

Monaco and Spain both proved to be disappointing from driver and team. In the south of France, Gene took exception to the tyre wall at Ste Devote and was out of the race with 24 laps completed. In front of his home crowd, he managed to stall the car on the grid and was retired.

An eighth place came in Canada where he managed a lap that was faster than the time he had set during any in his qualifying session. Starting from last place he produced one of his best drives of the season but was a considerable way back from the last points-winning position. A fourth dnf of the season came at Magny-Cours when the rain caught him out as he spun after 25 laps.

The British Grand Prix set him off on his most consistent part of the season with five successive finishes. At Silverstone he came home 15th, pushing Takagi into last spot during the final set of pits stops. In Austria he improved to 11th and was never out of contact with the rest of the middle order field in what was a very good drive. Germany brought even more improvement with a season's best grid position of 15th. He was lucky to remain running after whacking Villeneuve at the first corner, but he came through unscathed and ultimately finished ninth out of the 11 who completed the race.

A fourth completion came in Hungary. Although it was another safe drive for the Spaniard, he came home 17th and last, having made no impression on the race from 22nd on the grid. It was much the same in his next outing at Spa, improving to a 16th place finish and a lap down. At Monza he was involved in two incidents with Arrows cars, the latter when de la Rosa put him out of the race in the very first lap.

Gene drove probably his best race of the season in the wet/dry conditions affecting the Nurburgring during the European Grand Prix. Utilising one stop, he managed to drive through the first downpour on dries. His stop was timed perfectly and with cars retiring in front of him he found himself running in fifth place. The first point of his career was achieved in sixth place though when the charging Mika Hakkinen passed him in the run for home.

His 19th starting place in Malaysia was one of Marc's best positions of the season, and that's what he said when asked about it. It carried through to the start where he had a great get-away and catapulted himself into 12th place after the first corner and finished the race ninth. A gearbox failure finished his season in the final race of 1999, coming on lap 32 of the Japanese race.

Marc Gene will be back in the Minardi for year 2000. He is unlikely to be winning a race, nor is he likely to find a place on the podium, but remember he did score one more point in 1999 than former F1 and Cart World Champion Jacques Villeneuve!

Born: 29/03/74, Sabadell, Barcelona, Spain.

Grand Prix 1999 Record

Grand Prix	Grid	Qual Time	Fin	Laps	Race Time	Reason
Australian	22	1:37.013	r	25		spin
Brazilian	20	1:20.710	9	69	1:37:02.116	
San Marino	21	1:30.035	9	59	3 laps down	
Monaco	22	1:24.914	r	24		accident
Spanish	21	1:25.672	r	0		gearbox
Canadian	22	1:23.387	8	68	1 lap down	
French	19	1:46.324	r	25		spin
British	22	1:28.772	15	58	2 laps down	
Austrian	22	1:14.363	11	70	1 lap down	
German	15	1:45.331	9	45	1:23:46.912	
Hungarian	22	1:21.867	17	74	3 laps down	
Belgian	21	1:54.557	16	43	1 lap down	

Italian	20	1:25.695	r	0		accident
European	20	1:22.760	6	66	1:42:59.468	
Malaysian	19	1:43.563	9	55	1 lap down	
Japanese	20	1:41.529	r	31		gearbox

1999 Position Summary

Started:	16	Finished:	10
Pole Positions:	0	Fastest Laps:	0
Points:	1		
1st:	0	2nd:	0
3rd:	0	4th:	0
5th:	0	6th:	1

Grand Prix Career Record

Started:	16	(1999)
Completed:	10	62.50%
Retired:	6	37.50%
Points:	1	1999-17/1
Point Finishes:	1	
Pole Positions:	0	
Fastest Laps:	0	
1st-5th:	0	
6th:	1	1999 (Eur)

Year	Team	No.	Grand Prix
1999	Minardi-Ford	16	Aus r, Bra 9, San 9, Mon r, Esp r, Can 8, Fra r, GB 15, Aut 11, Ger 9, Hun 17, Bel 16, Ita r, Eur 6, Mal 9, Jap r

HAKKINEN, Mika   Finland

1999: McLaren Mercedes   *2000: McLaren Mercedes*

The anguish that Mika showed on the podium at Sepang in the penultimate race of the season was one of total frustration. It meant that, for the second successive season, he would have to effectively win the final race of the season to win, or in this case, retain the Drivers' Championship title. As Eddie and Michael celebrated a Ferrari one-two in Malaysia, Mika might well have been reflecting on a championship that should have been his with several races to spare. Too many times the Finn had made silly mistakes that might have cost him dearly, especially had not Michael ended his championship charge, embedded in Stowe at Silverstone. Justice was done though, because Mika was by far and above the pick of the bunch in 1999.

The stats speak for themselves – five wins, 11 pole positions, 10 podium appearances and 76 points, not to mention six fastest laps. Indeed, of the

11 races that Mika completed, he never once finished outside of a point-scoring position and was only outside of the top three on one occasion. That sort of consistency proved of paramount importance for Hakkinen, because of the consistency of his nearest challenger Eddie Irvine, who completed all but one of the races on the calendar.

Mika's early season form was key in all of this. Five straight pole positions provided an emphatic message as he dominated the qualifying grid in the season's opening encounters. Indeed his tally of 11 in one season bettered the nine he secured in his 1998 championship season and has only been surpassed by three drivers in the history of F1, and they went by the name of Mansell (14), Senna (13) and Prost (13). Not bad company!

Despite all that, by the time the German Grand Prix arrived Mika found himself trailing Eddie in the championship race – all because he had failed to make it count in four of those first ten races.

For the opening race of the season, reliability proved a problem and he suffered an early setback when he had a heavy crash in the Friday practice. A brilliant final run in qualifying saw him snatch his first pole of the season from his team-mate, David Coulthard, but a misfiring engine forced him into the T-car for the race. The Safety Car wiped out Mika's 17-second advantage after 13 laps and when the race restarted a throttle linkage problem forced him to retire.

Brazil was profitable. Ten points and a first win of the season put the nightmare of Melbourne to bed. Using the harder Bridgestone tyres, Mika led from the off but then dropped to third while suffering a gear change problem which somehow cured itself. Use of the pit lane allowed Mika to get ahead of arch-rival Schumacher Snr and on to the top step of the podium.

For the second time in three races, Mika saw victory slip from his grasp, this time at Imola. Having ousted team-mate Coulthard from pole by the narrowest of margins, he then disappeared into the distance at the race start, he was leading by more than 12 seconds when he edged on to the kerb at Targiardo and slammed into the pit lane wall, bringing his race to a premature end after just 17 laps. The first of several defining mistakes by the World Champion.

Another uncharacteristic mistake in Monaco cost more points, although he did keep his tally moving forward with a third place. Mika out-gunned Schuey senior for pole, which the German stole back as the race got under way with a terrific start. Mika held off the challenge of Irvine but eventually lost his second place when he took an unexpected detour along the escape road at Mirabeau.

Two consecutive victories in Spain and Canada saw Mika leapfrog over Michael in the Drivers' Championship. From his fifth successive pole –

snatched from Irvine on his final run – Mika stole the show and was never really troubled other than by his team-mate who he finished over six seconds ahead of. In Canada, the bubble burst as Michael Schumacher wrestled the top grid placing from Mika. But the Finn went into the lead after the German crashed on the 30th lap and he took advantage of the safety car to pit and take up the lead on lap 37. This opened a four-point lead over the Ferrari driver.

The French Grand Prix looked as though it was going to be a disaster. In deteriorating weather conditions Mika waited for an improvement, which didn't come, and could only manage a potentially disastrous 14th place on the grid. But for the race the Finn lived up to his nickname and by lap five was flying through the field to a point position and was up to second place when he suffered a spin on lap 38. Back down to seventh, he raced into a short lead by lap 60, only to lose out to Frentzen in the pit stops. Nevertheless a second place was achieved from a truly remarkable drive, made all the sweeter by extending his lead in the championship to eight points.

Back on pole position for the British Grand Prix, Mika looked to be in dominating form when he maintained the lead at the start, and then the restart. But then what proved to be a wheel hub assembly problem forced him into retirement. His first pit stop was almost 10 seconds as his crew had problems fitting his rear left wheel and he was back in again next time round to have it sorted. By the time he came out he had dropped to last and, after setting the fastest lap on number 28, the wheel came free and the McLaren three-wheeled to retirement. Mika maintained his championship lead since Michael Schumacher did not make the restarted race after his near season-ending crash had prompted the red flags.

In Austria Mika again set pole position and recorded the fastest lap, but when team-mate David Coulthard ran into the back of Mika at the second corner, it dented the Finn's championship challenge. Mika dropped to last but he got back on course and for the second time in the season found himself charging through the pack. This time he salvaged a third place, but saw his championship lead whittled to two points with Irvine being the pursuer.

A third successive pole and the eighth of the season was secured for the German Grand Prix but it was another bad race day for McLaren. The Finn maintained the lead at the start but retired on lap 26 after a rear-tyre failure saw him charge into the tyre barrier in what was almost like a re-run of Schumacher Snr's crash. Mika's day got worse as Irvine won the race and moved eight points clear in the championship.

Another pole at the Hungaroring was the start of a flawless performance by the Finn in Hungary, who was totally dominant from start to finish. He came in over 10 seconds in front of second place Coulthard, and with

Irvine finishing third, he reduced the championship gap to four points. At Spa it was pole again and a second successive McLaren front row and this time it was to prove a detriment to the Finn who had a poor start and found himself touching wheels with his team-mate as they went into the first corner at La Source. Mika found himself second, where he remained to score six points, which pushed him a point back in front of Irvine.

Monza meant pole again but a rather different story for Mika who, having made one of his best starts of the season, opened up an eight-second lead after 29 laps. But a basic error saw him spin off at the first chicane as he started his 30th lap, having selected first gear rather than second for entry to it. With the engine naturally stalling, the world saw Mika's frustration and then desperation as the aerial cameras pictured him in the bushes sobbing badly. His only consolation was that Irvine only managed one point and the two now shared the Drivers' Championship lead.

At the European GP, he found himself off the front row of the grid for only the third time all season. Starting third on the grid his afternoon went relatively pear shaped when he pitted early for wets when the rain started. It proved to be the wrong decision and cost places. After just four laps he re-pitted for dries and actually drove well to secure two points in fifth place, which took him into a similar championship lead.

Mika arrived at the new Sepang circuit knowing that if he won and if Irvine finished fifth or lower, he would win his second successive Drivers' Championship title. Malaysia was the real venue for sweet and sour. The Finn found Irvine and the returning Schumacher and team-mate Coulthard in front of him on the starting grid and that's how it stayed after the third corner. With Schumacher backing Mika up, Irvine was able to make the ground that netted him the race and kept Mika in third, but only after he had managed to get past Johnny Herbert following a splash and dash stop nine laps from home. Everything was set for a fascinating finale in Japan and so it proved, albeit the one-week disqualification of the two Ferraris from the Malaysian result, which, temporarily at least gave Mika an unassailable lead in the Drivers' Championship. The Finn wasn't celebrating early though, wisely as it proved when the result of the disqualification was reversed. This left Mika needing a win in the final race to ensure the title or he could also win by scoring four points or more than Irvine in the race.

In the lead up to the final race, the McLaren driver kept himself to himself as he concentrated on the task in hand. He found himself having to contend not just with Irvine but also Schuey, who had put it on notice that he was out to win. In many respects the battle over the two days of competition seemed to be between the German and the Finn with Mika hoping that Irvine wouldn't get the points he needed. Despite being ousted from pole position, the Finn produced his best get-away of the season and by the time the cars came out of the first corner his McLaren started to build a lead that was never going to be challenged. Reliability was then the key and it fitted the Finn's lock with the win that provided him with his second successive World Championship.

For the 2000 season, it is hard to look beyond Mika once again. If the field stays free of injuries then it may well be that Hakkinen will have his toughest battle for the championship yet. Certainly he will be made to pay dearly if he repeats the sort of errors he produced last season. It could even come down to the number of victories he takes during the year – it could be that close.

Born: 28/9/68, Helsinki, Finland.

Grand Prix 1999 Record

Grand Prix	Grid	Qual Time	Fin	Laps	Race Time	Reason
Australian	1	1:30.462	r	21		throttle
Brazilian	1	1:16.568	1	72	1:38:03.765	
San Marino	1	1:26.362	r	17		accident
Monaco	1	1:20.547	3	78	1:50:09.295	
Spanish	1	1:22.088	1	65	1:34:13.665	
Canadian	2	1:19.327	1	69	1:41:35.727	
French	14	1:44.368	2	72	1:58:35.435	
British	1	1:24.804	r	35		wheel hub
Austrian	1	1:10.954	3	71	1:28:34.720	
German	1	1:42.950	r	25		accident
Hungarian	1	1:18.156	1	77	1:46:23.536	
Belgian	1	1:50.329	2	44	1:25:53.526	
Italian	1	1:22.432	r	29		spin
European	3	1:20.376	5	66	1:42:57.264	
Malaysian	4	1:40.866	3	56	1:36:48.237	
Japanese	2	1:37.820	1	53	1:31:18.785	

1999 Position Summary

Started:	16	Finished:	11
Pole Positions:	11	Fastest Laps:	6
Points:	76		
1st:	5	2nd:	2
3rd:	3	4th:	0
5th:	1	6th:	0

Grand Prix Career Record

Started:	128	(1991-1999)
Completed:	79	61.72%
Retired:	49	38.28%

Points:	294	1991-15/2, 1992-8/11, 1993-15/4, 1994-4/26, 1995-7/17, 1996-5/31, 1997-5/27, 1998-1/100, 1999-1/76
Point Finishes:	59	46.09%
Pole Positions:	21	1997 (Lux), 1998 (Aus, Bra, Esp, Mon, Fra, GB, Ger, Hun, Bel), 1999 (Aus, Bra, San, Mon, Esp, GB, Aut, Ger, Hun, Bel, Ita)
Fastest Laps:	13	1997 (Ita), 1998 (Aus, Bra, Esp, Mon, Ita, Lux), 1999 ((Bra, Mon, GB, Aut, Bel, Eur)
1st:	14	1997 (Eur), 1998 (Aus, Bra, Esp, Mon, Aut, Ger, Lux, Jap), 1999 (Bra, Esp, Can, Hun, Jap)
2nd:	7	1994 (Bel), 1995 (Ita, Jap), 1998 (Arg, GB), 1999 (Fra, Bel)
3rd:	16	1993 (Jap), 1994 (San, GB, Ita, Por, Eur), 1996 (GB, Bel, Ita, Jap), 1997 (Aus, Ger), 1998 (Fra), 1999 (Mon, Aut, Mal)
4th:	8	1992 (Fra, Hun), 1994 (GB), 1996 (Bra, Hun), 1997 (Bra, Jap), 1998 (Ita)
5th:	9	1991 (San), 1992 (Por), 1995 (San), 1996 (Aus, Esp, Can, Fra), 1997 (Arg), 1999 (Eur)
6th:	6	1992 (Mex, GB, Bel), 1996 (Mon), 1997 (San), 1998 (Hun)

Year	Team	No.	Grand Prix
1991	Lotus-Judd	15	US r, Bra 9, San 5, Mon r, (Fra dnq), Can r, Mex 9, GB 12, Ger r, Hun 14, Bel r, Ita 14, Por 14, Esp r, Jap r, Aus 19
1992	Lotus-Ford	15	SA 9, Mex 6, Bra 10, (San dnq), Esp r, Mon r, Can r, Fra 4, GB 6, Ger r, Hun 4, Bel 6, Ita r, Por 5, Jap r, Aus 7
1993	McLaren-Ford	3	Por r, Jap 3, Aus r
1994	McLaren-Peugeot	15	Bra r, Pac r, San 3, Mon r, Esp r, Can r, Fra r, GB 3, Ger r, Bel 2, Ita 3, Por 3, Eur 3, Jap 7, Aus 12
1995	McLaren-Mercedes	15	Bra 4, Arg r, San 5, Esp r, Mon r, Can r, Fra 7, GB r, Ger r, Hun r, Bel r, Ita 2, Por r, Eur 8, Jap 2
1996	McLaren-Mercedes	16	Aus 5, Bra 4, Arg r, Eur 8, San 8, Mon 6, Esp 5, Can 5, Fra 5, GB 3, Ger r, Hun 4, Bel 3, Ita 3, Por r, Jap 3
1997	McLaren-Mercedes	17	Aus 3, Bra 4, Arg 5, San 6, Mon r, Esp 7, Can r, Fra r, GB r, Ger 3, Hun r, Bel dq, Ita 9, Aut r, Lux r, Jap 4, Eur 1

| 1998 | McLaren-Mercedes 16 | Aus 1, Bra 1, Arg 2, San r, Esp 1, Mon 1, Can r, Fra 3, GB 2, Aut 1, Ger 1, Hun 6, Bel r, Ita 4, Lux 1, Jap 1 |
| 1999 | McLaren-Mercedes 16 | Aus r, Bra 1, San r, Mon 3, Esp 1, Can 1, Fra 2, GB r, Aut 3, Ger r, Hun 1, Bel 2, Ita r, Eur 5, Mal 3, Jap 1 |

HEIDFELD, Nick   Germany

1999: F3000 (World Champion)   *2000: Prost Peugeot*

After a rapid rise through the ranks, Nick Heidfeld joins Jean Alesi in France as part of the Prost line-up for his first competitive race drive in Formula One. Nick does so coming off of the back of an exciting F3000 Championship in 1999 in which he won the International Championship driving for the West McLaren team. The latest in the conveyor belt of drivers coming out of Germany, Heidfeld is under contract to the McLaren team where he was test driver to Hakkinen and Coulthard in 1999, and if successful at Prost, can be expected to replace one of the current incumbents at some time in the future.

Nick started karting in 1988 at the age of nine and worked his way up through the ranks of regional championships to finish winner of the International CIK junior run in 1991. The following year he earned fifth place in the German Junior Karting Championship. Two years later he was winner of German Formula Ford 1600 German Championship with eight wins from nine races. He repeated the winning feat a year later, taking the FF1800 International German Championship with four victories and five podiums. In 1996 he drove in the German Formula 3 Championship, as a pilot of the Opel Team BSR. He finished third overall with three wins.

In 1997 he was signed as a Mercedes junior driver and became the West McLaren Mercedes test driver. He competed in the German Formula 3 Championship with Opel Team BSR and won the Monaco Grand Prix. In 1998 he was runner-up in the F3000 International Championship, winning at Monaco, Hockenheim and the Hungaroring before taking the title last season. Heidfeld dominated the F3000 Championship in 1999 and was literally in a league of his own, securing 59 points, 29 more than runner-up Jason Watt. Wins at Imola, Barcelona, Magny-Cours, and the A1-Ring were backed up by two second-place finishes (Budapest and Nurburgring). He suffered just one retirement in the season and fully deserves his chance on the Grand Prix circuit.

1999 F3000 Season Record

Grand Prix	Grid	Qual Time	Fin	Laps	Race Time	Reason
Italian	A2	1:39.189	1	42	1:11:29.942	
Monaco	A1	1:30.087	7	50	1:19:18.178	
Spanish	A1	1:32.491	1	44	1:13:16.982	
French	B1	1:27.376	1	49	1:25:56.738	
British	A2	1:38.165	3	40	1:07:52.998	
Austrian	B1	1:23.206	1	48	1:07:50.994	
German	A3	2:00.574	r	3		spun out
Hungarian	B2	1:29.659	2	52	1:19:44.468	
Belgian	A5	2:14.787	4	30	1:14:04.095	
European	B5	1:30.925	2	45	1:09:36.002	

For more details about Nick Heidfeld's season, F3000 and other motorsport competition check out the *Virgin Motor Sport 2000 Pocket Annual* by yours truly!

HERBERT, Johnny   Great Britain

1999: Stewart Ford   *2000: Jaguar Racing*

There can be little doubt about it. Before the 1999 season got underway, Johnny Herbert walked under a ladder, broke a dozen mirrors, killed a black cat and failed to touch wood at all the appropriate moments. There can be no other reason for ten season's worth of bad luck coming in the space of just one. But once all that wore off, his fortunes had the most dramatic of changes as he took the third Grand Prix win of his career – and Stewart's first ever – at the Nurburgring. As with his two wins in 1995, Johnny proved that it doesn't need the fastest car and the most dramatic driver to produce victory, but someone who can stay out of trouble and deliver the goods to the chequered flag.

Johnny started the season by not starting. Having qualified 13th for the race it proved more than unlucky for him as his engine caught fire on the grid after oil had leaked on the exhaust. The race start was stopped, only for Johnny to find that his team-mate had suffered the exact same problem and was taking the T-Car. So Melbourne wasn't a dnf it was a dns.

Qualifying would prove to be a problem throughout the season, with Johnny only managing to match his team-mate's efforts once, his only trip to the third row of the grid. In Brazil it was the fifth row but the race was over after 15 laps when his car suffered hydraulic problems. San Marino saw the ever-smiling Englishman fail to take the finish line when his engine went three laps from home. At that point he had been running fifth and looked set to secure his first points of the season. The only stroke of luck was that he was classified as 10th rather than dnf by the FIA.

Monaco, Spain. Suspension, transmission. Another two races and another two dnfs. In Monaco his retirement came at Mirabeau on lap 33 and in Spain on lap 41 – on both occasions he was running 11th. The Canadian air clearly did wonders to move away the cobwebs. Having qualified 10th, Johnny made a good start at the second start and moved up to seventh and then utilised a section of the race under the Safety Car to pit and get further ahead before holding off the Ferrari of Eddie Irvine to finish fifth and to claim his first points of the season. The French Grand Prix produced his best starting position to date – ninth – but four laps into the race a gearbox problem caused an extra early retirement.

Johnny's luck took a distinct turn for the better at his home Grand Prix with his car's reliability problems evaporating. However, for the most part he was still some way off the pace being set by team-mate Rubens Barrichello. At Silverstone he was unable to improve on his starting position and finished one place behind in 12th position. Those facts don't tell the story though as a great restart saw him move up and ultimately to sixth place until he was penalised with a 10-second Stop-Go penalty for passing Jean Alesi before permitted after the Safety Car had peeled off for the race to restart.

Sixth was where he lined up on the grid at the A1-Ring for the Austrian Grand Prix – by far his best start of the season using a new Series 3 engine. However, he lost his rear wing at the start and had to pit thanks to Mika Salo in the Ferrari. He rejoined in last place, ultimately finishing 14th out of the 15 cars that finished and four laps down. A season's worst 17th place was where he lined up in Germany but a flying start saw him immediately make up five places and with a steady drive he was running fifth and just five laps from the chequered flag before his gearbox called it a day and left him to be classified 11th.

Handling problems proved problematic at the Hungaroring, but he had a relatively steady run, despite dropping one position to finish 11th. The brakes and clutch were the official reasons for retirements in Spa and Monza as the Englishman chalked up his sixth and seventh dnfs of the season. Never demoralised, the ever-smiling Herbert would be positively grinning by the end of the European Grand Prix. Qualifying didn't hold any pointers to what was to come. Fourteenth was in fact Johnny's third worst starting position of the season. He had opted for a one stop strategy, however, and despite having to pit to change tyres as the conditions changed to wets, he was able to stay out longer than most and went into the lead on lap 50, driving the remaining 16 from the front to win by over half a minute.

What confidence it gave him! Not only did he out-qualify his team-mate to line-up a season's best place start of fifth at the Malaysian race, he maintained his race position to finish ahead of him fourth on the road. In the final race of the season he finished one position out of the points, but his final tally of 15 points for the season was consistent with what he has achieved during the previous four years of racing.

Johnny races the 2000 season as number two to new team-mate Eddie Irvine. The two should provide an enjoyable mix in the Jaguar team garage, and who could rule out another win for Herbert. Certainly his luck must get better.

Born: 27/6/64, Brentwood, Essex, England.

Grand Prix 1999 Record

Grand Prix	Grid	Qual Time	Fin	Laps	Race Time	Reason
Australian	13	1:32.991	–	–		dns
Brazilian	10	1:18.374	r	15		hydraulics
San Marino	12	1:28.246	10	58		engine
Monaco	13	1:22.248	r	32		suspension
Spanish	14	1:23.505	r	40		transmission
Canadian	10	1:20.829	5	69	1:41:38.532	
French	9	1:42.199	-	4		gearbox
British	11	1:26.873	12	60	1:33:47.853	
Austrian	6	1:12.488	14	67	4 laps down	
German	17	1:45.454	11	40		gearbox
Hungarian	10	1:19.389	11	76	1 lap down	
Belgian	10	1:52.164	r	27		brakes
Italian	15	1:24.594	r	40		clutch
European	14	1:21.379	1	66	1:41:54.314	
Malaysian	5	1:40.937	4	56	1:36:56.032	
Japanese	8	1:39.706	7	52	1 lap down	

1999 Position Summary

Contested:	15	Finished:	9
Pole Positions:	0	Fastest Laps:	0
Points:	15		
1st:	1	2nd:	0
3rd:	0	4th:	1
5th:	1	6th:	0

Grand Prix Career Record

Contested:	143	(1989-1999)
Completed:	81	56.64%
Retired:	62	43.36%
Points:	98	1989-14/5, 1992-14/2, 1993-9/11, 1995-4/45, 1996-14/4, 1997-10/15, 1998-15/1, 1999-8/15
Point Finishes:	29	20.28%
Pole Positions:	0	

Fastest Laps:	0		
1st:	3	1995 (GB, Ita), 1999 (Eur)	
2nd:	1	1995 (Esp)	
3rd:	3	1995 (Jap), 1996 (Mon), 1997 (Hun)	
4th:	11	1991 (Bra), 1993 (Bra, Eur, GB) 1995 (Arg, Mon, Ger, Hun), 1997 (Arg, Bel), 1999 (Mal)	
5th:	6	1989 (USA), 1993 (Bel), 1995 (Eur), 1997 (Esp, Can), 1999 (Can)	
6th:	5	1992 (SA, Fra), 1995 (Pac), 1997 (Jap), 1998 (Aus)	

Year	Team	No.	Grand Prix
1989	Benetton-Ford	5	Bra 4, San 11, Mon 14, (Can dnq), Mex 15, US 5
	Tyrrell-Ford	1	Bel r, (Por dnq)
1990	Lotus-Lamborghini	2	Jap r, Aus r
1991	Lotus-Judd	7	Mex 10, Fra 10, GB 14, Bel 7, (Can dnq), Por r, Jap r, Aus 11
1992	Lotus-Ford	16	SA 6, Mex 7, Bra r, Esp r, San r, Mon r, Can r, Fra 6, GB r, Ger r, Hun r, Bel 13, Ita r, Por r, Jap r, Aus 13
1993	Lotus-Ford	16	SA r, Bra 4, Eur 4, San 8, Esp r, Mon r, Can 10, Fra r, GB 4, Ger 10, Hun r, Bel 5, Ita r, Por r, Jap 11, Aus r
1994	Lotus-Mugen H.	13	Bra 7, Pac 7, San 10, Mon r, Esp r, Can 8, Fra 7, GB 11, Ger r, Hun r, Bel 12, Ita r, Por 11
	Ligier-Renault	1	Eur 8
	Benetton-Ford	2	Jap r, Aus r
1995	Benetton-Renault	17	Bra r, Arg 4, San 7, Esp 2, Mon 4, Can r, Fra r, GB 1, Ger 4, Hun 4, Bel 7, Ita 1, Por 7, Eur 5, Pac 6, Jap 3, Aus r
1996	Sauber-Ford	15	(Aus dns), Bra r, Arg 9, Eur 7, San r, Mon 3, Esp r, Can 7, Fra dq, GB 9, Ger r, Hun r, Bel r, Ita 9, Por 8, Jap 10
1997	Sauber-Petronas	17	Aus r, Bra 7, Arg 4, San r, Mon r, Esp 5, Can 5, Fra 8, GB r, Ger r, Hun 3, Bel 4, Ita r, Aut 8, Lux 7, Jap 6, Eur 8
1998	Sauber-Petronas	16	Aus 6, Bra r, Arg r, San r, Esp 7, Mon 7, Can r, Fra 8, GB r, Aut 8, Ger r, Hun 10, Bel r, Ita r, Lux r, Jap 10
1999	Stewart-Ford	15	(Aus dns), Bra r, San 10, Mon r, Esp r, Can 5, Fra r, GB 12, Aut 14, Ger 11, Hun 11, Bel r, Ita r, Eur 1, Mal 4, Jap 7

1999: Jordan Mugen Honda   *2000: Retired*

Running at the back and with no hope of making up lost ground, Damon turned into the pit lane on lap 22 of the Suzuka circuit and pulled into his Jordan garage and stepped out of the cockpit of a Formula 1 car in race circumstances for the last time. It was a sad end to what has been a glittering career full of highs, and unfortunately for Damon in his last season, lows. The post-mortems have inevitably been held with the inquests asking whether, having made the decision to retire at the end of the season, he should not have done so when he announced his intentions in the lead-up to the British Grand Prix.

The desire of Jordan to accumulate points in their bid to secure a best-ever third place in the Constructors' Cup were no doubt of paramount consideration, but the four points Damon contributed after his announcement didn't affect the final outcome – although that wasn't to be known at the time.

Two finishes in his first seven starts really marked Damon's cards for the early part of the season. In truth his performances in the opening races did not differ from those in the 1998 season, but whereas in 1998 he stormed to victory and a string of points successes in the final set of races, he was unable to carry it on or repeat it during 1999.

Clutch problems shattered Damon's qualifying runs in Melbourne and so the Englishman had to settle for ninth position on the grid and then had ill-fortune when Jarno Trulli tipped him into the gravel at the second chicane before the race was even a lap old. In Brazil things got marginally better but with the same result. Oil leaks and fires plagued his lead-up to qualifying where he had to settle for seventh place. A quick start saw Damon move up a place but then drop down to eighth before trying to manoeuvre past Wurz and suffer damage to his steering in the process, to put him out of the race after 10 laps.

Fortunes looked to have taken a distinct change for the better by the time the San Marino Grand Prix had run its course. Eighth on the grid had been engineered into a fourth place points finish. Hill might have mounted the podium had he been fractionally quicker than Barrichello in the pit lane. Monaco proved to be more disappointing, starting 17th on the grid after a shunt at Rascasse and then giving up the ghost as he entered Harbour. In the race he did little better and was clearly having a go to try and move up the order before tangling with Ralf Schumacher and going out at the chicane as early as the fourth lap. The dejection was there to be seen as a solemn-faced Hill walked waterside around the harbour hardly acknowledging the crowd around him.

Damon produced his second finish of the season in Spain but it will have been of scant reward that his overtaking move on Barrichello in the final stages of the race was probably the best of the race. It didn't get him into the points though as he came home seventh. The meetings in Canada (crash on lap 15) and France (engine misfire) saw Damon starting from the back ranks. Without being able to finish in either race, it left him pondering his future in F1. Despite the bad luck and car reliability problems, qualifying was proving that it was difficult to remain competitive. This was further compounded by the fact that his team-mate, Heinz-Harald Frentzen, was performing so well and among the points leaders.

In the lead-up to the British Grand Prix the talk centred on whether Damon would retire immediately, drive a farewell drive at Silverstone, or stay on and complete the season before bowing out. Eventually Damon opted for the third option and produced his best qualifying performance of the season to line up on the third row of the grid. The biggest cheer of the weekend came on lap 45 when, with the pit stops working to his advantage, Damon led his home Grand Prix, albeit for a single lap until he pitted. Nevertheless it was a great boost and he held the pace in chancing for a higher finish but in the end telemetry readings gave cause for concern and, despite slowing off, Hill came home in fifth position.

Austria provided a second successive finish for the first time in the season with an eighth. At least he looked on the pace, although unable to get past Jarno Trulli's Prost for much of the race. Retirement came after 13 laps in Germany after an excursion across the gravel left him unable to trust his brakes and he toured in to retire.

The Hungaroring has been the scene of some of Damon's greatest triumphs. Who could ever forget his second place for Arrows in 1997 having just been pipped for victory in the final straight? Indeed Damon had never finished outside the top four and has invariably been in the top two. This time round he came in sixth, just as he had qualified. Despite a small excursion late on, he put in some excellent laps to keep him up with those battling for points outside the podium.

The resurgence continued to Belgium where he produced his best qualifying performance of the season to line up on the second row alongside his team-mate Frentzen. He didn't get away quickly enough and had dropped to seventh by the first corner but managed to make up one place by the end of the race to get in the points. A point that took him to 360 in total and edge him one ahead of Jackie Stewart in the all-time list.

Struggling with car balance, Damon dropped to ninth for the start in Italy and, having suffered a failure in his power steering, did well to muscle the car home to 10th place. Damon entered the final European race amid speculation that it might be his last race. Certainly that seemed a likely scenario but one that depended on him helping his team Jordan to secure an unassailable third place in the Constructors' Cup. As it turned out all the planning was in vain when Damon suffered an electrical problem as his car pulled away from his seventh place on the grid and he had to retire almost before he had started. So, Damon travelled to Malaysia and lined up on the Sepang grid in ninth place. Once again though he didn't manage to complete the first lap when in the melee through the first set of corners he was shunted in the gearbox by Fisichella and once again found himself out of the race. And so to the final race in Japan, where his supporters would have hoped for a points scoring run in his finale. But twelfth place on the grid, left him needing a miracle that didn't happen and running at the back after a detour on to the grass Damon decided to call it a day and made that last call on the Jordan garage.

After eight years, 114 races, 22 wins, 360 points and a world championship England's most loved sportsman called it a day. His return to Formula 1, in whatever capacity, will be eagerly awaited.

Born: 17/9/60, Hampstead, London, England.

Grand Prix 1999 Record

Grand Prix	Grid	Qual Time	Fin	Laps	Race Time	Reason
Australian	9	1:32.695	r	0		accident
Brazilian	7	1:17.884	r	10		steering
San Marino	8	1:27.708	4	61	1:33:47.629	
Monaco	17	1:22.832	r	3		accident
Spanish	11	1:23.317	7	64	1:34:25.044	
Canadian	14	1:21.094	r	14		accident
French	18	1:45.334	r	31		misfire
British	6	1:26.099	5	60	1:33:08.750	
Austrian	11	1:12.901	8	70	1 lap down	
German	8	1:44.001	r	13		brakes
Hungarian	6	1:18.667	6	77	1:47.19.262	
Belgian	4	1:51.372	6	44	1:26:37.973	
Italian	9	1:23.979	10	53	1:17:59.182	
European	7	1:20.818	r	0		electrics
Malaysian	9	1:42.050	r	0		accident
Japanese	12	1:40.140	r	21		retired

1999 Position Summary

Started:	16	Finished:	7
Pole Positions:	0	Fastest Laps:	0
Points:	7		

1st:	0	2nd:	0
3rd:	0	4th:	1
5th:	1	6th:	2

Grand Prix Career Record

Started:	115	(1992-1999)
Completed:	77	66.96%
Retired:	38	33.04%
Points:	360	1993-3/69, 1994-2/91, 1995-2/69, 1996-1/97, 1997-12/7, 1998-6/20, 1999-11/7
Point Finishes:	56	48.70%
Pole Positions:	20	1993 (Fra, Por), 1994 (Fra, GB), 1995 (Bra, Mon, Fra, GB, Ger, Hun, Aus), 1996 (Bra, Arg, Eur, Esp, Can, GB, Ger, Ita, Por)
Fastest Laps:	19	1993 (GB, Ita, Por, Aus), 1994 (San, Fra, GB, Bel, Ita, Jap), 1995 (Esp, Hun, GB, Aus), 1996 (Bra, Eur, San, Ger, Hun)
1st:	22	1993 (Hun, Bel, Ita), 1994 (Esp, GB, Bel, Ita, Por, Jap), 1995 (Arg, San, Hun, Aus), 1996 (Aus, Bra, Arg, San, Can, Fra, Ger, Jap), 1998 (Bel)
2nd:	15	1993 (Bra, Eur, Mon, Fra), 1994 (Bra, Can, Fra, Hun, Eur), 1995 (Mon, Fra, Bel), 1996 (Hun, Por), 1997 (Hun)
3rd:	5	1993 (Can, Por, Aus), 1995 (Por, Pac)
4th:	7	1993 (Jap), 1995 (Esp), 1996 (Eur), 1998 (Ger, Hun, Jap), 1999 (San)
5th:	2	1996 (Bel), 1999 (Bel)
6th:	5	1994 (San), 1997 (GB), 1998 (Ita), 1999 (Hun, Bel)

Year	Team	No.	Grand Prix
1992	Brabham-Judd	2	GB 16, Hun 11 (dnq: Esp, San, Mon, Can, Fra, Ger)
1993	Williams-Renault	16	SA r, Bra 2, Eur 2, San r, Esp r, Mon 2, Can 3, Fra 2, GB r, Ger 15, Hun 1, Bel 1, Ita 1, Por 3, Jap 4, Aus 3
1994	Williams-Renault	16	Bra 2, Pac r, San 6, Mon r, Esp 1, Can 2, Fra 2, GB 1, Ger 8, Hun 2, Bel 1, Ita 1, Por 1, Eur 2, Jap 1, Aus r
1995	Williams-Renault	17	Bra r, Arg 1, San 1, Esp 4, Mon 2, Can r, Fra 2, GB r, Ger r, Hun 1, Bel 2, Ita r, Por 3, Eur r, Pac 3, Jap r, Aus 1
1996	Williams-Renault	16	Aus 1, Bra 1, Arg 1, Eur 4, San 1, Mon r, Esp r, Can 1, Fra 1, GB r, Ger 1, Hun 2, Bel 5, Ita r, Por 2, Jap 1

1997	Arrows-Yamaha	16	(Aus dns), Bra 17, Arg r, San r, Mon r, Esp r, Can 9, Fra 12, GB 6, Ger 8, Hun 2, Bel 13, Ita r, Aut 7, Lux 8, Jap 11, Eur r
1998	Jordan-Mugen H.	16	Aus 8, Bra dq, Arg 8, San r, Esp r, Mon 8, Can r, Fra r, GB r, Aut 7, Ger 4, Hun 4, Bel 1, Ita 6, Lux 9, Jap 4
1999	Jordan Mugen-H.	16	Aus r, Bra r, San 4, Mon r, Esp 7, Can r, Fra r, GB 5, Aut 8, Ger r, Hun 6, Bel 6, Ita 10, Eur r, Mal r, Jap r

IRVINE, Eddie   Great Britain

1999: Ferrari   *2000: Jaguar Racing*

After four years as a number two at Ferrari, Eddie lines up with the Jaguar Racing team as a number one in his own right. Backed by the undoubted talents of team manager Jackie Stewart, who managed the impossible in the three rookie years of the Stewart Team. Now with the full weight of the Ford Motor Company behind them, Jaguar will expect to take ever more prominent positions on the podium and will be charging Eddie with the responsibility to deliver.

Will the Ulsterman be able to come up with the goods? The simple answer is yes, and definitely if he can find that extra bit of speed that has been lacking from even last season which was his best by far, entering as he did the final race of the season with a four-point lead in the Drivers' Championship. The season ended without the points advantage that would have provided Irvine with his first championship.

What Eddie does take with him to Jaguar is an incredible record. He was the most consistent driver in 1999 with an amazing 94% completion record – 15 finishes from 16 starts – and only Mika Hakkinen had more podium placings.

Irvine's charge for the Drivers' Championship only really materialised because of the accident and broken leg that Michael Schumacher suffered at the halfway point of the season. Unavailable for seven races, Ferrari threw their weight behind him, during a period in which he only failed to score points at one race – The European Grand Prix. On Michael's return the conspiracy theories were out in force and we will probably only ever know whether he had the full support of Schumacher when he retires and the inevitable autobiography becomes available.

The season opened in perfect style for the Ulsterman as he confounded his critics with a flawless display. Having qualified sixth, he drove a near perfect race. At the start he moved up to third place and then into second on lap 14. Seven laps latter, after the safety car was recalled, Eddie took advantage of Hakkinen's throttle problems to take the lead, where he stayed to record his first ever victory in his 82nd race and after six years of trying. His ten points also moved him past the 100 mark for his all-time total.

Eddie again took sixth spot for the start of the Brazilian Grand Prix and made a place on the start and by lap 28 had moved up to third spot. However, pneumatic problems were hampering him and an extra pit stop to have his system re-set cost him two places. At least he earned two points to ensure he headed the Drivers' Championship for the second successive race.

Irvine's Ferrari proved reliable for most of the season and it was at Imola that he suffered his only retirement of the season. Having qualified fourth, he looked to be assured of a podium position when his engine failed on lap 47 while he was running third. That cost him his lead in the Drivers' Championship but he would regain it again later in the season. Monaco saw Eddie back on the podium again, this time as part of a Ferrari one-two. Having qualified fourth, he failed to build on that at the start but excellent pit-stop management and errors by those in front allowed him to follow his team-mate home for his best ever finish in Monte Carlo.

In Spain the positions were reversed, when he out-qualified Schumacher for only the fourth time in their pairing at Ferrari. Just when it looked like he might clinch his first ever pole position, he was nudged down to second place by Hakkinen. On the dirty side of the track there was two much wheel spin at the start, which saw him drop to fifth position before they turned into Elf, which he improved on to finish fourth.

The trip to Canada saw Irvine mount the podium steps again, when he consolidated his third spot on the grid with an identical finish, although he had been running second until he had a bad restart when the Safety Car peeled into the pits, which left him in third after a tussle with Coulthard. He did record the first fastest lap of his career in his charge to catch up to Coulthard in the final laps of the race.

The worsening weather conditions during qualifying at Magny-Cours for the French Grand Prix saw Eddie tumble down the starting grid like so many of the leading drivers. Seventeenth position and a trip through the gravel trap was all he had to show for his Saturday efforts. Race day proved little better and after a mixture of terrible pit stops and spins, it was perhaps surprising and maybe a bonus that he managed to pick up a point by coming home sixth.

The British Grand Prix marked a real change in his fortunes, albeit largely after the loss of Michael Schumacher for much of what remained of the season. Having qualified 4th and then watched his team-mate crash out at the start, Eddie made a good restart and finished second. The eight points elevated him into equal second place with his injured team-mate on 32 driver championship points.

Prior to the Austrian Grand Prix, Ferrari had stated that they were putting all their efforts behind the Ulsterman in his bid to win a championship crown for Ferrari. Irvine didn't disappoint with a tremendous drive to victory. Having qualified third, he stayed out to lap 44 before pitting – a move that got him in front of the two McLarens and just two points off the Drivers' Championship leadership. It was almost the same again when the teams arrived in Germany. Fifth on the grid, he fell to sixth after a bad start, but strategy and luck saw him into second place – behind team-mate Salo. The new Ferrari number two yielded and allowed Irvine to take a full set of points and the championship lead.

In Hungary, another front row start provided optimism but in the race he was faced with a multitude of minor problems and, with the tyres going off in his final stint, he ran off and lost a place to Coulthard. Despite that, his third place was enough to maintain his championship lead, albeit cut to just two points. The Belgian and Italian races brought disappointing qualifying performances but solid drives continued to keep the Brit in the points. At Spa he couldn't get to grips with the car and probably did well to secure a sixth place start. However, he used that as a platform to make a great start but still found himself stuck in fourth and unable to get past Frentzen and had to settle for three points. At Monza it was a similar story. Eighth on the grid, he was out-qualified by Ferrari stand-in Salo. As in Spa he improved his finishing position by two places. That sixth spot and one point was more than important as it, helped by Hakkinen's non-finish, put Eddie tied on 60 points with the Finn.

Things continued to go downhill when the Ulsterman arrived at the Nurburgring for the European-badged race. Starting ninth, his second worst position of the season, he might have been on the front row but for a spin on his final fast lap where he looked to be setting a good time. For the race he opted for the harder compound tyres and suffered, finishing a place outside the points. He was not helped when he pitted only to find that his pit-crew had only three tyres waiting to go on the car at the change. The only good news was that Hakkinen could only manage fifth and Eddie dropped two points behind him going into the final two races.

Irvine arrived in Malaysia knowing that Michael Schumacher was back from his enforced injury break and publicly sporting the team line that he would drive as number two to help Eddie in his bid to secure both championships for Ferrari. It must have brought a continuous wry smile to Eddie, but he knew that he had to produce the goods at the new Sepang circuit if he was going to take advantage of Schuey's support. With Schuey setting a blistering pole position, Eddie responded brilliantly to get his Ferrari on the front row alongside him. Eddie held his position at the start and then slipped past the yielding Schumacher to race into the lead. After the final pit stops, Eddie repeated the process in the final laps to take the chequered flag and 10 points to fire him into a four-point lead over Hakkinen. The subsequent disqualification and subsequent re-instatement of Irvine, following a supposedly illegal bargeboard, all added to the drama in the lead-up to the final race of the season.

Eddie was as phlegmatic as ever in the days and hours leading up to the championship showdown at Suzuka, a track well known to him from his days driving Japanese F3000. A victory on familiar macadam would have given him the title, but Michael was looking for a win and if that was the case then a fourth place was enough for the title no matter where Hakkinen finished. As it transpired, it turned into a bad weekend, as Eddie was never comfortable with the set-up of his car. Irvine was pushed to fifth on the grid and after Schuey lost the pole at the start, Hakkinen raced to victory. Eddie struggled through to a subdued third place, which wasn't enough. Despite a best ever finish of second place in the Drivers' Championship and points to ensure Ferrari won the Constructors' Cup, there was no disguising the disappointment.

The question to be answered is: was that Eddie's best chance of the championship? The 2000 season will be tough with many good drivers and many good teams. It could well be the closest run season for many a year and a repeat of the four wins he achieved in 1999 would go a long way to producing a championship title.

Born: 10/11/65, Newtownards, Northern Ireland.

Grand Prix 1999 Record

Grand Prix	Grid	Qual Time	Fin	Laps	Race Time	Reason
Australian	6	1:32.289	1	57	1:35:01.659	
Brazilian	6	1:17.843	5	71	1:35:23.103	
San Marino	4	1:26.993	r	46		engine
Monaco	4	1:21.011	2	78	1:50:02.288	
Spanish	2	1:22.219	4	65	1:34:43.847	
Canadian	3	1:19.440	3	69	1:41:37.524	
French	17	1:45.218	6	72	1:59:13.244	
British	4	1:25.677	2	60	1:32:31.973	
Austrian	3	1:11.973	1	71	1:28:12.438	
German	5	1:43.769	1	45	1:21:58.594	
Hungarian	2	1:18.263	3	77	1:46:50.784	
Belgian	6	1:51.895	4	44	1:26:28.005	
Italian	8	1:23.765	6	53	1:17:30.325	
European	9	1:20.842	7	66	1:43:00.997	
Malaysian	2	1:40.635	1	56	1:36:38.494	
Japanese	5	1:38.975	3	53	1:32:54.473	

1999 Position Summary

Started:	16	Finished:	15
Pole Positions:	0	Fastest Laps:	1
Points:	74		
1st:	4	2nd:	2
3rd:	3	4th:	2
5th:	1	6th:	2

Grand Prix Career Record

Started:	96	(1993-1999)
Completed:	61	63.54%
Retired:	35	36.46%
Points:	173	1993-20/1, 1994-14/6, 1995-12/10, 1996-10/11, 1997-7/24, 1998-4/47, 1999-2/74
Point Finishes:	41 ·	42.71%
Pole Positions:	0	
Fastest Laps:	1	1999 (Can)
1st:	4	1999 (Aus, Aut, Ger, Mal)
2nd:	6	1997 (Arg), 1998 (Fra, Ita, Jap), 1999 (Fra, Ita)
3rd:	14	1995 (Can), 1996 (Aus), 1997 (San, Mon, Fra, Jap), 1998 (Arg, San, Mon, Can, GB), 1999 (Can, Hun, Jap)
4th:	8	1994 (Eur), 1995 (Jap), 1996 (San), 1998 (Aus, San, Mon, Can, GB), 1999 (Esp, Bel)
5th:	6	1994 (Jap), 1995 (Esp), 1996 (Arg, Por), 1997 (Eur), 1999 (Bra)
6th:	5	1993 (Jap), 1994 (Esp), 1995 (Eur), 1999 (Fra, Ita)

Year	Team	No.	Grand Prix
1993	Jordan-Hart	2	Jap 6, Aus r
1994	Jordan-Hart	12	Bra r, Esp 6, Can r, Fra r, (GB dns), Ger r, Hun r, Bel 13, Ita r, Por 7, Eur 4, Jap 5, Aus r
1995	Jordan-Peugeot	17	Bra r, Arg r, San 8, Esp 5, Mon r, Can 3, Fra 9, GB r, Ger 9, Hun 13, Bel r, Ita r, Por 10, Eur 6, Pac 11, Jap 4, Aus r
1996	Ferrari	16	Aus 3, Bra 7, Arg 5, Eur r, San 4, Mon 7, Esp r, Can r, Fra r, GB r, Ger r, Hun r, Bel r, Ita r, Por 5, Jap r
1997	Ferrari	17	Aus r, Bra 16, Arg 2, San 3, Mon 3, Esp 12, Can r, Fra 3, GB r, Ger r, Hun 9, Bel 10, Ita 8, Aut r, Lux r, Jap 3, Eur 5

1998	Ferrari	16	Aus 4, Bra 8, Arg 3, San 3, Esp r, Mon 3, Can 3, Fra 2, GB 3, Aut 4, Ger 8, Hun r, Bel r, Ita 2, Lux 4, Jap 2
1999	Ferrari	16	Aus 1, Bra 5, San r, Mon 2, Esp 4, Can 3, Fra 6, GB 2, Aut 1, Ger 1, Hun 3, Bel 4, Ita 6, Eur 7, Mal 1, Jap 3

PANIS, Olivier   France

1999: Prost Peugeot   *2000: Test Driver (McLaren)*

The last race of the 1999 season saw Olivier Panis bow out of the F1 limelight for a time at least, if not forever. He has signed a deal with Mercedes that will see him drive for them in the new German DTM Touring Car series and also act as a test driver for the McLaren team. It was a season too far for Olivier, who perhaps missed the boat a little by showing such allegiance to the Ligier and then Prost team and you can't help wondering what he might have achieved had he moved on to another F1 set-up a couple of years ago. Certainly at the start of the 1999 season Panis himself said that it was 'now or never' as far as his F1 career was concerned.

One finish was all that Olivier had to show for his first five races. A run from 12th on the grid took him to a point-scoring sixth place in Brazil. It might have been better had he not been too eager to get away and suffer a Stop-Go penalty for a jump-start. Nevertheless another steady drive through the back ranks got him what was to be his first and only point for the next seven races. Five weeks earlier in the first race of the year he had an awful time, qualifying a hugely disappointing 20th and blaming the imbalance of the car for the problems. He had risen to ninth place by lap 23 when a problematic wheel nut forced him to retire.

Engine problems plagued the Frenchman the entire weekend of the San Marino Grand Prix. They forced him out of his car into the spare car for the qualifying session where he achieved 11th and then brought his race to an end when it failed on lap 49. In the early testing at Monaco the car and the driver performed well but after he had made a detour down an escape road and had assistance to get back running, he was penalised and had his best time discarded – the net effect was that he lined up 18th on the grid and completed 40 laps of the street circuit until his engine again let him down. Spain completed an unwanted hat trick of dnfs. This time low oil pressure halted his race, this after he had stalled the car on the start before joining the race a lap down.

The break to Canada failed to bring a massive change in fortunes although he completed the race in ninth place, after another Stop-Go penalty – this time for ignoring blue flags. A change of luck came in his home Grand Prix where Olivier got out early to set a time before the rain came and upset everybody else's qualifying. Panis though was sitting pretty on the second row with third place, by far his best starting position of the year. His start though wasn't quite quick enough and he fell to sixth and found himself off the pace and was eventually passed by another car to leave him crossing the line in eighth place.

Having qualified 15th at Silverstone, he had yet another engine problem on the grid and had to start the race from the pit lane in the T-car. However, he had some fortune when the red flags came out at the start and so he was able to resume his place on the grid for the restart. He wasn't able to make much impression at the back though and finished 13th out of the 16 cars that completed the race. In Austria at the A1-Ring he brought the car home tenth, despite having some problems early on.

The German Grand Prix must have brought a huge sigh of relief to Olivier and his team. He was looking competitive during the qualifying session and with a good final run secured seventh place on the grid. With a reasonable start he gave himself a good chance and spent much of the race in among the usual pack of cars trailing the front runners and was rewarded with his second point of the season when he finished sixth. The relief though looked to be short lived, as Olivier qualified 14th at Hungary and went on to finish 10th although some positive pit stop management secured him a finish a few places higher than he looked on schedule for.

By the time that the teams had arrived at Spa for the Belgian meeting, Panis knew that he no longer had a drive at Prost for the year 2000. With no immediate takers for his services, and a drive at one of the smaller teams looking like the only hope, the Frenchman was driving for his F1 future. In that respect 17th on the grid was no place to begin, but he wasn't helped by mechanical problems during qualifying. The car was reliable enough in the race where he moved up to 13th for the finish. Despite being classified 11th Panis didn't finish the Italian race, his engine failing on the final lap after he had put in one of his better, but still disappointing, qualifying performances on the previous day.

At the Nurburgring, Olivier looked on the pace early on and secured fifth place – his second best starting position of the season. After a reasonable start the weather worked against him and he lost a couple of places when the safety car peeled off for the restart. The decision to swap from drys to wets to drys during changeable conditions also worked against him but he lasted to the end for ninth.

Olivier only managed to get through five laps of the Malaysian Grand Prix when his engine spluttered to a stop. It hadn't been a great weekend for the Frenchman in his penultimate Prost race, having had little practice time after he crashed his car early on. Nevertheless his 12th place starting position was better than many of his season's qualifying positions. It wasn't to be a high profile finale in Japan, a reasonable qualifying run placed him a creditable sixth on the grid but an alternator failure ended his race and Prost career after just 19 laps.

A disappointing end to the season but F1 has a habit of throwing up amazing circumstances – just ask Mika Salo. Who knows? Perhaps, having originally had talks with the Arrows team, Olivier might get the opportunity to return to the Show in the coming months as part of the McLaren team. Don't bet against it totally. Remember that is how Hakkinen got his chance at McLaren in 1993 when the moves were engineered by the same Keke Rosberg!

Born: 2/9/66, Lyon, France.

Grand Prix 1999 Record

Grand Prix	Grid	Qual Time	Fin	Laps	Race Time	Reason
Australian	20	1:35.068	r	23		locked wheel nut
Brazilian	12	1:18.836	6	71	1:37:13.388	
San Marino	11	1:28.205	r	48		engine
Monaco	18	1:22.916	r	40		engine
Spanish	15	1:23.559	r	24		oil pressure
Canadian	15	1:21.252	9	68	1 lap down	
French	3	1:40.400	8	72	1:59:22.874	
British	15	1:27.543	13	60	1:33:50.636	
Austrian	18	1:13.457	10	70	1 lap down	
German	7	1:43.979	6	45	1:22.28.473	
Hungarian	14	1:19.841	10	76	1 lap down	
Belgian	17	1:53.148	13	44	1:27:24.600	
Italian	10	1:24.016	11	52	1 lap down	
European	5	1:20.638	9	65	1 lap down	
Malaysian	12	1:42.208	r	5		engine
Japanese	6	1:39.623	r	19		gearbox

1999 Position Summary

Started:	16	Finished:	11
Pole Positions:	0	Fastest Laps:	0
Points:	2		
1st:	0	2nd:	0
3rd:	0	4th:	0
5th:	0	6th:	2

Grand Prix Career Record

Started:	90	(1994-1999)
Completed:	61	67.78%
Retired:	29	32.22%

Points:	56	1994-11/9, 1995-8/16, 1996-9/13, 1997-9/16, 1999 -15/2
Point Finishes	19	21.11%
Pole Positions:	0	
Fastest Laps:	0	
1st:	1	1996 (Mon)
2nd:	3	1994 (Ger), 1995 (Aus), 1997 (Esp)
3rd:	1	1997 (Bra)
4th:	3	1995 (Can, GB), 1997 (Mon)
5th:	4	1994 (Aus), 1995 (Jap), 1996 (Hun), 1997 (Aus)
6th:	7	1994 (Hun), 1995 (Esp, Hun), 1996 (Bra), 1997 (Lux), 1999 (Bra, Ger)

Year	Team	No.	Grand Prix
1994	Ligier-Renault	16	Bra 11, Pac 9, San 11, Mon 9, Esp 7, Can 12, Fra r, GB 12, Ger 2, Hun 6, Bel 7, Ita 10, Por dq, Eur 9, Jap 11, Aus 5
1995	Ligier-Mugen H.	17	Bra r, Arg 7, San 9, Esp 6, Mon r, Can 4, Fra 8, GB 4, Ger r, Hun 6, Bel 9, Ita r, Por r, Eur r, Pac 8, Jap 5, Aus 2
1996	Ligier-Mugen H.	16	Aus 7, Bra 6, Arg 8, Eur r, San r, Mon 1, Esp r, Can r, Fra 7, GB r, Ger 7, Hun 5, Bel r, Ita r, Por 10, Jap 7
1997	Prost-Mugen H.	10	Aus 5, Bra 3, Arg r, San 8, Mon 4, Esp 2, Can 11, Lux 6, Jap r, Eur 7
1998	Prost-Peugeot	15	Aus 9, Bra r, Arg 15, San r, Esp 16, Mon r, Can r, Fra 11, GB r, Aut r, Ger 15, Hun 12, (Bel dns), Ita r, Lux 12, Jap 11
1999	Prost-Peugeot	16	Aus r, Bra 6, San r, Mon r, Esp r, Can 9, Fra 8, GB 13, Aut 10, Ger 6, Hun 10, Bel 13, Ita 11, Eur 9, Mal r, Jap r

SALO, Mika   Finland

1999: (BAR / Ferrari)   *2000: Sauber Petronas*

What an amazing comeback for Mika Salo. He started the season without a drive and ended it having led a race for Ferrari, a race that he could have won had he not played team-orders. He nevertheless secured a career best second place.

The first three of his nine races in 1999 came in a BAR car following an injury to the team's number two, Ricardo Zonta. Despite a lack of any meaningful testing, Mika turned up at Imola for the San Marino Grand Prix sporting BAR colours and was immediately plagued with problems during the practice and qualifying sessions, suffering with low fuel pressure and hydraulic failures on the car. Not surprisingly he only managed 19th on the grid, but this was achieved in the spare car which was set up for Villeneuve. The troubles continued during the race and in the end the car suffered an electrical failure three laps from home. He was still classified seventh and thus recorded the first ever 'classified finish' of a BAR car! Next up was Monaco where he improved in qualifying, putting the car into 12th until his brakes failed on the 37th lap. Having got close at Imola, Mika managed BAR's first arrival at the chequered flag in Spain when he drove home in ninth place, to be elevated by one position when Barrichello was disqualified.

With Zonta back for the Canadian race, Salo found himself out in the F1 wilderness until Michael Schumacher's crash at Silverstone led to him getting a surprise call-up from the Italian team. It was a surprise in that most expected Ferrari test driver Luca Badoer to get the nod, but Ferrari chiefs clearly thought that Mika would be able to handle the pressure that the Prancing Horse would bring to its new incumbent. And he handled it brilliantly. First time out in Austria he put the car on the fourth row and finished ninth, having had to make an early pit stop for a new nose after he crunched into Johnny Herbert during the start of the race. If that eased him into his seat then he had made himself more than comfortable for the German Grand Prix. First indications came in qualifying where he pulled the stops out to secure fourth place on the grid, and immediately powered his way through to second place as the cars roared away from the start line. Then on lap 25 he took the lead when Hakkinen had an accident, a position he held for a lap until he allowed team-mate Eddie Irvine through to lead the race. With Irvine winning, Salo maintained his position to complete a Ferrari one-two.

On the back of that the Hungarian meeting was a downright disappointment, only qualifying 18th and then struggling to keep the car on the course to come home 12th and two laps down, leaving everybody to wonder just exactly what was going on! Salo responded well though, finishing seventh in Spa from his ninth place start and then he secured his second Ferrari podium position by finishing third after an excellently timed pit stop had managed to get in and out of the traffic and then out ahead of Barrichello. The European Grand Prix proved to be his final race of the season, with Schuey Senior making his return for the Malaysian race. Unfortunately he couldn't go out in a blaze of glory, qualifying 12th and spinning out in the rain after 44 laps, having experienced brake problems.

Now married, Mika's exploits in 1999 re-established him in the minds of the F1 teams and it was no real surprise when Sauber turned to him to head up their 2000 challenge alongside Pedro Diniz. It will be another chance for Mika to sit in front of a Ferrari engine – in fact the one he used to such good effect in the 1999 season. He will also continue testing for Ferrari which should also be of great benefit to Salo, Sauber and Big Red. *Born: 30/11/66, Helsinki, Finland.*

Grand Prix 1999 Record

Grand Prix	Grid	Qual Time	Fin	Laps	Race Time	Reason
San Marino	19	1:29.451	7	59		electrics
Monaco	12	1:22.241	r	36		brakes
Spanish	16	1:23.683	8	64	1:35:21.065	
Austrian	7	1:12.514	9	70		1 lap down
German	4	1:43.577	2	45	1:21.59.601	
Hungarian	18	1:20.369	12	75	2 laps down	
Belgian	9	1:52.124	7	44	1:26:39.306	
Italian	6	1:23.657	3	53	1:17:14.855	
European	12	1:21.314	r	44		spun-out

1999 Position Summary

Started:	9	Finished:	7
Pole Positions:	0	Fastest Laps:	0
Points:	10		
1st:	0	2nd:	1
3rd:	1	4th:	0
5th:	0	6th:	0

Grand Prix Career Record

Started:	76	(1994-1999)
Completed:	43	56.58%
Retired:	33	43.42%
Points:	25	1995-14/5, 1996-13/5, 1997-16/2, 1998-13/3, 1999-10/10
Point Finishes:	10	13.16%
Pole Positions:	0	
Fastest Laps:	0	
1st:	0	
2nd:	1	1999 (Ger)
3rd:	1	1999 (Ita)
4th:	1	1998 (Mon)
5th:	5	1995 (Ita, Por), 1996 (Bra, Mon), 1997 (Mon)
6th:	2	1995 (Jap), 1996 (Aus)

Year	Team	No.	Grand Prix
1994	Lotus-Mugen H.	2	Jap 10, Aus r
1995	Tyrrell-Yamaha	17	Bra 7, Arg r, San r, Esp 10, Mon r, Can 8, Fra 15, GB 8, Ger r, Hun r, Bel 8, Ita 5, Por 13, Eur 10, Pac 12, Jap 6, Aus 5

1996	Tyrrell-Yamaha	16	Aus 6, Bra 5, Arg r, Eur dq, San r, Mon 5, Esp dq, Can r, Fra 10, GB 7, Ger 9, Hun r, Bel 7, Ita r, Por 11, Jap r
1997	Tyrrell-Ford	17	Aus r, Bra 13, Arg 8, San 9, Mon 5, Esp r, Can r, Fra r, GB r, Ger r, Hun 13, Bel 11, Ita r, Aut r, Lux 10, Jap r, Eur 12
1998	Arrows	15	Aus r, Bra r, Arg r, San 9, Esp r, Mon 4, Can r, Fra 13, GB r, Aut r, Ger 14, Hun r, (Bel dns), Ita r, Lux 14, Jap r
1999	BAR-Supertec	3	San 7, Mon r, Esp 8
	Ferrari	6	Aut 9, Ger 2, Hun 12, Bel 7, Ita 3, Eur r

SARRAZIN, Stephane   France

1999: (Minardi Ford)   *2000: –*

The F3000 driver and Prost test driver made his debut in Formula 1 last season driving Luca Badoer's Minardi after the Italian had damaged his hand. His only race of the season came in Brazil where he qualified 19th and was promoted to 18th when Villeneuve was penalised and moved to the back of the grid. During the race he managed to stay out of trouble, although nearly came to grief trying to pass Alex Zanardi. This experience finally took its toll when he had an argument with the final corner during his 32nd lap. His can point to the fact that he did out-qualify team-mate Gene despite not having driven the race-car until the Friday morning of practice.

Born: 2/11/74, France.

Grand Prix 1999 Record

Grand Prix	Grid	Qual Time	Fin	Laps	Race Time	Reason
Brazilian	18	1:20.016	r	31		accident

Grand Prix Career Record

Contested:	1	(1999)
Points:	0	
Point Finishes:	0	
Pole Positions:	0	
Fastest Laps:	0	
1st-6th:	0	

Year Team   No.   Grand Prix

Year	Team	No.	Grand Prix
1999	Minardi-Ford	1	Bra r

1999: Ferrari   *2000: Ferrari*

While I do not think that Michael Schumacher is quite the German automaton that many make him out to be – he makes too many mistakes for that tag to be accurate – you cannot help but admire his ability in a racing car. He started the season as the Ferrari number one and went into the penultimate race of the season as an effective number two. Forget the technical result of the Malaysian Grand Prix. First, second, disqualifications and appeals not-withstanding, Schuey all but won that race by driving slowly! He proved beyond any doubt that when he is at the front he can do what he wants and dictate a race to suit his, and at that time, the team's needs.

I do not rate him as the best driver of all time. Maybe that will come, but he is, without a shadow of a doubt, the most adaptive to any situation. This of course all came in his first race back after an enforced absence after he suffered a broken leg at Silverstone six races earlier. Don't forget Michael drove the final two races with a steel plate in his leg – the implications of that should he have had another crash during the weekend, don't bear thinking about.

His late return certainly swung the Constructors' Cup balance Ferrari's way but I don't really think that deep down he was committed to Irvine's Drivers' Championship cause. That is a title he wants to win in a Ferrari for himself. But this is his fifth year driving the Prancing Horse and if he is to justify the claims that he is one of the best ever, then now is the year to deliver. But can he and will he? At $25 million a year you might argue that it doesn't matter. An injury free season is vital and if he can take the consistent finishing his team-mate Irvine showed throughout last season then the title is very definitely on. As far as the 1999 season went, it came to a painful end when he crashed out and broke his right leg at Silverstone. To that point he had only managed to secure one pole position (Canada) but had won in San Marino and Monaco.

A good start to the season had been needed but it effectively mirrored the poor progress that had been made when the 1998 season had got underway. In Melbourne for the opener he managed to get close to the qualifying pace but ultimately lined up on the second row of the grid in third. If he was disappointed with that he was even more so when the cars passed him by on the formation lap when he was unable to select first gear and was forced to start from the back row. Although he made up ground through the ranks during the race, up to 4th by lap 22, the gear problems had reoccurred and on lap 26 he went off and suffered a puncture and some wing damage. After repairs he came out last but kept running to finish as the last running driver in 8th position. Despite this he still managed to record the day's fastest lap as he closed on the pack in the closing laps!

In Brazil Schuey again found himself on the second row of the grid, but marginally worse in fourth place, which became an instant third at the start when Coulthard stalled. He passed Hakkinen and then gained the lead on lap 27 when the teams started making pit stops. The German took his only pit stop on lap 38 and came out in second place behind a resurgent Hakkinen, where he stayed to collect his first points of the season.

The first two races on the European calendar produced Michael's first two and only wins of the season in quick succession – his lowest number of maximum pointers since 1993. At Imola he qualified third despite using a new revised front wing. He remained in third, moving to second when Hakkinen crashed out and then using his pit stops to get ahead of leader Coulthard on lap 36 to give him his second victory at San Marino and his first in Ferrari red. Things showed an even bigger improvement on the streets of Monte Carlo, where Michael began second and produced a fantastic start to gain first spot by the first turn. From there on he was half a second per lap faster and finished over 30 seconds ahead of his team-mate. With the 20 points that the two victories provided the German had leap-frogged into the championship lead, eight points ahead of Hakkinen. The victory at Monaco was his 16th win since joining Ferrari in 1996 and eclipsed Niki Lauda's previous record of 15.

A fourth successive podium position came in Spain, but only after he had been out-qualified by his number two Eddie Irvine, for only the fourth time during their spell together at Ferrari. It was a position that cost him vital time as the race leaders pulled away and he had to settle for third after Irvine allowed him to pass and take the spot he had held.

Michael's first pole position of the year came in Montreal, when he kept Hakkinen at bay in the qualifying session with a three-hundredths of a second margin. In the race, the Ferrari performed better than the rival McLaren and Michael was able to open up a lead. Just days before Schumacher had talked about the fact that he usually made one mistake a year. It came on lap 30 as he slid sideways into the wall as he exited the final corner. With his error went his championship lead, which Hakkinen took with a four-point advantage.

Back on European macadam Schuey managed to scrape sixth place on the grid in the rain at Magny-Cours. Race day fared little better, with Michael improving on his position by a single place, but losing more ground in the Drivers' Championship. It was to be his last race for some time. Having qualified on the front row for the British Grand Prix, he didn't make the best of starts and found himself behind Irvine as the pair headed into the 90 degree right-hander at Stowe. Irvine allowed the

Ferrari number one the line but as Schumacher approached the corner he suffered a failure in his rear brakes while travelling at 190 mph and continued across the gravel trap to hit the tyre wall at around 66 mph at an estimated peak g-force of 50! There is little doubt Michael's life was saved by safety improvements carried out over the past four years and it can be considered lucky that the impact resulted in 'just' broken tibia and fibula in his right leg. It was an accident that need not have happend because, as the slowing McLaren's showed, the race had already been red flagged for trouble on the grid, as Michael attempted his passing move on Irvine.

Transported during the halted race to the Emergency Centre, the patient later underwent orthopaedic surgery in Northampton General Hospital and, after a few days recuperation, was flown back to his home in Switzerland.

The talk then was of his recovery which was aided by his remarkable fitness. By 20th August he took his first lap back in a Ferrari but was clearly still limping and ultimately expressed that he had been suffering some pain. With speculation that he would not return until the 2000 season, the German declared himself fit for the Malaysian Grand Prix. This turn-around was all the more remarkable as it came on the back of a further test at Marinello, home of Ferrari, where he hadn't performed to his expectations. But a further test saw him race 250 miles and set the fastest ever lap time at the Marinello test circuit at that point. He was back and we will probably never know just who persuaded him to have another go. Of course, the story would not have been complete had he not qualified for the race in pole position – which he duly did in some style, being nearly one second faster than his front-row team-mate Eddie Irvine. Now, however, Schuey was playing the number two to his team-mate in a bid to let Irvine take the Drivers' Championship and to help Ferrari win the Constructors' Cup. He did it quite brilliantly, holding the hopeful Hakkinen up and twice allowing Irvine to pass him to ultimately take the win and secure a Ferrari one-two on the new circuit.

A couple of hours later came the ensuing disqualification and appeal, with his subsequent re-instatement a week later. It was all an unnecessary attraction in the lead-up to the final race of the season where the German committed himself to winning the race and with it the Constructors' Cup for Ferrari. A third pole position of the season set the tone, but a lethargic start saw him drop to second as champion elect Mika Hakkinen took the lead and remained there to the end. Schuey came in second and, with Irvine third, the Constructors' Cup was Ferrari's.

On reflection I wonder how much Michael's return at Sepang was to get him knowledge of the new circuit. Certainly he would be arriving there this year at a disadvantage to his main rivals had he not made the return.

Only he knows. Nevertheless he reached several more milestones in 1999. One of those was to bring his all-time points total to 570. If he collects 41 points in 2000 then he will edge above Ayrton Senna and take second place in the all-time points list.

At home the German post office released a 9.5DM stamp with his image on it. That may be an indication that he will take some licking this season. *Born: 3/1/69, Kerpen, Germany.*

Grand Prix 1999 Record

Grand Prix	Grid	Qual Time	Fin	Laps	Race Time	Reason
Australian	3	1:31.781	8	56	1:35:16.505	
Brazilian	4	1:17.578	2	72	1:38:08.710	
San Marino	3	1:26.538	1	62	1:33:44.792	
Monaco	2	1:20.611	1	78	1:49:31.812	
Spanish	4	1:22.277	3	65	1:34:24.510	
Canadian	1	1:19.298	r	29		accident
French	6	1:41.127	5	72	1:59:12.224	
British	2	1:25.223	r			dns
Malaysian	1	1:39.688	2	56	1:36:39.534	
Japanese	1	1:37.470	2	53	1:31:23.800	

1999 Position Summary

Started:	9	Finished:	8
Pole Positions:	3	Fastest Laps:	5
Points:	44		
1st:	2	2nd:	3
3rd:	1	4th:	0
5th:	1	6th:	0

Grand Prix Career Record

Started:	126	(1991-1999)
Completed:	93	73.81%
Retired:	33	26.19%
Points:	570	1991-12/4, 1992-3/53, 1993-4/52, 1994-1/92, 1995-1/102, 1996-3/59, 1997-dq/78, 1998-2/86, 1999-5/44
Point Finishes:	86	68.25%
Pole Positions:	23	1994 (Mon, Esp, Can, Hun, Eur, Jap), 1995 (San, Esp, Can, Jap), 1996 (San, Mon, Fra, Hun), 1997 (Can, Fra, Hun), 1998 (Ita, Lux, Jap), 1999 (Can, Mal, Jap)

Fastest Laps:	39	1992 (Bel, Aus), 1993 (Bra, Esp, Can, Fra, Ger), 1994 (Bra, Pac, Mon, Esp, Can, Hun, Eur, Aus), 1995 (Bra, Arg, Can, Fra, Ger, Eur, Pac, Jap), 1996 (Esp, Ita), 1997 (Mon, Fra, GB), 1998 (San, Can, GB, Hun, Bel, Jap), 1999 (Aus, San, Esp, Mal, Jap)
1st:	35	1992 (Bel), 1993 (Por), 1994 (Bra, Pac, San, Can, Mon, Ger, Hun, Eur), 1995 (Bra, Esp, Mon, Fra, Ger, Bel, Eur, Pac, Jap), 1996 (Esp, Bel, Ita), 1997 (Mon, Can, Fra, Bel, Jap), 1998 (Arg, Can, Fra, GB, Hun, Ita), 1999 (San, Mon)
2nd:	22	1992 (Esp, Can, Aus), 1993 (San, Can, GB, Ger, Bel), 1994 (Esp, Jap), 1996 (Por), 1996 (Eur, San, Jap), 1997 (Aus, San, Ger), 1998 (San, Lux), 1999 (Bra, Mal, Jap)
3rd:	14	1992 (Mex, Bra, Ger, Ita), 1993 (Bra, Esp, Fra), 1995 (Arg), 1996 (Bra, Por), 1998 (Bra, Esp, Aut), 1999 (Esp)
4th:	6	1992 (SA, Mon, GB), 1996 (Ger), 1997 (Esp, Hun)
5th:	5	1991 (Ita), 1995 (Can), 1997 (Bra), 1998 (Ger), 1999 (Fra)
6th:	4	1991 (Por, Esp), 1997 (Ita, Aut)

Year	Team	No.	Grand Prix
1991	Jordan-Ford	1	Bel r
	Benetton-Ford	5	Ita 5, Por 6, Esp 6, Jap r, Aus r
1992	Benetton-Ford	16	SA 4, Mex 3, Bra 3, Esp 2, San r, Mon 4, Can 2, Fra r, GB 4, Ger 3, Hun r, Bel 1, Ita 3, Por 7, Jap r, Aus 2
1993	Benetton-Ford	16	SA r, Bra 3, Eur r, San 2, Esp 3, Mon r, Can 2, Fra 3, GB 2, Ger 2, Hun r, Bel 2, Ita r, Por 1, Jap r, Aus r
1994	Benetton-Ford	14	Bra 1, Pac 1, San 1, Mon 1, Esp 2, Can 1, Fra 1, GB dq, Ger r, Hun 1, Bel dq, Eur 1, Jap 2, Aus r
1995	Benetton-Renault	17	Bra 1, Arg 3, San r, Esp 1, Mon 1, Can 5, Fra 1, GB r, Ger 1, Hun 11, Bel 1, Ita r, Por 2, Eur 1, Pac 1, Jap 1, Aus r
1996	Ferrari	15	Aus r, Bra 3, Arg r, Eur 2, San 2, Mon r, Esp 1, Can r, (Fra dns), GB r, Ger 4, Hun 9, Bel 1, Ita 1, Por 3, Jap 2
1997	Ferrari	17	Aus 2, Bra 5, Arg r, San 2, Mon 1, Esp 4, Can 1, Fra 1, GB r, Ger 2, Hun 4, Bel 1, Ita 6, Aut 6, Lux r, Jap 1, Eur r

| 1998 | Ferrari | 16 | Aus r, Bra 3, Arg 1, San 2, Esp 3, Mon 10, Can 1, Fra 1, GB 1, Aut 3, Ger 5, Hun 1, Bel r, Ita 1, Lux 2, Jap r |
| 1999 | Ferrari | 9 | Aus 8, Bra 2, San 1, Mon 1, Esp 3, Can r, Fra 5, (GB dns), Mal 2, Jap 2 |

SCHUMACHER, Ralf   Germany

1999: Williams Supertec   *2000: Williams BMW*

Take your pick for the 1999 Driver of the Year, but for my money you could do worse than plump for the younger, more affable, member of the Schumacher family. In a car that was, by the Williams team's own admission, difficult and uncompetitive, Ralf worked wonders. What's more he is clearly happy with his lot and exudes confidence. He clearly likes the spotlight and one of my memories of the 1999 season was his reaction to the crowd as he walked along the Harbour at Monaco after crashing out late on. Ralf clearly has the ability to emulate the achievements of his brother and, given a more competitive package – as Williams will surely deliver in due course – he could well do so.

As for the 1999 season? Despite some variable qualifying positions, Schuey Junior provided some consistently good finishes. In his first ten races for the Williams team he never qualified higher than eighth but scored points in each of his seven finishes. Indeed, several of his drives produced the best individual performances of the season according to this and many other observers. Many of his performances where based around some quite excellent starts that more often than not moved him up a number of places before the first corner was being negotiated. All this in a car that is still a long way short of the one that had brought previous championship success, and in which he was able to produce a 75% race completion rate.

A great start to the season came in Melbourne with third place secured from the fourth row of the grid. Having cruised up a few places at the start, he couldn't get past fellow countryman Frentzen and inherited his podium position when the McLaren dropped out of the race. Ralf missed out on the podium in Brazil, but his drive from 11th on the grid to a fourth place finish and a second points finish was another blinder. The races at Imola and Monte Carlo produced a couple of dnfs. For the San Marino race Ralf got away quickly and converted his ninth place starting position to fifth only for an engine fire to bring matters to an abrupt end before the half way mark. Monaco provided his worst starting position of the year – 16th – and after being shunted by Damon Hill early on – he made a mistake coming out of Loews and crashed.

The next four races all produced points finishes, albeit with just one place on the podium. In Spain another great start saw him move up a few positions from his 10th place on the grid and then some of the old Williams pit-stop magic re-appeared and his two stops were largely responsible for him moving up to fifth and two points. In Canada the finish was better but from a worse grid position. In fact the Montreal circuit probably gave Ralf his hardest qualifying session of the season and saw him being outdone on the grid by his team-mate Zanardi, not least because of a close encounter with a pit-wall and much too close attention by Zonta when he was in the spare car. However, the German rose to the challenge and had gained five places inside the first four laps and hit fourth with five laps remaining. After the race he was hit with a record fine for speeding in the pit lane. He had to pay close on £8,000 for being 28mph over the speed limit!

At Magny-Cours Ralf equalled his previous worst starting position of 16th, although this time the reason lay in the wet weather conditions that created such an upset with the whole qualifying process. In the race he moved up to sixth place by his first pit stop and, as the rain came down, took advantage of a spin by Alesi and pit-stops to fourth with just a handful of laps remaining, passing his brother in the process!

The podium was revisited at Silverstone and the manner in which Junior held off the charging Frentzen for the final laps of the race was one of the highlights of the meeting. Remember that his brother had just had a serious accident at the first start. Once again it was ability out of the blocks that helped his cause, this time moving from eighth to fifth. The number eight spot was again filled for the Austrian grid, but an uncharacteristic mistake while trying to hold off the storming Diniz caused him to spin out with just eight laps gone.

For his home Grand Prix at Hockenheim the car's set-up proved most problematic; according to Ralf, its handling, especially during braking, was awful and so he had to settle for the sixth row to start from. However, he was soon through the pack, and taking advantage of attrition to Stewart and McLaren cars, he found himself once again in the points – this time just shy of the bottom step of the podium. In Hungary 16th on the grid for the third time was indicative of what was probably the worst weekend of the season to that point for Ralf. However, steady progress saw him up through the middle order but he couldn't get through those at the front and had to settle for ninth and his first finish outside the points in 1999.

For the final part of the season Ralf put on a superb display which was in no small part helped by a great improvement in his qualifying performances which put him much higher up the order on a regular basis. Fifth on the grid in Spa was matched with a same place finish although he had run as high as third and was ultimately hindered by Salo in the

Ferrari. It was fifth on the grid again in Italy with a more than convincing performance in which he equalled his best ever finish by coming home in second place, just a few seconds behind Frentzen. For the European race Ralf produced his best qualifying run to date when he qualified fourth, a position he mirrored in the race in which the conditions were constantly changing, and in which, during the wet periods, he pushed hard while those around him took the more cautious route.

Ralf qualified eighth in Malaysia despite having a difficult time with his car in the practice sessions which limited his time on the circuit, and this probably reflected in his spin which ended his race after just seven laps. In the final race of the season he started ninth, but this was achieved in the T-Car after he twice went off in practice. He made an immediate improvement on that at the start, moving up two places in typical fashion and with a couple of retirements in front of him, he finished the season where he had started it, in the points.

His tally of 35 championship points ensured him of sixth place in the Drivers' Championship, nine points behind his older brother. He should improve on that tally during 2000, but is probably a season or two off being a serious contender for the title.

Born: 30/6/75, Huerth, Germany.

Grand Prix 1999 Record

Grand Prix	Grid	Qual Time	Fin	Laps	Race Time	Reason
Australian	8	1:32.691	3	57	1:35:08.671	
Brazilian	11	1:18.506	4	71	1:36:22.860	
San Marino	9	1:27.770	r	28		engine
Monaco	16	1:22.719	r	54		accident
Spanish	10	1:23.303	5	65	1:35:40.873	
Canadian	13	1:21.081	4	69	1:41:38.119	
French	16	1:45.189	4	72	1:59:09.818	
British	8	1:26.438	3	60	1:32:57.555	
Austrian	8	1:12.515	r	8		spin
German	11	1:44.468	4	45	1:22:11.403	
Hungarian	16	1:19.945	9	76	1 lap down	
Belgian	5	1:51.414	5	44	1:26:31.124	
Italian	5	1:23.636	2	53	1:17:06.195	
European	4	1:20.444	4	66	1:42:33.822	
Malaysian	8	1:41.558	r	7		spun-out
Japanese	9	1:39.717	5	53	1:32:58.279	

1999 Position Summary

Started:	16	Finished:	12
Pole Positions:	0	Fastest Laps:	1

Points:	35		
1st:	0	2nd:	1
3rd:	2	4th:	5
5th:	3	6th:	0

Grand Prix Career Record

Started:	49	(1997-1999)	
Completed:	28	57.14%	
Retired:	21	42.86%	
Points:	62	1997-11/13, 1998-10/14, 1999-6/35	
Point Finishes:	22	44.90%	
Pole Positions:	0		
Fastest Laps:	1	1999 (Ita)	
1st:	0		
2nd:	2	1998 (Bel), 1999 (Ita)	
3rd:	4	1997 (Arg), 1998 (Ita), 1999 (Aus, Bra)	
4th:	5	1999 (Bra, Can, Fra, Ger, Eur)	
5th:	8	1997 (GB, Ger, Hun, Aut), 1998 (Aut), 1999 (Esp, Bel, Jap)	
6th:	3	1997 (Fra), 1998 (GB, Ger)	

Year	Team	No.	Grand Prix
1997	Jordan-Peugeot	17	Aus r, Bra r, Arg 3, San r, Mon r, Esp r, Can r, Fra 6, GB 5, Ger 5, Hun 5, Bel r, Ita r, Aut 5, Lux r, Jap 9, Eur r
1998	Jordan-Mugen H.	16	Aus r, Bra r, Arg r, San 7, Esp 11, Mon r, Can r, Fra 16, GB 6, Aut 5, Ger 6, Hun 9, Bel 2, Ita 3, Lux r, Jap r
1999	Williams-Supertec	16	Aus 3, Bra 4, San r, Mon r, Esp 5, Can 4, Fra 4, GB 3, Aut r, Ger 4, Hun 9, Bel 5, Ita 2, Eur 4, Mal r, Jap 5

TAKAGI, Toranosuke   Japan

1999: Arrows   *2000: –*

After a reasonable debut year in the fast fading Tyrrell car in 1998, Takagi was one of the last of the crop of 1999 drivers to get the call to race when he got the nod from Arrows. His initial arrival in F1 was heralded by those in the know, who suggested he had the ability to become on of the best racers to come out of the Land of the Rising Sun. He was always going to struggle to prove it in Tyrrell's final year and in truth last year with an uncompetitive Arrows car.

In qualifying there weren't many drivers who fared as badly. He was more often than not lining up on the last row of the grid and his 17th place starting position in the first race of the season proved to be the loftiest of the season. Nevertheless the season started very brightly for Tiger, who got his car home just outside of the points in the opening two races of the season. In Australia he finished seventh, his best ever finish in F1 despite being a place and under two seconds behind his Arrows team-mate, but recording his best ever finish in Formula 1. In Brazil he finished eighth, although this lofty position was as much due to the attrition in front of him as to his driving prowess.

After two finishes there followed two retirements with hydraulic and engine failures at San Marino and then Monaco, the former while he was running a fairly safe eighth, while the latter occurred while he was under a Stop-Go penalty for failing to give way to faster cars on the track.

For the Spanish race he finished 13th and was elevated one position after Barrichello was excluded from the race result. He then fell to a transmission problem in Montreal after 41 laps of the Canadian race. The French Grand Prix saw Takagi start from the very last spot on the grid and then make up half the field to finish 11th, only then to be excluded from the race because he used tyres originally named for his team-mate Pedro de la Rosa. At Silverstone he was the last of the finishers, coming in 16th albeit two laps down on the race winner.

As the season moved into its second half, Tiger recorded three consecutive dnfs. In Austria and Germany engine failures caused retirement in the early stages of both races, while in Hungary a broken drive shaft was the culprit – as with the previous two failures they came within the first 26 laps of the race.

The dnfs continued for the remainder of the season, the clutch going at the start in Spa, a spin accounting for him at Monza while he spun on dries in the wet at the Nurburgring two-thirds of the way through the European Grand Prix. A sixth successive dnf came in Malaysia when his Arrows drive shaft went on lap seven, after he had started in last place. It was another gearbox problem that ended his season in Japan, having completed 43 laps of the race.

Tiger has decided no to return to F1 for the 2000 season – opting instead to compete in the Japanese Formula Nippon competition.
Born: 12/2/74, Shizuoka, Japan.

Grand Prix 1999 Record

Grand Prix	Grid	Qual Time	Fin	Laps	Race Time	Reason
Australian	17	1:34.182	7	57	1:36:27.947	
Brazilian	19	1:20.096	8	69	1:36:10.072	
San Marino	20	1:29.656	r	29		hydraulics
Monaco	19	1:23.290	r	36		engine
Spanish	20	1:25.280	12	62	1:34:38.929	

Canadian	19	1:21.693	r	41		transmission
French	22	1:48.322	dq			dq – illegal tyres
British	19	1:28.037	16	58	2 laps down	
Austrian	20	1:13.641	r	25		engine
German	22	1:46.209	r	15		engine
Hungarian	21	1:21.675	r	26		drive shaft
Belgian	19	1:54.099	r	0		clutch
Italian	22	1:26.509	r	35		spin
European	21	1:23.401	r	42		accident
Malaysian	22	1:44.637	r	7		drive shaft
Japanese	19	1:41.067	r	43		gearbox

1999 Position Summary

Started:	16	Finished:	5
Pole Positions:	0	Fastest Laps:	0
Points:	0		
1st-6th:	0		

Grand Prix Career Record

Started:	32	(1998-1999)
Completed:	13	40.63%
Retired:	19	59.38%
Points:	0	
Pole Positions:	0	
Fastest Laps:	0	
1st-6th:	0	
Best:	7th	1999 (Aus)

Year	Team	No.	Grand Prix
1998	Tyrrell-Ford	16	Aus r, Bra r, Arg 12, San r, Esp 13, Mon 11, Can r, Fra r, GB 9, Aut r, Ger 13, Hun 14, Bel r, Ita 9, Lux 16, Jap r
1999	Arrows	16	Aus 7, Bra 8, San r, Mon r, Esp 12, Can r, Fra dq, GB 16, Aut r, Ger r, Hun r, Bel r, Ita r, Eur r, Mal r, Jap r

TRULLI, Jarno   Italy

1999: Prost Peugeot   *2000: Jordan Mugen-Honda*

Jarno Trulli has developed rapidly as an F1 driver. Last season was only his third full season behind the Grand Prix wheel and it was no surprise that his name was being bandied around the paddocks as a driver the top teams were interested in during the later stages of last season. As it turned out, it was Eddie Jordan who secured his services and the Ulsterman may just have pulled off a coup similar to that when he signed Trulli's new team-mate, Heinz-Harald Frentzen, at the start of the 1999 season.

Trulli has in fact been under contract to Benetton who 'leased' him out to Prost initially due to the fact they were concentrating their efforts on Fisichella and Wurz. The validity of their contract does seem to have been drawn into question and it may well be the subject of negotiation and litigation during the 2000 season. Whatever the outcome, the short-term is sorted with Jarno donning the yellow of Jordan.

The 1999 season didn't get off to the sort of start expected of Jarno. Three mid-range qualifications were joined by an unwanted trio of dnfs. In fact in the first three races the Italian only managed to complete 46 racing laps. In Australia he qualified 12th and started the race at a good pace and ran third for a period in the first half of the race as the pit stops started to unfold. After he pitted he had to come in again after his fuel cap failed to close and after 25 laps went off into the gravel after trying to avoid the debutante Marc Gene. Thirteenth on the grid in Brazil proved unlucky as this time Jarno's race lasted just 21 laps when the gearbox on his Prost gave out – this after moving up into the top ten. It failed to get any better when The Show returned to Europe. Having qualified 14th at San Marino and starting in the T-Car, he couldn't get his first lap in before he clashed with another new boy, Pedro de la Rosa.

Monaco saw a definite change in fortunes for Jarno. Having qualified seventh, he was looking good for his first point of the season, running sixth, until a differential problem occurred and he had to settle for seventh. He had to wait only until the next race though to secure that elusive first point. For the Spanish run he qualified ninth and was running fifth before Ralf Schumacher took him on the final round of pit stops to nudge him down to sixth – but a points finish.

In Canada the Italian got his second no-lapper of the season. Starting ninth again he clashed with Barrichello and Alesi in the rush for the first corner and was out. In France, for Prost's home race, Trulli came home seventh having run eighth – his grid position – for most of the race. Qualifying took a turn for the worse at the British and Austrian Grands Prix but lowly positions were converted into more respectable ninth and seventh place finishes by the completion of the races. In Germany his engine lasted 10 laps before giving up the ghost before he got back into finishing ways in Hungary with an eighth place that was one lap down on the leaders.

A twelfth place finish in Belgium was identical to his grid position at both Spa and the ensuing Italian race, the latter lasting just 29 laps when a gearbox problem produced a retirement at his home Grand Prix. It they had been mediocre performances then there was no such charge following a quite brilliant second place at the European Grand Prix. Jarno qualified

10th and then timed his three pit stops perfectly for fuel and wet/dry tyre changes. The first after 28 laps put him into second place where he effectively remained as the conditions took their toll on those around him. It was the Italian's best ever Grand Prix finish, his previous high being fourth in Germany in 1997.

The Malaysian meeting drew Jarno's worst qualifying performance of the season out of him, starting 18th at the new circuit. Citing grip problems, it was his engine that let him down at the start when it failed on the formation lap, this after it had failed during the earlier warm-up session. The season ended on a low note as he completed just three laps of the Suzuka circuit in Japan before his engine gave way, this after having qualified seventh.

All-in-all it wasn't a great season for Jarno and perhaps that is why, despite the pit talk, some teams may have had question marks over his ability. Not so Eddie Jordan, who has an uncanny knack of being proved right when it comes to drivers!

Born: 13/7/74, Pescara, Italy.

Grand Prix 1999 Record

Grand Prix	Grid	Qual Time	Fin	Laps	Race Time	Reason
Australian	12	1:32.971	r	25		accident
Brazilian	13	1:18.684	r	21		gearbox
San Marino	14	1:28.403	r	0		accident
Monaco	7	1:21.769	7	77	1:50:05.845	
Spanish	9	1:23.194	6	64	1:34:24.028	
Canadian	9	1:20.557	r	0		accident
French	8	1:42.096	7	72	1:59:22.114	
British	14	1:27.227	9	60	1:33:42.189	
Austrian	13	1:12.999	7	70	1 lap down	
German	9	1:44.209	r	10		engine
Hungarian	13	1:19.788	8	76	1 lap down	
Belgian	12	1:52.644	12	44	1:27:19.211	
Italian	12	1:24.293	r	29		gearbox
European	10	1:20.965	2	66	1:42.16.933	
Malaysian	18	1:42.948	–	–		dns
Japanese	7	1:39.644	r	3	engine	

1999 Position Summary

Started:	15	Finished:	8
Pole Positions:	0	Fastest Laps:	0
Points:	7		
1st:	0	2nd:	1
3rd:	0	4th:	0
5th:	0	6th:	1

Grand Prix Career Record

Started:	44	(1997-1999)
Completed:	25	56.82%
Retired:	19	43.18%
Points	11	1997-15/3, 1998-15/1, 1999-11/7
Point Finishes:	4	9.09%
Pole Positions:	0	
Fastest Laps:	0	
1st:	0	
2nd:	1	1999 (Eur)
3rd:	0	
4th:	1	1997 (Ger)
5th:	0	
6th:	2	1998 (Lux), 1999 (Esp)

Year	Team	No.	Grand Prix
1997	Minardi-Hart	6	Aus 9, Bra 12, Arg 9, San dns, Mon r, Esp 15, Can r
	Prost-Mugen H.	7	Fra 10, GB 8, Ger 4, Hun 7, Bel 15, Ita 10, Aut r
1998	Prost-Peugeot	16	Aus r, Bra r, Arg 11, San r, Esp 9, Mon r, Can r, Fra r, GB r, Aut 10, Ger 12, Hun r, Bel 6, Ita 13, Lux r, Jap 12
1999	Prost-Peugeot	15	Aus r, Bra r, San r, Mon 7, Esp 6, Can r, Fra 7, GB 9, Aut 7, Ger r, Hun 8, Bel 12, Ita r, Eur 2, Mal dns, Jap r

VILLENEUVE, Jacques   Canada

1999: BAR Supertec   *2000: BAR Honda*

Jacques Villeneuve is realistic enough to know that the first season at the newly formed BAR team was not going to be quite the bed of roses some of those involved with the team were trying to make out it was going to be. But he will have started the season feeling relatively comfortable, not least because his agent, Craig Pollock, was heading up the team and it had the multi-million pound backing of the British American Tobacco company. That said, he knows he has enough ability to have expected a better season than the quite dismal one he experienced in 1999.

Jacques isn't just a good driver, he is a great driver. CART champion in 1995, F1 Drivers' Championship runner-up in 1996 and F1 Drivers' Champion in 1997. Clearly it was the package that was the problem in 1997. Indeed a look at the results clearly confirms this point. Jacques didn't manage to get his car to the finish line in the first 11 races and the reasons for this included three gearbox failures, a rear wing failure, a hydraulic problem, an oil leak, a faulty clutch and a mangled drive shaft. Only in France did the Canadian spin out, while he was the victim of an accident in Germany.

However, despite the reliability problems, Jacques was often quite competitive in the car and this reflected in his qualifying performances which, apart from one blip, saw him mostly in the front half of the grid and included a fifth and sixth place in San Marino and Spain respectively. Indeed, the most likely reason he didn't get past the chequered flag in the first set of races was that he was driving the car not just to its limit but probably beyond it.

Having qualified 11th in his first race in the BAR, Jacques' Australian Grand Prix lasted just 13 laps when his rear wing suffered a failure and forced him off the road, after he had managed to force his way into seventh place. In Brazil he wasn't able to get on the pace at all and originally qualified in 16th place before he was relegated to the back of the grid when a fuel irregularity was discovered by the officials. However, after a slow start he worked his way through the back markers and was eighth when a hydraulic failure occurred on lap 49.

A stunning final run at Imola saw Jacques put his BAR fifth on the grid for the San Marino race, but as the race got underway the Canadian couldn't engage his gearbox and was left stranded on the grid. On the street circuit of Monaco, Villeneuve saw his car into eighth place on the grid but an oil leak saw him retire before he reached the halfway point of the race. Another gearbox problem saw a third successive creditable grid position, sixth, not taken advantage of.

Looking to please on home territory in Canada, Jacques could not get the set-up of his car to work and found himself towards the back of the grid and lost control towards the end of his 35th lap, crashing out while in eighth place. Back in Europe, Jacques looked set to get his first finish of the season, but spun out while trying to catch up to the Safety Car, having taken advantage of its appearance to pop into the pits for a fuel and tyre change.

The British and Austrian Grands Prix both saw Villeneuve start from ninth place but again provided dnfs. At Silverstone he found that again his gearbox would not operate as the cars got underway but was proffered some good fortune when the race was black-flagged. Rushing to get in the spare car he was able to retake his grid position and was running seventh when his gearbox let him down for the third time. At the A1-Ring a sterling drive saw him move as high as fifth but he had dropped to sixth when his drive shaft broke just ten laps from home.

The gravel trap at the first corner was where Jacques finished the German race after Marc Gene had pushed him off the track as the cars got away from the start, and his bad luck continued at the Hungaroring when his clutch disengaged itself and forced him out.

The relief that came in Spa when Jacques finished his first race in the BAR must have been immense even though it came during a weekend when the BAR team were presented by a continuous stream of problems with their cars. Indeed, virtually every previous meeting had been better in terms of performance and competitiveness – but such is Formula 1! A crash at Eau Rouge meant that the Canadian couldn't improve on the 11th place time he had set earlier. Having opted for a one-stop strategy, Villeneuve commented after the race that the car was almost impossible to drive full of fuel and, although he finished one lap down on the leader, he did finish.

The first finish set him off on a succession of them. Eighth place was achieved in Italy – this time finishing on the same lap as the race winner Frentzen. Despite a spin in the rain during the early stages of the European Grand Prix, Villeneuve stayed out and was eventually classified 10th, despite not finishing the race with a clutch failure. Tenth was where he started the Malaysian GP, and he had made a place after the first set of stops. Tussling with Wurz he suffered a spin and, although he got back on the road, the effect on his car was long lasting and he was forced to retire after 48 laps with hydraulic problems. He finished the season with a finish, recording a ninth place in Japan having started 11th on the grid.

No championship points in the season for Jacques will not have gone down well with him and, at the season's end, the rumours about a possible trade back to Williams were starting to circulate. From my point of view the worst thing about the whole season was the general absence of Jacques himself from the cameras. Naturally coverage centres on the race winners but none ever seem to offer the same clarity of vision of the Canadian. His state-it-like-it-was reflections on races and situations have always been the highlight of his races when he has been running at the front. Soon may he return, but that may be a long time off in BAR colours, whatever the livery.

Born: 9/4/71, St Jean-sur-Richelieu, Quebec, Canada.

Grand Prix 1999 Record

Grand Prix	Grid	Qual Time	Fin	Laps	Race Time	Reason
Australian	11	1:32.888	r	13		rear wing failure
Brazilian	21	Time ignored	r	49		hydraulics
San Marino	5	1:27.313	r	0		gearbox
Monaco	8	1:21.827	r	32		oil leak
Spanish	6	1:22.703	r	40		gearbox
Canadian	16	1:21.302	r	34		accident
French	12	1:43.748	r	25		spin

British	9	1:26.719	r	29		gearbox
Austrian	9	1:12.833	r	34		drive shaft
German	12	1:44.508	r	0		accident
Hungarian	9	1:19.127	r	60		clutch
Belgian	11	1:52.235	15	43	1 lap down	
Italian	11	1:24.188	8	53	1:17:44.720	
European	8	1:20.825	10	61		clutch
Malaysian	10	1:42.087	r	48		hydraulics
Japanese	11	1:39.732	9	52	1 lap down	

1999 Position Summary

Started:	16	Finished:	4
Pole Positions:	0	Fastest Laps:	0
Points:	0		
1st-6th:	0		

Grand Prix Career Record

Started:	65	(1996-1999)
Completed:	42	64.62%
Retired:	23	35.38%
Points:	180	1996-2/78, 1997-1/81, 1998-5/21
Point Finishes:	31	47.69%
Pole Positions:	13	1996 (Aus, Bel, Jap), 1997 (Aus, Bra, Arg, San, Esp, GB, Bel, Aut, Jap, Eur)
Fastest Laps:	9	1996 (Aus, Can, Fra, GB, Por, Jap), 1997 (Bra, Bel, Aut)
1st:	11	1996 (Eur, GB, Hun, Por), 1997 (Bra, Arg, Esp, GB, Hun, Aut, Lux)
2nd:	5	1996 (Aus, Arg, Can, Fra, Bel)
3rd:	5	1996 (Esp, Ger), 1997 (Eur), 1998 (Ger, Hun)
4th:	3	1997 (Fra), 1998 (San, Fra)
5th:	4	1997 (Bel, Ita), 1998 (Aut, Mon)
6th:	3	1998 (Esp, Aut, Jap)

Year	Team	No.	Grand Prix
1996	Williams-Renault	16	Aus 2, Bra r, Arg 2, Eur 1, San 11, Mon r, Esp 3, Can 2, Fra 2, GB 1, Ger 3, Hun 1, Bel 2, Ita 7, Por 1, Jap r
1997	Williams-Renault	17	Aus r, Bra 1, Arg 1, San r, Mon r, Esp 1, Can r, Fra 4, GB 1, Ger r, Hun 1, Bel 5, Ita 5, Aut 1, Lux 1, Jap dq, Eur 3

1998 Williams-Mecachrome
16 Aus 5, Bra 7, Arg r, San 4, Esp 6, Mon 5,
Can 10, Fra 4, GB 7, Aut 6, Ger 3, Hun 3,
Bel r, Ita r, Lux 8, Jap 6
1999 BAR-Supertec   16 Aus r, Bra r, San r, Mon r, Esp r, Can r,
Fra r, GB r, Aut r, Ger r, Hun r, Bel 15,
Ita 8, Eur 10, Mal r, Jap 9

WURZ, Alexander   Austria

1999: Benetton Playlife   *2000: Benetton Playlife*

Like team-mate Giancarlo Fisichella, Alexander Wurz, in terms of points, experienced his worst season in three years of Formula 1 racing. Despite being a reasonably consistent finisher (62.5%) he could only contribute three of Benetton's 16 points in 1999. All too often he was starting just too far down the grid to be able to make it into the points on any sort of regular basis.

He weighed in at the start of the season as the heaviest of all the drivers at 82.5kg and the early races didn't provide too much for the lanky Austrian to shout about. After eight races he had recorded just four finishes and a single championship point. At Melbourne he qualified 10th and then yo-yoed up and down between 14th and eighth before a suspension failure put him out at the halfway point in the race. In Brazil he improved his grid position by two places to finish a place outside the points after coming together with Damon Hill and thereafter suffered all sorts of handling problems. San Marino didn't lift the early season gloom after a terrible 17th place on the grid when plagued by brake problems during the qualifying session. Things didn't get any better in the race and after five laps he was shunted out by Pedro de la Rosa.

The first point of the season was won at Monaco where, despite a loose rear wing, he managed to move up from his 10th place starting position to sixth place with just six laps remaining. Spain brought the worst grid position of the year, where lack of grip on the Catalunya circuit saw him start in 18th place. Having gained places at the start, the big Austrian traversed the grass as early as the fourth lap and finished 10th, largely due to retirements in front of him.

An accident on the first lap of the Canadian Grand Prix meant that Alex didn't even record a lap for his trans-Atlantic travels, this after he had avoided the first-corner smash that caught quite a few out. It was a second dnf when the show returned to Europe for the French meeting. Starting an unlucky 13th, he managed to spin out while trying to catch up the touring Safety Car. This, as much as anything, typified the sort of season Wurz was having.

Another poor 18th place on the grid was where Alex started the British Grand Prix and, in a fairly uneventful race for him, he moved up to 10th place, thus mirroring the performance in Spain four races earlier. Things took a distinct turn for the better for his home Grand Prix in Austria where he recorded his highest finish to date and picked up his second set of points of the season. Starting 10th on the grid, he got ahead of his team-mate after the first set of pit stops. He moved up to fifth place with 15 laps remaining and there he stayed until the chequered flag. Alex completed his third consecutive finish of the season (the only time he achieved it all year) by running to seventh place for the German Grand Prix. Starting 13th he had a good start and immediately moved up to eighth and looked to be on target for a point until, as he chased Panis, he couldn't get past him. Another seventh place came at the Hungaroring, mirroring his grid position. This was after he and Villeneuve had come together at the start. The resultant minor damage affected his car and prevented him from making any improvement on his position.

The set-up created problems for Alex at Spa, where he only managed to improve by one place on his grid position. In Italy his race came to an end with an electrical failure after 11 laps. A minor improvement to 11th place on the grid for the European race didn't improve his luck as he sent Diniz flying while trying to avoid a slowing Hill at the start. The final two races brought two more pointless finishes for a disappointing end to the season.

The 2000 season is sure to be an important one for Alex if he has ambitions to maintain a position with Benetton.

Born: 15/2/74, Waithofen, Austria.

Grand Prix 1999 Record

Grand Prix	Grid	Qual Time	Fin	Laps	Race Time	Reason
Australian	10	1:32.789	r	28		suspension
Brazilian	9	1:18.334	7	70	1:36:12.021	
San Marino	17	1:28.765	r	5		accident
Monaco	10	1:21.968	6	77	1:49:47.799	
Spanish	18	1:23.824	10	64	1:35:29.548	
Canadian	11	1:21.000	r	0		accident
French	13	1:44.319	r	25		spin
British	18	1:28.010	10	60	1:33:42.267	
Austrian	10	1:12.850	5	71	1:29:18.796	
German	13	1:44.522	7	45	1:22:31.927	
Hungarian	7	1:18.733	7	77	1:47.24.548	
Belgian	15	1:52.847	14	44	1:27:40.802	
Italian	14	1:24.593	r	11		electronics
European	11	1:21.144	r	0		accident

| Malaysian | 7 | 1:41.444 | 8 | 56 | 1:37:39.428 |
| Japanese | 15 | 1:40.303 | 10 | 52 | 1 lap down |

1999 Position Summary

Started:	16	Finished:	10
Pole Positions:	0	Fastest Laps:	0
Points:	3		
1st:	0	2nd:	0
3rd:	0	4th:	0
5th:	1	6th:	1

Grand Prix Career Record

Started:	35	(1997-1999)
Completed:	23	65.71%
Retired:	12	34.29%
Points:	24	1997-14/4, 1998-7/17, 1999-13/3
Point Finishes:	9	25.71%
Pole Positions:	0	
Fastest Laps:	1	1998 (Arg)
1st:	0	
2nd:	0	
3rd:	1	1997 (GB)
4th:	5	1998 (Bra, Arg, Esp, Can, GB)
5th:	2	1998 (Fra), 1999 (Aut)
6th:	1	1999 (Mon)

Year	Team	No.	Grand Prix
1997	Benetton-Renault	3	Can r, Fra r, GB 3
1998	Benetton-Playlife	16	Aus 7, Bra 4, Arg 4, San r, Esp 4, Mon r, Can 4, Fra 5, GB 4, Aut 9, Ger 11, Hun 16, Bel r, Ita r, Lux 7, Jap 9
1999	Benetton-Playlife	16	Aus r, Bra 7, San r, Mon 6, Esp 10, Can r, Fra r, GB 10, Aut 5, Ger 7, Hun 7, Bel 14, Ita r, Eur r, Mal 8, Jap 10

ZANARDI, Alex   Italy

1999: Williams Supertec   *2000: Williams BMW*

Will he or won't he? By the time you read this you may already know the answer, but at the time of writing the future of Alex Zanardi at Williams was very much in the balance.

Like Jacques Villeneuve three years previously, Alessandro Zanardi joined the Williams team as CART champion. There, however, the comparison ends. In his first year Villeneuve finished second in the championship and went on to take the F1 Drivers' title the following year. Alex never looked like even winning a race in 1999 in what was a dismal season for the likeable Italian. There perhaps lies the rub. His happy-go-lucky attitude, even after races in which he hadn't performed well, probably wouldn't have sat well with his employers. Despite a three-year contract with the Williams team the rumours were rife by the end of the season of a possible swap move to the BAR team. At the time of going to press that hadn't materialised but in F1 you never say never.

Alex was in fact making his return to F1 in 1999 and his form reflected more what he had shown in his previous spell in a Formula 1 car. In 20 races from 1991 to 1994 he collected one point and, apart from a sudden surge of form at the Italian Grand Prix, never looked like adding to it during 1999. Qualifying was inevitably a problem. In the first ten races he only once managed to get in the top five rows when he qualified 10th in Imola and in that period an eighth place was the best he managed from just three finishes.

In Melbourne for his Williams debut, Zanardi suffered a hellish weekend, experiencing car problems and then qualifying 15th nearly a second behind his team-mate Ralf Schumacher – also in his first Williams race. The Italian gained a place on the first lap but then lost four places when he got off line on his second lap, which caused him to pit eventually. Back out, his race came to an abrupt end after 20 laps when he spun out after an accident. In Brazil things didn't look any brighter. He lost a place on the grid, starting 16th (after Villeneuve had been sent to the back of the grid), although there were mitigating circumstances in that he had missed much of the Friday practice due to sensor problems with his car. This reappeared early in qualifying and an engine failure curtailed his efforts using the T-car. During the race the differential started to suffer problems and after several diversions into the pits, he retired after 43 laps.

San Marino provided that aforementioned 10th place on the grid. He drove a largely uneventful race, climbing up the field and was on the verge of securing his first point in a Williams after Johnny Herbert had retired. But the luckless Zanardi spun on the oil left behind by Herbert's misfortune, and found himself spinning out of the race with just two laps to go and was eventually classified 11th. Monaco provided his first finish in the top ten and was again indicative of the freakish luck the Italian was having. Having made a good start, his seat came adrift in the cockpit and, as he struggled to reach the pedals, he lost places and one spin saw him fall to 16th place. Nevertheless he battled on and finished eighth.

At Catalunya in Spain Alex couldn't get his set-up right. The car proved difficult for him to handle and he made his worst grid position of the year – 17th. From here he moved through the field and was an unlucky 13th when he pitted and had a gearbox failure as he tried to re-join the race.

The gearbox problems trailed Zanardi across the Atlantic to Montreal where he had another dnf. He managed to twice spin off and the gravel traps probably added to his gearbox problems. His retirement came when he was running eighth and after he had experienced a Stop-Go penalty.

The French meeting produced a third successive retirement when his engine failed, probably due to the torrential rain getting into his airbox, as early as the 26th lap. Relief came at Silverstone where Zanardi got the car home, improving two places on his grid position to finish 11th – nevertheless disappointing given the major aerodynamic improvements that the Williams factory had made to the car.

Running out of fuel during a race is almost a crime, but that was what happened to the Italian in Austria where a radio failure and unseen pit board saw him grind to a halt after just 35 laps. That was the first of three successive non-finishes (his second such unwanted hat trick of the season) although those in Germany and Hungary were down to mechanical problems. Qualifying performances again lacked sparkle and he started nearer the back of the pack than the front.

There was considerable improvement over the next two races where Alex looked competitive for the first time in the season. Eighth on the grid at Spa was his best starting position of the season and was matched by his finish, even though he wasn't helped by fuel rig problems when he pitted. Even that was bettered in Italy where he looked the type of driver you expect as CART champion. From fourth he had a terrific start and was soon running second, dropping to third. Pursued by his team-mate, Alex yielded to him on lap 18 when he started to experience his floorboard coming loose, an irritation that surely cost him his first points in a Williams when he had to settle for seventh place – his best finish of the season. He was unable to build on that relative success though and at the European race had his worst qualifying performance of the season. Starting 18th, he was soon running at the back of the pack, retiring on lap 10 after a tangle with de la Rosa.

Hydraulic problems prevented Alex from getting in laps during the set-up sessions at Sepang and a spin on his last flying lap in qualifying meant that he couldn't improve on the 16th position he had set himself. The Italian finished 10th in the race, and was later elevated to eighth, after the Ferraris were ousted, just one lap down, after he had trailed the leaders by no less than four laps. At the start he was walloped in the rear and had to have an extra stop to clear gravel from his radiators after he had taken a detour. If he hoped to finish the season on the up then there was more disappointment when, qualifying 16th in Japan, his season spluttered to a finish on his very first lap as his car's engine died on him.

Likeable yes, lucky no. Alex had a terrible season where anything that could happen or could go wrong just about did. The incident at Monza,

where a loose floorboard robbed him of a certain point, just typified matters. You feel that Williams have to stick with him because he simply cannot be so unfortunate during the 2000 season. One thing is for sure, it must be a make or break year for Alex in terms of his F1 future.
Born: 23/10/66, Bologna, Italy.

Grand Prix 1999 Record

Grand Prix	Grid	Qual Time	Fin	Laps	Race Time	Reason
Australian	15	1:33.549	r	20		accident
Brazilian	16	1:19.462	r	43		differential
San Marino	10	1:28.142	11	58		spin
Monaco	11	1:22.152	8	76	1:49:49.514	
Spanish	17	1:23.703	r	24		gearbox
Canadian	12	1:21.076	r	50		gearbox
French	15	1:44.912	r	26		engine
British	13	1:27.223	11	60	1:33:47.268	
Austrian	14	1:13.101	r	35		out of fuel
German	14	1:45.034	r	21		differential
Hungarian	15	1:19.924	r	10		differential
Belgian	8	1:52.014	8	44	1:26:50.079	
Italian	4	1:23.432	7	53	1:17:30.970	
European	18	1:22.284	r	10		accident
Malaysian	16	1:42.885	10	55	1 lap down	
Japanese	16	1:40.403	r	0		electrics

1999 Position Summary

Started:	16	Finished:	6
Pole Positions:	0	Fastest Laps:	0
Points:	0		
1st-6th:	0		

Grand Prix Career Record

Started:	41	(1991-1999)
Completed:	18	43.90%
Retired:	23	56.10%
Points:	1	1993-20/1
Point Finishes:	1	2.44%
Pole Positions:	0	
Fastest Laps:	0	
1st-5th:	0	
6th:	1	1993 (Bra)

Year	Team	No.	Grand Prix
1991	Jordan-Ford	3	Esp 9, Jap r, Aus 9
1992	Minardi-Lamborghini		
		1	(GB dnq), Ger r, (Hun dnq)
1993	Lotus-Ford	11	SA r, Bra 6, Eur 8, San r, Esp 14, Mon 7, Can 11, Fra r, GB r, Ger r, Hun r, (Bel dns)
1994	Lotus-Mugen H.	10	Esp 9, Can 15, Fra r, GB r, Ger r, Hun 13, Ita r, Eur 16, Jap 13, Aus r
1999	Williams-Supertec	16	Aus r, Bra r, San 11, Mon 8, Esp r, Can r, Fra r, GB 11, Aut r, Ger r, Hun r, Bel 8, Ita 7, Eur r, Mal 10, Jap r

ZONTA, Ricardo   Brazil

1999: BAR Supertec   *2000: BAR Honda*

At the end of his first season in F1, Brazilian Ricardo Zonta could point to the fact that he had successfully finished more races than his team-mate and former F1 World Champion Jacques Villeneuve. He managed the feat by driving in three less races. However, he was still looking to claim his first championship point, but came close to achieving it on a couple of occasions – something that will be an early target in 2000.

His first retirement of the season came in the first race in Australia in crazy circumstances. It was down to his engine overheating, caused by tear-off strips from his helmet finding their way into the engine cooling ducts after he discarded them! This was just nine laps from home in his first ever Formula 1 race when he was looking set to make it home, running around 10th position. His performance in qualifying in Melbourne – 19th – was, on reflection perhaps not surprising given the problems he experienced during the lead-up to the session and his general lack of miles in the car itself. Disappointment came when Ricardo had to sit out his home race in Brazil after a huge accident in the Saturday morning practice session left him with minor injuries. It was in truth a terrifying accident, as he careered into an unprotected barrier at over 100 mph. The general consensus was that recent improvements to the cockpit and its surrounding padding saved his life and left him nursing 'just' a number of chipped bones and damaged tendons in his left foot. His injuries meant that he had to sit out the San Marino, Monaco and Spanish meetings as he recovered to full fitness in time to make a return in Canada, where he did better in qualifying but went off into a wall on his second lap after the restart.

However, his third race in the BAR brought him his first career finish. A season's best qualifying performance at Magny-Cours put him on to tenth place on the grid in France and he managed to drive through the rain to come home in ninth place after the full 72 laps. A suspension failure threw him off the track at Silverstone after 41 laps but he chalked up a second finish for the season, albeit it on a technicality, when he was classified 15th in Austria despite being eight laps down, having coasted to a halt after his clutch failed. It was another dnf in Germany when his engine decided it had had enough after 20 laps, this after having to pit for a new nose cone after he ran into the back of a Minardi.

The Hungarian outing provided another finish – this time just two laps down from the race winner. He came home in 13th place, after having to make an extra stop after one trip into the pits had to be prematurely aborted when his fuel rig developed a problem. Gearbox and suspension problems provided early retirements at Spa and Monza. At the former he had managed to get to 14th on the grid, his second highest starting position of the year, but he stalled his car on the grid and was already a lap down by the time his mechanics got him on his way. In Italy he developed suspension problems that created vibration throughout the car and forced him out after 25 laps. At the Nurburgring he finished eighth – his best position of the season – while in Malaysia he secured his second best grid position of the season – 13th. At Sepang he took a spin on the first lap but managed to recover his car but had to retire on his seventh circuit when he developed a water leak causing his engine to blow. He completed the year by driving home in 12th place in Japan, one lap down on the leaders.

Born: 23/3/76, Curibita, Brazil.

Grand Prix 1999 Record

Grand Prix	Grid	Qual Time	Fin	Laps	Race Time	Reason
Australian	19	1:34.412	r	48		overheating
Brazilian	–	–	–	–		dns
Canadian	17	1:21.467	r	2		accident
French	10	1:42.228	9	72	1:59:53.107	
British	16	1:27.699	r	41		suspension
Austrian	15	1:13.172	15	63	8 laps down	dnf
German	18	1:45.460	r	20		engine
Hungarian	17	1:20.060	13	75	2 laps down	
Belgian	14	1:52.840	r	33		gearbox
Italian	18	1:25.114	r	25		wheel bearing
European	17	1:22.267	8	65	1 lap down	
Malaysian	13	1:42.310	r	6		water leak
Japanese	18	1:40.861	12	52	1 lap down	

1999 Position Summary

Contested:	12	Finished:	5
Pole Positions:	0	Fastest Laps:	0
Points:	0		
1st-6th:	0	Best–8th Eur	

Year	Team	No.	Grand Prix
1999	BAR Supertec	13	Aus r, Bra r, Can r, Fra 9, GB r, Aut 15, Ger r, Hun 13, Bel r, Ita r, Eur 8, Mal r, Jap 12

Teams 2000

Introduction

These pages contain details of the 11 teams that will contest the Y2K Formula 1 season. I am indebted to the teams for help in supplying the information. Due to deadlines and car launch dates it has not been possible to provide a completely up-to-date set of details. In this cases specifications are as given for the 1999 cars. However, as the regulations governing cars have not changed significantly in the past year most of the information remains relative.

Arrows

Arrows Grand Prix
Arrows Grand Prix International
TWR Group Ltd, Leafield Technical Centre,
Leafield, Witney, Oxon, OX8 5PF
Tel: +44 (0)1993 871000   Fax : +44 (0)1993 871100

Chairman and	
Team Principle:	Tom Walkinshaw
Technical Director:	Mike Coughlan
Chief Designer:	Eghbal Hamidy
Team Manager:	Steve Nielsen
Chief Mechanic:	Stuart Cowie
Drivers:	Marc Gene (2nd year)
	tba
Mechanics:	Greg Baker (Gene)
	Dave Crabtree
	Phil Traves (Spare)

Brief History

1977: Arrows Grand Prix founded. 1978: Riccardo Patrese scores Arrows' first point with sixth at Long Beach; Patrese takes second in Sweden. 1981: Patrese takes first pole position at Long Beach. 1989: Arrows open new $10 million technical centre in Milton Keynes. 1989: Arrows are bought by Wataru Ohashi's Footwork Corporation. 1995:

Jackie Oliver takes control after Footwork pull out. 1996: Tom Walkinshaw buys controlling interest in team and relocates works; reigning World Champion Damon Hill signs for team. 1997: Damon Hill equals team's best ever finish – 2nd after leading Hungarian Grand Prix.

Grand Prix Record

Contested:	337	as Arrows and Footwork
Cars Started:	633	Completed: 325 Retired: 308
Victories:	0	Best Finish: 2nd – 5 times
Pole Positions:	1	
Fastest Laps:	0	
Constructors' World Titles:	0	Best: 4th 1988
Drivers' World Championships:	0	Best: =7th 1988
Most Points in a Season:	23	1988
Total Constructors' Cup Points:	157	
Average Points/Grand Prix:	0.49	

Review

The last two years for Arrows seem to have been a case of one step forward, two steps back. Just nine finishes combined from their two drivers left them bottom of the completion table with just 31.25%. It was a sorry state of affairs for a team that looked to be going forward at pace in 1997. The arrival of Prince Malik Ado Ibrahim, a Nigerian businessman whose consortium bought a share in the team prior to the start of the 1999 season, failed to have the desired effect off the track while the pairing of new boy Pedro de la Rosa with Tora 'Tiger' Takagi, in his first year out of rookie school, only produced a single championship point in it.

The Arrows own-brand V10 engine was never competitive and invariably its two drivers occupied the last row of the grid, although both drivers managed one 17th place start apiece, with Takagi's coming in the opening race in Australia and de la Rosa a few weeks later in Brazil.

De la Rosa at least got his F1 career off to an encouraging start finishing in sixth place in Melbourne to earn what was to prove to be his and his team's only point of the season. Takagi followed him home in seventh place. On that first showing there would have been a good deal of optimism in the camp, but apart from the Japanese driver finishing eighth in Brazil, that was as good as it was going to get.

Reliability, especially with the V10 power-pack, was invariably a problem and was a main reason why Takagi failed to finish any of the last set of eight races. It was virtually an identical story for the team's Spanish driver in his second half of the season with only a 15th place in Hungary breaking up the boredom of dnfs, although a 13th place finish did bring the season to a close in Japan.

At the French Grand Prix both Arrows drivers were placed ahead of the Minardi drivers on the grid despite the fact that neither Arrows man made it inside the 107% rule. A curious decision, made because they were quicker in practice!

Before the season had ended Ibrahim had resigned from the Board and the team opted to ditch its own in-house engine in favour of the Renault-sourced Supertec engines for the 2000 season. They should help provide the reliability so badly missing in 1999 but probably not much more.

Drivers and Results 1999

Driver	Races	Com	Ret	Dnq	HP	Pts	Psn	Comp%
de la Rosa, P.	16	5	11	0	6	1	17/24	31.25
Takagi, T.	16	5	11	0	7	0	–	31.25
Aggregate	32	10	21	0	6	1	9/11	31.25

			Pedro de la Rosa			**Toransuke Takagi**	
	Grand Prix	*Gd*	*P*	*Details*	*Gd*	*P*	*Details*
1	Australian	18	6	1:36:25.976	17	7	1:36:27.947
2	Brazilian	17	r	hydraulics	19	8	1:36:10.072
3	San Marino	18	r	suspension	20	r	hydraulics
4	Monaco	21	r	gearbox	19	r	engine
5	Spanish	19	11	1:34:41.268	20	12	1:34:38.929
6	Canadian	20	r	transmission	19	r	transmission
7	French	21	11	1 lap down	22	dq	illegal tyres
8	British	20	r	gearbox	19	16	2 laps down
9	Austrian	21	r	brakes	20	r	engine
10	German	20	r	accident	22	r	engine
11	Hungarian	20	15	2 laps down	21	r	drive shaft
12	Belgian	22	r	transmission	19	r	clutch
13	Italian	21	r	accident damage	22	r	spin
14	European	22	r	gearbox	21	r	accident
15	Malaysian	20	r	engine	22	r	drive shaft
16	Japanese	21	13	2 laps down	19	r	gearbox

Arrows A21 Specifications

Engine   **Supertec FB02**

Cylinders: 10 cylinders (71 degree angle)

Valves: 40 – pneumatically controlled

Dimensions: 623 mm (length), 542 mm (width), 395 mm (height)

Management:	Magneti Marelli electronic engine management and static ignition
Cylinder:	Head – aluminium. Block – thin aluminium

Car

Chassis:	Arrows manufactured Carbon Monocoque
Suspension:	Pushrod operated five damper system with dynamic dampers
Steering:	Arrows
Cooling system:	Secan oil and water radiators
Transmission:	Arrows 6-speed semi-automatic, in-line configuration
Clutch:	AP Racing (Carbon)
Brakes:	AP Arrows callipers
Instruments:	Arrows/TAG Data Display
Gearbox:	Arrows
Fuel System:	Arrows/ATL – 130 litres capacity
Dimensions:	Front Track: 1465 mm Rear Track: 1410 mm
	Wheelbase: 2995 mm Overall: 5140 mm

Engines 1978-99

1978-83: Ford. 1984-86: BMW Turbo. 1987-88: Megatron Turbo. 1989-90: Ford Turbo. 1991: Porsche. 1992-94: Mugen-Honda. 1995-96: Hart. 1997: Arrows 1998-99

Drivers 1989-99

1989: D.Warwick, E.Cheever & M.Donnelly. 1990: M.Alboreto & I.Capelli. 1991: M.Alboreto, A.Caffi & S.Johansson. 1992: M.Alboreto & A.Suzuki. 1993: D.Warwick & A.Suzuki. 1994: C.Fittipaldi & G.Morbidelli 1995: G.Morbidelli, T.Inoue & M.Papis. 1996: J.Verstappen & R.Rosset. 1997: D.Hill & P.Diniz. 1998: P.Diniz & M.Salo. 1999: P.de la Rosa & T.Takagi.

Constructors' Cup Record

Year-Position/Points:1978-9/11; 1979-9/5; 1980-7/11; 1981-8/10; 1982-10/5; 1983-10/4; 1984-9/6; 1985-8/14; 1986-10/1; 1987-6/11; 1988-4/23; 1989-7/13; 1990-9/2; 1992-7/6; 1993-9/4; 1994-9/9; 1995-8/5; 1996-9/1; 1997-8/9; 1998-7/6; 1999-9/1.

Grand Prix Best Performance

2nd position five times: 1978 Swe (Patrese), 1980 USA (Patrese), 1981 San (Patrese), 1985 San (Boutsen), 1997 Hun (Damon Hill).

BAR

British American Racing
Brackley, Northamptonshire, NN13 7BD
Tel: +44 (0)1280 844000   Fax: +44 (0)1280 844001
Chairman: Martin Broughton
Vice-Chairman: Adrian Reynard
MD: Craig Pollock
Tech. Director: Malcolm Oastler
Chief Engineer: Steve Farrell
Team Manager: Robert Synge
Drivers: Jacques Villeneuve (2nd year)
                         Ricardo Zonta (2nd year)
Race Engineers: Jock Clear (Villeneuve)
                         Mick Cook (Zonta)
Test Driver: Darren Manning

Brief History

1997: BAR team announced in December. 1998: Tyrrell acquired by BAR for £22 million. 1999: Team enter F1 but fail to score point in debut season.

Grand Prix Record

Contested:	16	
Cars Started:	31	Completed: 11 Retired: 20
Victories:	0	Best Finish: 7th 1999
Pole Positions:	0	Best Grid: 5th 1999
Fastest Laps:	0	
Constructors' World Titles:	0	Best: 11th 1999
Drivers' World Championships:	0	
Most Points in a Season:	0	
Total Constructors' Cup Points:	0	
Average Points/Grand Prix:	0.0	

Review

How do you gauge the success or failure of the BAR team in its first season? Had this been any other team then the fact they had got through the first season, unscathed and producing some consistent finishes, would have led to a reasonable end of term report. But this was no normal team. It had huge backing, a long lead-up and there was even talk of a win in its first race, let alone season. Then there were conflicts with the governing FIA about the team's wish to run both of its cars with different livery. Added to this they had in the form of Jacques Villeneuve the services of the 1998 F1 World Champion who had also won the CART championship the previous year.

Not only did BAR fail to even look like securing a win in its debut season, Villeneuve had to wait to the 12th race of the season to even get the car home, while the team's first finish of the season was recorded by Mika Salo, who was a stand-in for rookie Ricardo Zonta who was recovering from an injury sustained in qualifying at Brazil, where he ran into an unprotected barrier at over 100 mph.

A simple glance down the team's results shows that their package did not have the reliability, something that had become ever apparent in the 1999 pre-season testing.

In Villeneuve's first five races he suffered a rear wing failure, two gearbox failures, an oil leak and hydraulic problems. An accident and spin were then followed by more mechanical problems right up until the Belgian Grand Prix when the Canada secured his first BAR finish, albeit a lap down in 15th place.

Neither Zonta nor Salo suffered these problems. This was probably mainly due to the fact that Jacques was pushing the car a lot harder. This fact was reflected in his qualifying performances which saw him get as high as a fifth starting position in Imola. Equally, the former champion was often running close to the pack behind the leaders before something on his car gave.

As mentioned already, Salo produced the team's first two finishes in his three races, before Zonta recorded his first classification in France. Zonta followed this up with a few more and the team's first double finish came in the final European race of the season with Zonta classified eighth a lap down, and Jacques 10th, although he had retired with a clutch problem so in truth both cars didn't make it past the chequered flag all season. The team also suffered its first qualifying disqualification, when Jacques had his times wiped out after a fuel check showed that his Elf fuel didn't match the approved sample given to the officials prior to qualifying. The team later reported that the use of a new fuel tank had contaminated its fuel supply.

The team ran the Renault-badged Supertec engines in its first season but almost before it was underway they had announced that Honda would be supplying their power for the 2000 season. That will be another learaning process for the team, but one that will have long term benefits.

Given the overall performance it wasn't surprising that rumours regarding Jacques' future at BAR were circulating, especially given internal political wrangling that at one point looked to have forced manager Craig Pollock out. But they were seemingly resolved and Villeneuve announced that he would be honouring his contract for 2000.

Drivers and Results 1999

Driver	Races	Com	Ret	Dnq	HP	Pts	Psn	Comp%
Villeneuve, J.	16	4	12	0	8	0	–	25.00
Zonta, R.	12	5	7	0	8	0	–	41.67
Salo, M.	3	2	1	0	7	0	–	66.67
Aggregate	31	11	20	0	7	0	–	35.48

		Jacques Villeneuve			**Zonta/Salo***		
	Grand Prix	Gd	P	*Details*	Gd	P	*Details*
1	Australian	11	r	rear wing failure	19	r	overheating
2	Brazilian	21	r	hydraulics	–	–	dns
3	San Marino*	5	r	gearbox	19	7	electrics
4	Monaco*	8	r	oil leak	12	r	brakes
5	Spanish*	6	r	gearbox	16	8	1:35:21.065
6	Canadian	16	r	accident	17	r	accident
7	French	12	r	spin	10	9	1:59:53.107
8	British	9	r	gearbox	16	r	suspension
9	Austrian	9	r	drive shaft	15	15	8 laps down dnf
10	German	12	r	accident	18	r	engine
11	Hungarian	9	r	clutch	17	13	2 laps down
12	Belgian	11	15	1 lap down	14	r	gearbox
13	Italian	11	8	1:17:44.720	18	r	wheel bearing
14	European	8	10	clutch	17	8	1 lap down
15	Malaysian	10	r	hydraulics	13	r	water leak
16	Japanese	11	9	1 lap down	18	12	1 lap down

BAR Honda 02 Specifications

Car

Chassis:	Moulded carbon fibre and honeycomb composite structure
Gearbox:	Triple-plate carbon
Transmission:	Gearbox Reynard/Xtrac longitudinal, six-speed unit Gear selection by sequential, semi-automatic, hydraulic activation. Reynard drive shafts
Steering:	Reynard-developed, rack and pinion

Suspension:	Front: Reynard pushrod-activated torsion springs and damper units, rockers, mechanical anti-roll bar
	Rear: Reynard pushrod-activated combined spring and damper units, rockers, mechanical anti-roll bar
Dampers	Koni (developed exclusively for BAR)
Brakes:	Brakes AP Racing. 2 x 6-piston callipers – front and rear
Wheels:	Wheels OZ forged magnesium Front: 305 mm/12.0 in wide. Rear: 348 mm/13.7 in wide
Fuel Tank:	ATL Kevlar-reinforced rubber bladder. 100 litres capacity
Instrumentation:	Pi Research Intelligent Instrumentation set in steering wheel, integrated digital display with real-time/microwave telemetry
Dimensions :	Length: 4470 mm Wheelbase: 3020 mm
	Width: 1800 mm Height: 950 mm
	Front/Rear track 1800 mm

• *Detail based on 1999 BAR 01.*

Benetton

Mild Seven Benetton Playlife
Benetton Formula Limited
Whiteways Technical Centre, Enstone,
Chipping Norton, Oxon, OX7 4EE
Tel: +44 (0)1608 678000   Fax: +44 (0)1608 678800

Chairman/CEO:	Rocco Benetton
Tech. Director:	Pat Symonds
Team Manager:	Mark Owen
Chief Mechanic:	Mick Ainsley-Cowlishaw
Chief Designer:	Tim Densham
Drivers:	Giancarlo Fisichella (3rd year)
	Alexander Wurz (3rd year)
Race Engineers:	Alan Permane/Mark Herd (Fisichella)
	Christian Silk/Rod Nelson (Wurz)

Brief History

(*Team name Toleman 1981-85*). 1986: Benetton Formula 1 established after taking over the Toleman team. 1987: Gerhard Berger wins in Mexico to give Benetton their first victory. 1990: Nelson Piquet leads home fellow Brazilian Roberto Moreno for first one-two. 1992: Michael Schumacher wins his first Grand Prix in Belgium. 1994: Michael Schumacher wins the Drivers' World Championship. 1995: Michael Schumacher wins second Drivers' World Championship and Benetton win first Constructors' World Championship.

Grand Prix Record

Contested:	(226/57)	283	as Benetton & Toleman
Cars Started:	(451/94)	545	Completed: 325 Retired: 220
Victories:	(27/0)	27	
Pole Positions:	(16/0)	16	
Fastest Laps:	(36/2)	38	
Constructors' World Titles:		1	1995
Drivers' World Championships:		2	1994, 1995
Most Points in a Season:		137	1995
Total Constructors' Cup Points:		847.5	(821.5/26)
Average Points/Grand Prix:		2.99	

Review

Benetton spent another year in the F1 wilderness, never looking as though they would capture the form they had in the mid-Nineties. But then they had Michael Schumacher and the best power pack of the decade in Renault engines. While both their drivers have hinted at flashes of brilliance, Alexander Wurz had a poor 1999 while Giancarlo Fisichella – probably the pick of the two – doesn't seem to be able to handle the pressure on the occasions when he gets in front and is in with a chance of his first Grand Prix win.

For the 1999 season the design of the B199 was radically changed from the unsuccessful B198 – the most notable change being the introduction of a new Front Torque Transfer (FTT) system to aid with braking and handling. This immediately brought protest from several teams over its legality and continued to court controversy throughout the season.

The B199 was more often than not reliable but was invariably off the pace in qualifying, leaving both drivers to struggle through the mid-pack. Wurz was invariably in the lower orders on the starting grid, achieving a season's best starting position of seventh, twice – in Hungary and Malaysia. Fisichella was more consistent in getting his Supertec powered car towards the front order but as equally as likely to line-up towards the rear. His season's best – fourth – came in Hungary.

In terms of points then it was the Italian who was by far the most consistent, contributing 13 of his team's 16 Constructors' Cup total, with six of those coming for his second place finish in Canada, a race which he could have won, had he been able to hold his nerve. Curiously the team didn't run their FTT system there as they deemed it unsuitable for the circuit! Despite this, the portents at the start of the season looked reasonable for the team. Giancarlo got the season off to a points win for the Benetton team, qualifying a reasonable seventh and finishing fourth – encouraging enough although a suspension failure after 28 laps ended Wurz's hopes. The roles were reversed in the next race with Wurz completing the race in seventh place and Fisichella unable to build on his fifth place start when his clutch ended his race at half distance. The cars had looked more than competitive, which the team put down to adjusting the weight and its distribution on the car, making them a more balanced drive for their pilots.

Giancarlo showed the more consistent form over the next four races, securing two fifths, a ninth in Spain and then a tremendous second in Canada. Wurz on the other hand only secured his first point in Monaco and was involved in the accident at the start which put him out of the Canadian race. After the euphoria of Canada, Giancarlo spun-out at Magny-Cours to bring his run of good form to an end – indeed it virtually ended it for the season with him unable to score another point from that juncture on, despite a couple of good qualifying performances that had seen him in the second and third rows. Alex used the British GP as the starting point to secure five successive finishes, with a season best fifth place coming in Austria.

The team will be looking for a change in fortune for the 2000 season. They suffered a blow in late November when Nick Wirth resigned from his role of Chief Designer – a move due to the differing ideas as to the future directions of the car's development. He has been replaced by Tim Densham, who joined Benetton from Honda. Getting back into the top four of the Constructors' Championship must be the first aim but they seem unlikely to achieve this in 2000.

Drivers and Results 1999

Driver	Races	Com	Ret	Dnq		HP	Pts	Psn	Comp%
Fisichella, G.	16	10	6	0		2	13	9/24	62.50
Wurz, A.	16	10	6	0		5	3	13/24	62.50
Aggregate	32	20	12	0		2	16	6/11	62.50

		Giancarlo Fisichella				**Alexander Wurz**		
	Grand Prix	Gd	P	*Details*		Gd	P	*Details*
1	Australian	7	4	1:35:35.077		10	r	suspension
2	Brazilian	5	r	clutch		9	7	1:36:12.021
3	San Marino	16	5	1:34:27.002		17	r	accident
4	Monaco	9	5	1:49:32.705		10	6	1:49:47.799

5	Spanish	13	9	1:35:22.704	18	10	1:35:29.548
6	Canadian	7	2	1:41:36.509	11	r	accident
7	French	7	r	spin	13	r	spin
8	British	17	7	1:33:24.758	18	10	1:33:42.267
9	Austrian	12	12	3 laps - engine	10	5	1:29:18.796
10	German	10	r	suspension	13	7	1:22:31.927
11	Hungarian	4	r	fuel pressure	7	7	1:47.24.548
12	Belgian	13	11	1:27:15.252	15	14	1:27:40.802
13	Italian	17	r	accident	14	r	electronics
14	European	6	r	spun-out	11	r	accident
15	Malaysian	11	11	4 laps down	7	8	1:37:39.428
16	Japanese	14	14	engine	15	10	1 lap down

Benetton B200 Specifications

Engine: **Playlife FB02 3.0 V10**

Cylinders: 10 cylinders (71 degree angle), 3000 cc

Valves: 40 – pneumatically controlled

Dimensions: 623 mm (length), 542 mm (width), 395 mm (height)

Management: Magneti Marelli electronic engine management and static ignition

Cylinder: Head – aluminium. Block – thin aluminium
Car

Chassis: Carbon fibre composite monocoque manufactured by Benetton Formula 1 Racing Team. Engine installed as fully stressed member attached to the rearmost monocoque bulkhead.

Suspension: Front: Carbon fibre top and bottom wishbones operating a titanium rocker via a push rod system. Torsion bar and damper untis mounted internally in the monocoque. Rear: Carbon fibre top and steel lower wishbones, operating coil spring damper units, mounted on top of the magnesium gearbox.

Transmission: Benetton semi-automatic six-speed gearbox. Triple-plate clutch

Fuel System: ATL rubber fuel cell mounted within monocoque structure behind cockpit

Oil System: Oil tank within bell-housing providing two gallon/nine litres capacity

Cooling System: Separate water and cooling radiators in each sidepod

Electrical: Hardware and software developed jointly by Benetton and Magneti Marelli

Braking systems: Carbon fibre discs and pads

Engines 1981-00

(1981-85: Toleman.) 1981-85: Hart Turbo. 1986: BMW Turbo. 1987: Ford Turbo. 1988-94: Ford. 1995-97: Renault. 1998-00: Playlife (Renault).

Drivers 1989-00

1989: A.Nannini, J.Herbert & E.Pirro. 1990: A.Nannini, N.Piquet & R.Moreno. 1991: N.Piquet, R.Moreno & M.Schumacher. 1992: M.Schumacher & M.Brundle. 1993: M.Schumacher & R.Patrese. 1994: M.Schumacher, J.Verstappen, J.J.Lehto & J.Herbert. 1995: M.Schumacher & J.Herbert. 1996-97: J.Alesi & G.Berger. 1998-00: G.Fisichella & A.Wurz.

Constructors' Cup Record

Year-Position/Points: (Toleman) 1983-9/10; 1984-7/16; (Benetton) 1986-6/19; 1987-5/28; 1988-3/39; 1989-4/39; 1990-3/71; 1991-4/38.5; 1992-3/91; 1993-3/72; 1994-2/103; 1995-1/137; 1996-3/68; 1997-3/67; 1998-5/33; 1999-6/16.

Grand Prix Wins

1986 Mex (Berger); 1989 Jap (Nannini); 1990 Jap (Piquet), Aus (Piquet); 1991 Can (Piquet); 1992 Bel (M.Schumacher); 1993 Por (M.Schumacher); 1994 Bra, Pac, San, Mon, Can, Fra, Hun, Eur (all M.Schumacher); 1995 Bra, Esp, Mon, Fra (all M.Schumacher), GB (Herbert), Ger, Bel (both M.Schumacher), Ita (Herbert), Eur, Pac, Jap (all M.Schumacher); 1997 Ger (G.Berger).

Ferrari

Scuderia Ferrari Marlboro

Ferrari SpR
Via Ascari 55-57, 41053 Maranello, Modena, Italy
Tel: +39 0536 949 111   Fax: +39 0536 949 436
Chairman: Luca Di Montezemolo
Team Principal: Jean Todt
Tech. Director: Ross Brawn
TD Engine: Paolo Martinelli

Team Manager:	Stefano Domenicali
Chief Designer:	Rory Byrne
Chief Engineer:	Ignazio Lunetta
Engine TD:	Paolo Martinelli
Drivers:	Michael Schumacher (5th year)
	Rubens Barrichello (1st year)
Engineers:	Luca Baldisseri (Schumacher)
	Carlo Cantoni (Barrichello)
Test Driver:	Luca Badoer
Sponsors:	Philip Morris, Shell, Fiat, FedEx, Tic/Tac, Tim,
	Bridgestone, Magneti Marelli

Brief History

1929: Enzo Ferrari forms his company. 1947: Franco Cortese wins the Grand Prix of Rome to record Ferrari's first race win. 1951: Jose Gonzalez records Ferrari's first Formula 1 victory. 1952: Alberto Ascari wins the Drivers' World Championship in a Ferrari. 1953: Ascari wins back-to-back titles driving for the Modena-based team. 1956: Juan-Manuel Fangio wins World Championship with Ferrari. 1958: Mike Hawthorn becomes the third Ferrari driver to win the title. 1961: Phil Hill leads Ferrari to the 'double' of both Drivers' and Constructors' titles. 1964: John Surtees takes the World Championship in a Ferrari. 1969: Lowest ever Ferrari score of seven points achieved in Constructors' World Championship. 1975: Niki Lauda takes title in a Ferrari ahead of Emerson Fittipaldi. 1977: Lauda repeats his success of two years earlier. 1979: Jody Scheckter wins his only World Championship driving a Ferrari. 1983: Ferrari win their eight Constructors' Cup. 1999: Ferrari win first Constructors' Cup title since 1983.

Grand Prix Record

Contested:	619	including Lancia-Ferrari
Cars Started:	1426	Completed: 907 Retired: 519
Victories:	125	
Pole Positions:	127	
Fastest Laps:	139	
Constructors' World Titles:	9	1961, 1964, 1975, 1976, 1977, 1979, 1982, 1983, 1999
Drivers' World Championships:	9	1952, 1953, 1956, 1958, 1961, 1964, 1975, 1977, 1979
Most Points in a Season:	133	1998
Total Constructors' Cup Points:	2321.5	
Average Points/Grand Prix:	3.75	

The irony could not have been lost on anyone in Formula 1 that the driver they employed in a contractual support role to Michael Schumacher should have posed their main thrust towards the Drivers' Championship and with it the Constructors' Cup. The broken leg that Michael Schumacher suffered prior to the start at Silverstone forced the role on Eddie Irvine, but when Shuey returned he played the support role to Irvine as the team pushed towards glory, ultimately by taking the Constructors' Cup for the first time since 1983. There was also another hero in this amazing saga, Mika Salo, who covered for Michael in the six races he missed and did so quite brilliantly, contributing points and cover for Irvine on their charge towards glory.

Despite not seeming ever to have the full support of the Ferrari team throughout the season, Eddie was magnificent and his performance mirrored the words in these pages in last season's annual. He produced a near flawless performance throughout having just one retirement from 16 races to give him a 93.75% completion rate. In amongst this he scored points on a metronomic basis, only once finishing outside the points. Much of this was down to his improvement in qualifying where he was consistently strong.

Ferrari provided their drivers with an incredibly reliable package. The team completed 87.50% of their races, far ahead of their nearest rival Jordan who managed 65.63%. It was this ability to continually get cars home and more often than not, get them home in the points that really sustained the Ferrari challenge and ultimately won them the Constructors' title. Incredibly Ferrari lost just one car in the whole season due to a component failure!

The signs were not great at the start of the season, however. Even though Irvine provided a season opening win in Melbourne the Ferrari team must have been anxious about how the McLarens had dominated them in almost all aspects of the weekend. The chink in the armour was the Mercedes-powered cars' lack of reliability. Although they dominated the grid in the early part of the season, they struggled to get cars home. Ferrari took advantage of this fact.

In Australia Schuey was strangely off the pace finishing eighth from a third place grid start, while Eddie brought the bacon home with a terrific win. It was another scoring double in Brazil, this time Michael finishing higher but in second place. Back in Europe Michael recorded successive victories in San Marino and Monaco while Irvine suffered his only retirement of the season in the former, when his engine failed, but came home second in Monaco to give Ferrari their first one-two finish of the season and their first ever in Monaco.

Ferrari's victory at Imola was their first for 16 years on 'home-turf', since Patrick Tambay won in 1983. The win sent the scarlet hordes that were packed into the Autodromo Enzo e Dino Ferrari into raptures. Schuey's win at Monaco was his 16th victory since joining Ferrari in 1996 and eclipsed Niki Lauda's previous record of 15.

In Spain, Eddie out-qualified Michael for only the fourth time since they were team-mates at Ferrari but the German managed to finish one position ahead of him, in third place. It was a podium in Canada though, but it was a dnf for Michael whose error exiting the final corner of the circuit saw him slide into the wall and out of the race. Ferrari had to settle for fifth and sixth in France and then looked to be handed a mortal wound when Michael crashed out of the race, and six races of the season, when he crashed into the wall at Stowe on the first lap, to leave him with a broken tib and fib in his right leg. Eddie completed the race and came home a creditable second, after which the team pledged their support for him (what else could they do?) in his efforts to win the championship. The team also announced that Mika Salo, and not test driver Luca Badoer, would be Shuey's replacement while he was out injured.

Eddie took up the team's rallying cry with maximum points in Austria and Germany while Salo backed the Ulsterman up superbly to finish a career best second place at Hockenheim and thus record the team's second one-two of the season. Mika managed one more podium finish, third in Italy, in his remaining races but had done enough to keep Ferrari in the hunt for the Constructors' Cup by the time Michael announced that he would return for the Malaysian GP. In the meantime Eddie continued to pick up points but at a slower rate. He also recorded his only finish outside the points when he ran home seventh at the European meeting.

In among all this Eddie announced he had signed for the Jaguar Racing team (Stewart) with Barrichello making the reverse trip to Ferrari for the year 2000.

Michael's return for Sepang was surrounded by controversy. Was he pushed to return, was he really going to help Eddie and play the back-up role, was he really ready? Yes, yes, yes were the answers as the German maestro produced an impeccable display of driving. Not only did he take pole position at Sepang, with Eddie second to give Ferrari their first front row of the season, he continually backed up the McLarens and twice allowed Eddie past to take victory, with him assuring maximum team points to place both Irvine and Ferrari in the lead in both championships going into the final race.

But then it seemed disaster had struck. Following post-race scrutineering, both cars were deemed to have illegal bargeboards and were disqualified. Hakkinen was elevated to first place and looked to have been awarded the Drivers' Championship and McLaren the Constructors'

Cup by default. A fraught Ross Brawn seemed to admit the mistake after the race but immediately lodged an appeal. Six days later, the Race Stewards' decision was over-turned by an FIA tribunal and it was game on for the final race of the season.

In Japan, Michael announced his intention to drive for a win, which would mean that if Eddie finished fourth or above he was sure of the championship. Schuey qualified on pole, but Eddie couldn't make better than fifth place and when Hakkinen took the lead at the start the Ulsterman's fate seemed sealed and he had to settle for second place in the Drivers' Championship, his career-best tally of 74 points, two down on Hakkinen. But with the Ferrari drivers coming home second and third, the team were delighted at ousting McLaren to take the Constructors' Championship.

For 2000 Michael Schumacher will bear the brunt of the Ferrari challenge. He will not have been unhappy that Eddie failed to take the Drivers' title in a Ferrari as this is probably an honour he wants to reserve for himself. This is year five for the German behind the wheel of the Prancing Horse and he is now beyond his three year target of achieving his aim. The arrival of Rubens Barrichello adds spice to the plot. The Brazilian is not contracted as a number two to Schuey in the way that Irvine was, thus he is free to race his own race. Equally, Rubens, on results, has always been the number one driver in his previous teams – Jordan and Stewart. Their own battles will be fascinating to watch, providing Barrichello can get enough testing hours in the car. There could be plenty of red mist!

Drivers and Results 1999

Driver	Races	Com	Ret	Dnq	HP	Pts	Psn	Comp%
Schumacher, M.	9	8	1	0	1	44	5/24	88.89
Irvine, E.	16	15	1	0	1	74	2/24	93.97
Salo, M.	6	5	1	0	2	10	10/24	83.88
Aggregate	31	28	3	0	1	128	1/11	90.32

	M.Schumacher/Salo*			**Eddie Irvine**		
	Grand Prix	Gd	P	Details	Gd	P	Details
1	Australian	3	8	1:35:16.505	6	1	1:35:01.659
2	Brazilian	4	2	1:38:08.710	6	5	1:35:23.103
3	San Marino	3	1	1:33:44.792	4	r	engine
4	Monaco	2	1	1:49:31.812	4	2	1:50:02.288
5	Spanish	4	3	1:34:24.510	2	4	1:34:43.847
6	Canadian	1	r	accident	3	3	1:41:37.524
7	French	6	5	1:59:12.224	17	6	1:59:13.244
8	British	2	–	dns	4	2	1:32:31.973

9	Austrian*	7	9	1 lap down	3	1	1:28:12.438
10	German*	4	2	1:21.59.601	5	1	1:21:58.594
11	Hungarian*	18	12	2 laps down	2	3	1:46:50.784
12	Belgian*	9	7	1:26:39.306	6	4	1:26:28.005
13	Italian*	6	3	1:17:14.855	8	6	1:17:30.325
14	European*	12	r	spun-out	9	7	1:43:00.997
15	Malaysian	1	2	1:36:39.534	2	1	1:36:38.494
16	Japanese	1	2	1:31:23.800	5	3	1:32:54.473

Ferrari Specifications

Engine: **Ferrari 3.0 V10**
Cylinders: V10 – 40 valves
Injection: Magneti Marelli
Electronics: Magneti Marelli
Car
Gearbox: Ferrari longitudinal gearbox
Clutch: Manual command on steering wheel
Suspension: Independent push-rod activated torsion springs
Dampers: Ferrari
Brakes: Brembo
Instruments: Magneti Marelli
Brakes: Brembo
Clutch: AP/Sachs

Engines 1950-00

1950-80: Ferrari. 1981-88: Ferrari Turbo. 1989-00: Ferrari.

Drivers 1989-00

1989: N.Mansell & G.Berger. 1990: A.Prost & N.Mansell. 1991: A.Prost, J.Alesi & G.Morbidelli. 1992: J.Alesi, I.Capelli & N.Larini. 1993: J.Alesi & G.Berger. 1994: J.Alesi, G.Berger & N.Larini. 1995: J.Alesi & G.Berger. 1996-99: M.Schumacher & E.Irvine. 2000: M.Schumacher & R.Barrichello.

Constructors' Cup Record

Year-Position/Points: 1958-2/40 (57); 1959-2/32 (38); 1960-3/26 (27); 1961-1/40 (52); 1962-5/18; 1963-4/26; 1964-1/45 (49); 1965-4/26 (27); 1966-2/31 (32); 1967-4/20; 1968-4/32; 1969-5/7; 1970-2/52 (55); 1971-3/33; 1972-4/33; 1973-6/12; 1974-2/65; 1975-1/72.5; 1976-1/83; 1977-1/95 (97); 1978-2/58; 1979-1/113; 1980-10/8; 1981-5/34; 1982-1/74;

1983-1/89; 1984-2/57.5; 1985-2/82; 1986-4/33; 1987-4/53; 1988-2/65; 1989-3/59; 1990-2/110; 1991-3/55.5; 1992-4/21; 1993-4/28; 1994-3/71; 1995-3/73; 1996-2/70; 1997-2/102; 1998-2/133; 1999-1/128.

Grand Prix Wins

1951 GB (Gonzalez), Ger (Ascari), Ita (Ascari); 1952 Swi (Taruffi), Bel, GB, Ger, Hol, Ita (all Ascari); 1953 Arg, Hol, Bel (all Ascari), Fra (Hawthorn), GB (Ascari), Ger (Farina), Swi (Ascari); 1954 GB (Gonzalez), Esp (Hawthorn); 1955 Mon (Trintignant); 1956 Arg (Musso/Fangio), Bel (Collins), Fra (Collins), GB (Fangio), Ger (Fangio); 1958 Fra (Hawthorn), GB (Collins); 1959 Fra (Brooks), Ger (Brooks); 1960 Ita (G.Hill); 1961 Hol (von Trips), Bel (G.Hill), Fra (Baghetti), GB (von Trips), Ita (G.Hill); 1963 Ger (Surtees); 1964 Ger (Surtees), Aut (Bandini), Ita (Surtees); 1966 Bel (Surtees), Ita (Scarfiotti); 1968 Fra (Ickx); 1970 Aut (Ickx), Ita (Regazzoni), Can (Ickx), Mex (Ickx); 1971 SA (Andretti), Hol (Ickx); 1972 Ger (Ickx); 1974 Esp (Lauda), Hol (Lauda), Ger (Regazzoni); 1975 Mon, Bel, Swe, Fra (all Lauda), Ita (Regazzoni), USA (Lauda); 1976 Bra (Lauda), SA (Lauda), Long Beach (Regazzoni), Bel, Mon, GB (all Lauda); 1977 Bra (Reutemann), SA (Lauda), Ger (Lauda), Hol (Lauda); 1978 Bra, Long Beach, GB TP, USA (all Reutemann), Can (G.Villeneuve); 1979 SA (G.Villeneuve), Long Beach (G.Villeneuve), Bel, Mon, Ita (all Scheckter), USA (G.Villeneuve); 1981 Mon (G.Villeneuve), Esp (G.Villeneuve); 1982 San (Pironi), Hol (Pironi), Ger (Tambay); 1983 San (Tambay), Can (Arnoux), Ger (Arnoux); 1984 Bel (Alboreto); 1985 Can (Alboreto), Ger (Alboreto); 1987 Jap (Berger), Aus (Berger); 1988 Ita (Berger); 1989 Bra (Mansell), Hun (Mansell), Por (Berger); 1990 Bra, Fra, GB (all Prost), Por (Mansell), Esp (Prost); 1994 Ger (Berger); 1995 Can (Alesi); 1996 Esp, Bel, Ita (all M.Schumacher); 1997 Mon, Can, Fra, Bel, Jap (all M.Schumacher); 1998 Arg, Can, Fra, GB, Hun, Ita (all M.Schumacher). 1999: Aus (Irvine), San, Esp (M.Schumacher), Aut, Ger, Mal (all Irvine).

Jaguar Racing

Jaguar Racing Ltd
Bradbourne Drive, Tilbrook, Milton Keynes, Bucks., MK7 8BJ
Tel: +44 (0)1908 279700   Fax: +44 (0)1908 279763

CEO:	Jackie Stewart OBE
COO:	Paul Stewart
Tech. Director:	Gary Anderson
Team Manager:	Dave Stubbs
Race Director:	Andy Miller
Chief Designer:	John Russell
Chief Mechanic:	Dave Redding
Drivers:	Eddie Irvine (1st year)
	Johnny Herbert (2nd year)
Engineers:	Robin Gearing (Irvine)
	Andy Le Fleming (Herbert)
Test Driver:	Luciano Burti
Sponsors:	HSBC, MCI Worldcom, Hewlett Packard, Lear, Bridgestone

Brief History

1996: Stewart Grand Prix formed. 1997: First season F1 racing. Finished 2nd in Monaco Grand Prix. 1999: Johnny Herbert wins first Stewart Grand Prix. Ford buy Stewart team. 2000: Stewart F1 renamed Jaguar Racing.

Grand Prix Record

Contested:	49	
Cars Started:	95	Completed: 41 Retired: 54
Victories:	1	
Pole Positions:	1	
Fastest Laps:	0	
Constructors' World Titles:	0	Best: 4th 1999
Drivers' World Championships:	0	Best: 7th 1999
Most Points in a Season:	36	1999
Total Constructors' Cup Points:	47	
Average Points/Grand Prix	0.96	

As the teams arrived in Imola for the San Marino Grand Prix the Stewart team were given a huge boost when Ford confirmed that they would be channelling all their resources into an exclusive technical partnership with the team. They also added that they would be vacating their position as the sport's major off-the-shelf engine suppliers from the end of the season. Immediately the rumours started that the team would be re-badged with the Jaguar marque for the year 2000 – something that was neither denied or confirmed at that point, but which was confirmed with the unveiling of new livery before the 1999 season had run its full course.

The backing of Ford had always been a fundamental part of the Stewart team's arrival in Formula 1. Indeed so much so that the team hardly looked like a rookie team in their first year of competition in 1997. But the money and backing are just a small part of the story that has been an amazing success. The Stewart family and their staff have produced miracles in the three years of running under the family name and in no small part was it due to hard work, endeavour and bravery. Anyone who saw the TV documentary of their first season in F1 will be left with the memory of Jackie Stewart on the phone seeking the cash to keep his dream alive. Now they are probably queuing up with the money. How wonderful also that the team achieved its first Grand Prix victory last year while still running the Stewart tartan. How wonderful also that it was achieved by Johnny Herbert, especially in the wake of the announcement that the team's ever-present driver Rubens Barrichello was Ferrari bound. Indeed it marked an exciting end of the Stewart branded team and their season finish. It was bitter sweet for Johnny who suffered the worst possible luck in the opening half of the season, with only two finishes from his first seven races with retirements all being down to matters outside of his control. The second of those finishes brought his first points of the season, with a fifth place in Canada.

Qualifying for both cars had been consistent, Rubens invariably inside the top four rows with Johnny averaging the fifth row. The Brazilian seemed to have the more reliable car, finishing fifth in Australia and suffering the first of his four mechanical related failures of the season in Brazil. His first podium finish came in San Marino and he secured the team's first ever pole position in the rain at Magny-Cours, converting that to his second third place of the season. Johnny managed a set of four straight finishes starting at Silverstone, but in truth they were all at the back end of the finishers. Then after two more mechanical failures coming at Spa and Monza, Johnny showed how good he is at staying out of trouble to secure maximum points and that first ever Stewart 'W'. While those around him fell to the conditions, Johnny rode the attrition to take victory while Rubens made it a near perfect day at the office to take third place.

As the season entered its final phase the news broke that Rubens would be moving to Ferrari for the 2000 season and the persistent rumours finally came true with Eddie Irvine announcing his place in the Jaguar Team where he would be partnering Johnny Herbert. The question then was whether Irvine would be bringing the Number 1 with him as World Champion – a neat way for Jaguar to start off their term of office.

The last points of the season came in Malaysia with Johnny taking fourth and Rubens fifth, which were then temporarily lifted to second and third until the Ferrari appeal was upheld. The other bonus for the team was the sight of Sir Frank Williams wearing Tartan trousers after Jackie Stewart enforced the forfeit on the Williams team boss after a bet in which he said Stewart would not win a race in 1999. The season ended in Japan with both drivers making it to the finish line but outside the points in seventh and eighth with Johnny again coming home first.

Despite the Jaguar name the bulk of the Stewart personnel remains in place. They start a new era having ended the three-year one finishing fourth in the Constructors' Cup, and will be looking to break into the top three in the year ahead.

Drivers and Results 1999

Driver	Races	Com	Ret	Dnq	HP	Pts	Psn	Comp%
Barrichello, R.	16	11	4	0	3	21	7/24	68.75
Herbert, J.	15	9	6	0	1	15	8/24	60.00
Aggregate	31	20	10	0	1	36	4/11	64.52

			Rubens Barrichello			**Johnny Herbert**	
	Grand Prix	Gd	P	Details	Gd	P	Details
1	Australian	4	5	1:35:56.357	13	–	dns
2	Brazilian	3	r	engine	10	r	hydraulics
3	San Marino	6	3	1:33:46.721	12	10	engine
4	Monaco	5	9	suspension	13	r	suspension
5	Spanish	7	dq	(from 8th pos)	14	r	transmission
6	Canadian	5	r	accident damage	10	5	1:41:38.532
7	French	1	3	1:59:07.775	9	r	gearbox
8	British	7	8	1:33:38.734	11	12	1:33:47.853
9	Austrian	5	r	engine	6	14	4 laps down
10	German	6	r	hydraulics	17	11	gearbox
11	Hungarian	8	5	1:47.07.344	10	11	1 lap down
12	Belgian	7	10	1:27:03.799	10	r	brakes
13	Italian	7	4	1:17:20.553	15	r	clutch
14	European	15	3	1:42:17.180	14	1	1:41:54.314

173

| 15 | Malaysian | 6 | 5 | 1:37:10.790 | 5 | 4 | 1:36:56.032 |
| 16 | Japanese | 13 | 8 | 1 lap down | 8 | 7 | 1 lap down |

Jaguar Cosworth 01 Specifications

Engine:	**Ford Cosworth V10 CR-2**
Cylinders:	10 (72 degree) – 40 valves
Capacity:	3000 cc
Management:	Visteon
Lubrication:	Dry sump
Ignition:	Cosworth Racing
Spark Plugs:	Champion
Weight:	100 kg
Dimensions:	569 mm (length), 506 mm (width), 485 mm (height)
Car	
Chassis:	Carbon fibre monocoque designed and built in-house, carrying engine as fully-stressed member
Transmission:	Stewart magnesium-cased six-speed gearbox, longitudinally mounted. High-pressure hydraulic system for power shift and clutch operation. Integrated centralised oil system
Clutch:	AP Racing triple-plate pull-type clutch
Suspension:	Upper and lower carbon wishbones and pushrods. Stewart/Penske damper layout. Torsion bar springing (front)/coil springing (rear)
Brakes:	AP Racing lithium alloy six-piston callipers (front). Twin AP Racing six-piston callipers (rear)
Brake Pads:	Carbone Industrie carbon fibre discs and pads
Wheels:	BBS forged magnesium
Electronics:	Visteon VCS single box. Integrated engine/chassis electronic control systems
Dimensions:	Front Track: 1598 mm
	Rear Track: 1424 mm
	Height: 1080 mm

Engines 1997-00

1997-00: Ford Cosworth.

Drivers 1997-00

1997-98: R.Barrichello, J.Magnussen & J. Verstappen; 1999: R.Barrichello & J.Herbert. 2000: E.Irvine & J.Herbert.

Year-Position/Points: 1997-9/6; 1998-8/5; 1999-4/36.

Grand Prix Wins

1997 Eur (Herbert).

Jordan

Benson & Hedges Jordan

Jordan Grand Prix Ltd
Buckingham Road, Silverstone, Towcester, Northants, NN12 8JT
Tel: +44 (0)1327 857153   Fax: +44 (0)1327 858120

Chairman:	Eddie Jordan
Managing Director:	Trevor Foster
Team Manager:	Jim Vale
Designer:	Mike Gascoyne
Chief Mechanic:	Tim Edwards
Drivers:	Heinz-Harald Frentzen (2nd year)
	Jarno Trulli (1st year)
Race Engineers:	Andy Stevenson (Frentzen)
	Nick Burrows (Trulli)

Brief History

1980: Eddie Jordan forms Jordan Motor Racing Team. 1987: Johnny Herbert wins British Formula 3 Championship driving a Jordan. 1988: Jean Alesi takes the International F3000 title for Jordan. 1990: Jordan F1 formed. 1991: Jordan score their first F1 points with Andrea de Cesaris fourth in Canada. 1993: Jordan signs a deal to use Hart engines until the end of the 1994 season. 1995: Exclusive deal with Peugeot engines. 1998: Switch to Mugen-Honda engines. Jordan win first Grand Prix with Damon Hill's victory at Spa – Jordan's 127th F1 race. Ralf Schumacher finishes in second place for first one-two finish.1999: Team achieve highest position in Constructors' and Drivers' Championship – 3rd.

Grand Prix Record

Contested:	146		
Cars Started:	284	Completed: 152	Retired: 132
Victories:	3		
Pole Positions:	2		
Fastest Laps:	2		
Constructors' World Titles:	0	Best: 3rd 1999	
Drivers' World Championships:	0	Best: 3rd 1999	
Most Points in a Season:	61	1999	
Total Constructors' Cup Points:	216		
Average Points/Grand Prix:	1.48		

Review

The Jordan team went into the 1999 season cock-a-hoop after their first ever victory had come in the previous season, a year which included three podium positions. They had finished fourth, in the Constructors' Cup, just four points behind Williams and team leader Eddie Jordan was optimistic that they could have the sort of season that would see them break into the top three, and at the very least, cement them as one of the four top teams. And so it proved, with third position secured before the final race of the season in Japan. Now they have to repeat that feat yet again, although improving on it will probably prove a little more than their ambitions can realise, for this season at least.

Heading up the season was Damon Hill, who had secured that maiden win, but he had, by his own standards, a dismal year. It concluded with him securing just four point finishes, and left him openly frustrated in that he simply could not be competitive in racing situations. The new rules and changes in car design had clearly had a greater effect on Hill than anyone else. Having announced his retirement at the end of 1999 at the mid-point, he lost his zest for the race and after its conclusion admitted that he would have been too scared to race on.

The trump card for Jordan though was the inspired signing of Heinz-Harald Frentzen. Competitive at Sauber in his early Grand Prix days, he was largely disappointing during his time at Williams. Yet he waltzed into Jordan and started to drive as though he had been there all his life, so much so, that with three races of the season remaining he had helped all but achieve Eddie Jordan's desire and was in serious contention for the Drivers' Championship.

By the completion of the French GP, Damon had managed just two finishes and simply hadn't been able to get his act together in qualifying. There was already much talk of retirement. Heinz-Harald on the other hand had been setting a terrific pace and this in turn must have been putting pressure on Damon. In his first Jordan race he qualified fifth and finished second and added a second podium position in the next race in Brazil. A spin and two mechanical problems meant that by the French race he had secured just three finishes from three starts. But by the end of it he had secured his first Jordan victory, using the bad weather conditions to his advantage. It was made more special as HH had just come out of hospital following an injury and according to boss Eddie Jordan they made their own forecast on the weather by having a member of their own staff stationed a couple of miles from the track to tell them what was on its way, and were thus able to schedule their one stop to coincide with the Safety Car and keep them on course for the 'W'.

After the race Damon announced he would be retiring at the end of the season, and perhaps that took the load off his shoulders as his performances in the short term showed a distinct improvement. With the exception of Austria he was always inside the top ten on the grid and had three points finishes. The first came in the very next race at Silverstone, where the team used a new gearbox on the cars, and where Damon actually led the race for one lap! He came home tenth at Monza and it was to be his last finish of the season and his career. Before that at Spa for the Belgian Grand Prix both Damon and Heinz-Harald qualified in the top four (fourth and third respectively) – the first time Jordan had achieved this in four years.

Not surprisingly the win also further boosted HH's form and up to and including the European race he was in scintillating form, never outside the top four and finishing all but one race. He achieved a second season win for the team and at the European GP, secured the team's second ever pole position. Unfortunately the German couldn't hold on it when he suffered an electronics failure after 32 laps. Damon had opted for a left foot braking system at the European meeting, the first time in his career he had gone this way. Problems with the car's electric system though, meant that he didn't complete even the first lap.

The team went into the final two races looking to secure third place in the Constructors' Cup and with HH having an outside chance of the Drivers' Championship. The latter goal evaporated when HH failed to finish but the single point and failure of others ensured that the third place went to Jordan and the team showed their pleasure in the traditional manner! The final race of the season ended on a sweet and sour note with Damon retiring out of frustration after a trip off the macadam had left him in last place and a long way back while Heinz-Harald continued into the points to finish fourth and increase Jordan's Constructors' Cup points tally to 61, 25 points ahead of the fourth-placed Stewart team.

For season 2000 Jordan look as though they will continue to be competitive but will probably need to show the same sort of form at the very least to maintain their new found top-three status as there is likely to be big pressure from the Jaguar Racing team (Stewart). Heinz-Harald will be looking to build on his impressive form, which saw him finish third in the Drivers' Championship and should record more podium positions and wins. He will be partnered by the impressive Jarno Trulli, another driver who may well show that Eddie Jordan has struck gold once again.

Drivers and Results 1999

Driver	Races	Com	Ret	Dnq	HP	Pts	Psn	Comp%
Hill, D.	16	7	9	0	4	7	11/24	43.75
Frentzen, H-H.	16	13	3	0	1	54	3/24	81.25
Aggregate	32	20	12	0	1	61	3/11	62.50

			Damon Hill		**Heinz-Harald Frentzen**		
	Grand Prix	Gd	P	*Details*	Gd	P	*Details*
1	Australian	9	r	accident	5	2	1:35:02.686
2	Brazilian	7	r	steering	8	3	1:35:58.877
3	San Marino	8	4	1:33:47.629	7	r	spin
4	Monaco	17	r	accident	6	4	1:50:25.821
5	Spanish	11	7	1:34:25.044	8	r	differential
6	Canadian	14	r	accident	6	11	brakes
7	French	18	r	misfire	5	1	1:58:24.343
8	British	6	5	1:33:08.750	5	4	1:32:57.933
9	Austrian	11	8	1 lap down	4	4	1:29.05.241
10	German	8	r	brakes	2	3	1:22:03.789
11	Hungarian	6	6	1:47.19.262	5	4	1:46:55.351
12	Belgian	4	6	1:26:37.973	3	3	1:26:16.490
13	Italian	9	10	1:17:59.182	2	1	1:17:02.923
14	European	7	r	electrics	1	r	electronics
15	Malaysian	9	r	accident	14	6	1:37:13.378
16	Japanese	12	r	retired	4	4	1:32:57.420

Jordan Mugen-Honda EJ10 Specifications

Engine:	**Mugen-Honda MF301HE**
Cylinders:	V10 (72 degrees)
Valves:	40 – 4 per cylinder, with pneumatic return
Injection:	Honda PGM-F1
Ignition System:	Honda PGM-IG
Capacity:	3000 cc
Dimensions:	under 620 mm (length), under 520mm (width)

Car

Chassis:	Full carbon fibre composite monocoque
Suspension:	Composite pushrods activating gearbox mounted Penske dampers and torsion bars, unequal length aerodynamic wishbones, composite top wishbone, titanium fabricated uprights and front/back anti-roll bar
Transmission:	In-house Jordan GP design. Six-speed and reverse longitudinal gearbox with electro-hydraulic sequential gear change
Clutch:	Triple plate Jordan/Sacks racing clutch
Brakes:	Brembo braking system
Clutch:	Triple plate Jordan/Sachs racing clutch
Fuel/Oil System:	In-house
Cooling System:	In-house
Electrical:	In-house
Dimensions:	Length: 4550 mm Wheelbase: 3050 mm
	Front Track: 1500 mm Rear Track: 1418 mm
	Height: 950 mm

Engines 1991-00

1991: Ford. 1992: Yamaha. 1993-94: Hart. 1995-97: Peugeot. 1998-00: Mugen-Honda.

Drivers 1991-00

1991: A.de Cesaris, B.Gachot, R.Moreno, M.Schumacher & A.Zanardi. 1992: S.Modena & M.Gugelmin. 1993: R.Barrichello, I.Capelli, T.Boutsen, M.Apicella, E.Nespatti & E.Irvine. 1994: R.Barrichello, E.Irvine, A.Suzuki & A.de Cesaris. 1995: R.Barrichello & E.Irvine. 1996: R.Barrichello & M.Brundle. 1997: R.Schumacher & G.Fisichella. 1998: D.Hill & R.Schumacher.1999: D.Hill & H-H. Frentzen. 2000: H-H. Frentzen & J.Trulli.

Constructors' Cup Record

Year-Position/Points: 1991-5/13; 1992-11/1; 1993-10/3; 1994-5/28; 1995-6/21; 1996-5/22; 1997-5/33; 1998-4/34; 1999-3/61.

Grand Prix Wins

1998 Bel (D.Hill). 1999 Fra, Ita (Frentzen).

McLaren

West McLaren Mercedes

McLaren International Ltd
Unit 1A, Kingswey Business Park, Albert Drive, Woking,
Surrey, GU21 5SA
Tel: +44 (0)1483 728211   Fax: +44 (0)1483 720157

Managing Director:	Ron Dennis
Tech. Director:	Adrian Newey
Team Manager:	Dave Ryan
Chief Designer:	Neil Oatley
Chief Mechanic:	Mike Negline
Drivers:	Mika Hakkinen (7th year)
	David Coulthard (5th year)
Third Driver:	Olivier Panis
Race Engineers:	Mark Slade (Hakkinen)
	Pat Fry (Coulthard)

Brief History

1959: Bruce McLaren makes his F1 debut driving for the Cooper works
team. 1963: Bruce McLaren Motor Racing Ltd founded. 1966: McLaren
make their Grand Prix debut at Monaco. 1968: Bruce McLaren wins in
Belgium for his own team's first F1 victory. McLaren finish second
behind Lotus in Constructors' World Championship. 1970: Bruce
McLaren killed at Goodwood while testing a CanAm sportscar. 1973:
Emerson Fittipaldi leads McLaren to the Drivers' and Constructors'
Championship double. 1976: James Hunt takes the Drivers' World
Championship by a point from Niki Lauda. 1984: Niki Lauda beats team-
mate Alain Prost by just half a point to take the Drivers' title. 1985: Alain
Prost takes the title ahead of Michele Alboreto. 1986: Prost retains his
title after Nigel Mansell goes out in the final race at Adelaide. 1988:
Senna takes the title by three points from Prost. McLaren post a record
Constructors' Championship score of 199 points. 1989: Prost takes the
title from Senna by 16 points for another McLaren double. 1990: Senna
regains the title from Prost by seven points. 1991: Senna wins his third
World Drivers' Championship. 1998: McLaren win Constructors' Cup
and driver Mika Hakkinen wins his first Drivers' Championship. 1999:
Hakkinen retains Drivers' Championship.

Grand Prix Record

Contested:	492	
Cars Started:	1036	Completed: 673 Retired: 363
Victories:	123	
Pole Positions:	103	
Fastest Laps:	89	
Constructors' World Titles:	8	1974, 1984, 1985, 1988, 1989, 1990, 1991, 1998
Drivers' World Championships:	11	1974, 1976, 1984, 1985, 1986, 1988, 1989, 1990, 1991, 1998, 1999
Most Points in a Season:	199	(1988)
Total Constructors' Cup Points:	2327.5	
Average Points/Grand Prix:	7.73	

Review

Having taken the Formula 1 world by storm in 1998, pretty much the same was expected of the McLaren team in 1999. With an increasingly confident Mika Hakkinen starting the season as World Champion and without doubt the fastest driver in the sport and an expected resurgence of David Coulthard in the second car they seemed to be in prime position. All this of course, packaged in a new Newey-designed car powered by the latest Mercedes V10.

After first practice and the qualifying run at the first meeting in Melbourne, all the other teams' fears looked to be realised as McLaren were simply awesome and looked set to blow any pretenders to their crowns well and truly away. However, it didn't quite work out like that in the first part of the season. Indeed the team recorded just one finish out of its first two races in Australia and Brazil.

The reliability that had characterised the McLarens during the 1998 season seemed to have evaporated when their MP4-14 chassis moved from the testing environment on to the race track for real. There had been some concern about this prior to the start of the season with consideration being given to continuing with the 1998 championship-winning M4-13 chassis until the European season got underway. The team though opted for the additional performance the new design would bring with a view to the long term benefits of development during the first two races, rather than the possible short term gain of using what they knew.

After Hakkinen and Coulthard had set the pace in qualifying on the front row of the grid for the Australian Grand Prix, their races petered out early on. DC's lasted just 13 laps when his gear stuck – this after being forced into the T-Car before the start – while Hakkinen fared only a little better and coasted out of contention after 21 laps when his throttle failed.

DC had been forced into the spare after his clutch had burned out on the grid, leaving him to join the race three laps down. Five weeks later the McLaren mechanics must have been living on their nerves when he retired from the Brazilian race early on when his gearbox failed on him. The fears they held for Hakkinen didn't materialise though as he crossed the finish line in first place.

The qualifying form continued with McLaren back to the start of the European circuit. At the San Marino race, it was another one-two on the grid for Hakkinen and Coulthard respectively. DC used the Imola circuit to record his first finish of the season racing home in second place, while Hakkinen had an accident after 17 laps. DC had led until his pit stop but then lost places behind Barrichello when he emerged, a fact that probably cost him victory.

McLaren's dominance on the grid continued to be the talking point for the season. Indeed Hakkinen would record 11 pole positions for the 16 races while both cars would occupy the front row on no less than five occasions. The first break from those one-two starts came at Monaco, with Coulthard 'only' achieving third place, but failing to finish thanks to an oil leak. Mika though had a bad start and then erred so had to settle for third place at the flag.

The one-two sequence re-appeared in Spain – this time to signal the first time of the season that both McLarens made it to the finish. They did it in style too, securing maximum points racing across the line in first and second place with Mika again taking the top honours.

The trip to Canada was made with the team seemingly having put to bed the reliability problems. Where the team had been strong in set-up it now struggled as both drivers couldn't find the right balance. It clearly affected Hakkinen most who for the first time in the season found himself off pole position. Coulthard found himself in fourth place – his worst starting position all season. Hakkinen kept his place at the start and took advantage of race-leader Michael Schumacher's crash to take the lead and ultimately victory. DC on the other hand had a tangle with Irvine late on which pushed him back out of the points, for what was to prove to be the only time he would be out of the points when finishing in the season.

A look at the stats showed Mika qualified 14th for the French Grand Prix, as the weather conspired against him, even though DC managed a very creditable fourth on the grid. There the fortunes changed with an alternator ending DC's charge after nine laps and with Mika making a terrific run to claw back places and finish second. That 14th place was the spur the Finn needed as he set off to secure poles in the next six races for McLaren! Unfortunately he could only convert one of those into a 10-

point victory, that in Hungary. More worryingly for the team at that time was that out of those six races, he only managed three finishes. For McLaren, Hakkinen's pole at the German Grand Prix was the 100th in their history.

In stark contrast DC was never off the front two rows and managed to claw back points with what were to be his only victories of the season, those coming at Silverstone and Spa.

The fact that McLaren hadn't wrapped up both titles by the time the Italian race had run its course was not because of reliability – something that seemed to have been largely solved – but because of silly errors by the normally cool Finn, whose selection of wrong gear going into the chicane at Monza threw him out of the race. DC on the other hand, had been securing a steady stream of points and left the team in a position such that they were really unable to throw their hat into the ring with just one of their drivers, requesting that one or the other was the main contender. Team Manager Ron Dennis re-affirmed his belief that the drivers are there to race and that is what they were going to do, until it was impossible for one of them to take the Drivers' Championship.

With just a couple of races remaining things were somewhat tighter than they had been at the same stage in 1998. After the European Grand Prix DC was 14 points behind Hakkinen who himself had 62 points, just two more than second placed Irvine. In the challenge for the Constructors' Cup McLaren's lead over Ferrari was eight points and they therefore needed to ensure that both of their drivers were as competitive as possible while the cars remained reliable from start to finish.

Hakkinen collected points at both the European and then Malaysian circuits while DC spun out at the first and suffered fuel pressure problems at the latter. With Ferrari coming home one and two in the latter race, it looked as though both championships would go down to the final race in Japan, although DC was now out of the running in the Drivers' Championship. Then with both Ferraris disqualified and, with Mika elevated to first from third, both championships were seemingly retained by McLaren. However, experience put on hold any celebrations and when, a week later, the Ferrari appeals were upheld, the situation at the immediate end of the Sepang race was restored, much to the chagrin of Ron Dennis. Not least because it re-established Ferrari as the front runner for the Constructors' Cup.

However McLaren travelled to Suzuka knowing that a Mika win would give him the Drivers' Championship while the team needed to score four points more than Ferrari to retain the Constructors' Cup. As it was, McLaren secured one of the two titles with Mika and his team providing a peerless performance to come home in first place. However, Ferrari's second and third place meant that they retained their four points advantage in the Constructors' Championship.

Before that final showdown had been reached McLaren announced they had re-signed their drivers for the year 2000. Importantly, the winning working partnership they have forged with Mercedes was further cemented when they announced that Daimler/Chrysler had acquired an option to acquire 40 per cent of the shares in the TAG McLaren Group of companies. As 1999 drew to a close the team annouced that former Prost driver Olivier Panis was joining the team as designated Third Driver to help with testing and to provide experienced cover for prime drivers Hakkinen and Coulthard.

The bottom line is that McLaren will remain one of the teams to beat in the 2000 season and will continue to dominate the championship until someone can start forcing Mika Hakkinen off the front row on a regular basis.

Drivers and Results 1999

Driver	Races	Com	Ret	Dnq	HP	Pts	Psn	Comp%
Hakkinen, M.	16	11	5	0	1	76	1/24	68.75
Coulthard, D.	16	9	7	0	1	48	4/24	56.25
Aggregate	32	20	12	0	1	124	2/11	62.50

			Mika Hakkinen			**David Coulthard**	
	Grand Prix	Gd	P	Details	Gd	P	Details
1	Australian	1	r	throttle	2	r	gear stuck
2	Brazilian	1	1	1:38:03.765	2	r	gearbox
3	San Marino	1	r	accident	2	2	1:33:49.057
4	Monaco	1	3	1:50:09.295	3	r	oil leak
5	Spanish	1	1	1:34:13.665	3	2	1:34:19.903
6	Canadian	2	1	1:41:35.727	4	7	1:41:40.731
7	French	14	2	1:58:35.435	4	r	alternator
8	British	1	r	wheel hub	3	1	1:32:30.144
9	Austrian	1	3	1:28:34.720	2	2	1:28:12.751
10	German	1	r	accident	3	5	1:22:15.417
11	Hungarian	1	1	1:46:23.536	3	2	1:46:33.242
12	Belgian	1	2	1:25:53.526	2	1	1:25:43.057
13	Italian	1	r	spin	3	5	1:17:21.085
14	European	3	5	1:42:57.264	2	r	spun-out
15	Malaysian	4	3	1:36:48.237	3	r	fuel pressure
16	Japanese	2	1	1:31:18.785	3	r	hydraulics

McLaren MP4-15 Specifications

Engine:	**2000 Mercedes-Benz F0110J V10**
Type:	72-degree V10
Cylinders:	10 – 4 valves per cylinder, 2 camshafts per bank
Cylinder Block:	Cast aluminium alloy, wet liners
Cylinder Head:	One piece sand cast aluminium alloy
Crankshaft:	Steel
Oil System:	Dry sump
Injection:	TAG electronic system
Spark Plugs:	NGK
Capacity:	2998 cc
Car	**MP4-15**
Chassis:	McLaren moulded carbon fibre/aluminium honeycombed composite incorporating front, rear, side impact structures. Integral safety fuel cell
Transmission:	McLaren longitudinal six-speed semi-automatic. Control by TAG electronic system. McLaren drive shafts and CV assemblies
Suspension:	Front and rear: inboard torsion bar/damper system operated by pushrod and bellcrank with a double wishbone system.
Dampers:	McLaren
Brakes:	AP Racing callipers
Race Wheels:	Enkei
Bodywork:	One-piece side pod and engine cover. Separate floor section, structural nose with integral front wing.
Lubricants:	Mobile 1 engine oil
Fuel:	Mobil unleaded
Electronics:	TAG Electronic Management System 2000 integrated engine and chassis control and data acquisition system. Electronic dashboard, ignition coils, alternator voltage control, sensors, data analysis and telemetry systems supplied by TAG Electronic Systems.
Radios:	Kenwood

Engines 1966-00

1966-82: Ford. 1983-87: TAG-Porsche Turbo. 1988: Honda Turbo. 1989-92: Honda. 1993: Ford. 1994: Peugeot. 1995-00: Mercedes.

Drivers 1989-00

1989: A.Prost & A.Senna. 1990: A.Senna & G.Berger. 1991: A.Senna & G.Berger. 1992: A.Senna & G.Berger. 1993: A.Senna, M.Andretti & M.Hakkinen. 1994: M.Hakkinen, M.Brundle & P.Alliot. 1995: M.Hakkinen, N.Mansell, M.Blundell & J.Magnussen. 1996-00: M. Hakkinen & D. Coulthard.

Constructors' Cup Record

Year-Position/Points: 1966-9/2; 1966-10/1; 1967-10/3; 1968-2/49; 1968-10/3; 1969-4/38 (40); 1970-4/35; 1971-6/10; 1972-3/47 (49); 1973-3/58; 1974-1 /73 (75); 1975-3/53; 1976-2/74 (75); 1977-3/60;1978-8/15; 1979-7/15;1980-7/11; 1981-6/28; 1982-2/69; 1983-5/34; 1984-1/143.5; 1985-1/90; 1986-2/87; 1987-2/76; 1988-1/199; 1989-1/141; 1990-1/121; 1991-1/139; 1992-2/99; 1993-2/84; 1994-4/42; 1995-4/30; 1996-4/49; 1997-4/63; 1998-1/156; 1999-2/124.

Grand Prix Wins

1968 Bel (McLaren), Ita, Can (Hulme); 1969 Mex (Hulme); 1972 SA (Hulme); 1973 Swe (Hulme), GB (Revson), Can (Revson); 1974 Arg (Hulme), Bra, Bel, Can (all Fittipaldi); 1975 Arg (Fittipaldi), Esp (Mass), GB (Fittipaldi); 1976 Esp, Fra, Ger, Can, USA (all Hunt); 1977 GB, USA, Jap (all Hunt); 1981 GB (Watson); 1982 Long Beach (Lauda), Bel (Watson), Detroit (Watson), GB (Lauda); 1983 Long Beach (Watson); 1984 Bra (Prost), SA (Lauda), San (Prost), Fra (Lauda), Mon (Prost), GB (Lauda), Ger (Prost), Aut (Lauda), Hol (Prost), Ita (Lauda), Eur (Prost), Por (Prost); 1985 Bra, Mon, GB, Aut (all Prost), Hol (Lauda), Ita (Prost); 1986 San, Mon, Aut, Aus (all Prost); 1987 Bra, Bel, Por (all Prost); 1988 Bra (Prost), San (Senna), Mon (Prost), Mex (Prost), Can (Senna), Detroit (Senna), Fra (Prost), GB, Ger, Hun, Bel (all Senna), Por (Prost), Esp (Prost), Jap (Senna), Aus (Prost); 1989 San, Mon, Mex (all Senna), USA, Fra, GB (all Prost), Ger (Senna), Bel (Senna), Ita (Prost), Esp (Senna); 1990 USA (Senna), Mon (Senna), Can (Senna), Ger (Senna), Bel (Senna), Ita (Senna); 1991 USA, Bra, San, Mon, Hun, Bel (all Senna), Jap (Berger), Aus (Senna); 1992 Mon (Senna), Can (Berger), Hun (Senna), Ita (Senna), Aus (Berger); 1993 Bra, Eur, Mon, Jap, Aus (all Senna); 1997 Aus, Ita (Coulthard), Eur (Hakkinen); 1998 Aus, Bra, Esp, Mon, Aut, Ger, Luxembourg, Jap (all Hakkinen), San (Coulthard). 1999 Bra, Esp, Can (all Hakkinen), GB (Coulthard), Hun (Hakkinen), Bel (Coulthard), Jap (Hakkinen).

Minardi

Telefonica Minardi Fondmetal

Minardi Team SpA, Via Spallanzani 21, 48018 Faenza, Ravenna, Italy
Tel: +39 0546 696111   Fax: +39 0546 620998

Chariman/MD:	Gabriele Rumi
Team Manager:	Cesare Fiorio
Tech. Director:	Gustav Brunner
Tech. Coord:	Gabriele Tredozi
Logistics:	Giovanni Minardi
Chief Designer:	George Ryton
Chief	
Aerodynamicist:	Jean-Claude Migeot
Drivers:	Marc Gene (2nd Year)
	tbc
Mechanic:	Paolo Piancasselli (Gene)
Test Driver:	Gaston Mazzacane

Brief History

1979: Minardi formed by Gian Carlo Minardi. 1985: Minardi make their Formula 1 debut in Brazil. 1988: Pierluigi Martini picks up Minardi's first points with sixth in Detroit. 1990: Minardi record their only front row start with Martini behind Gerhard Berger in America. 1993: Christian Fittipaldi takes Minardi's highest placing thus far of fourth in South Africa. Minardi's best finish of seventh with seven points in the Constructors' World Championship.

Grand Prix Results

Contested:	237	
Cars Started:	433	Completed: 188 Retired: 245
Victories:	0	Best Finish: 4th – three times
Pole Positions:	0	
Fastest Laps:	0	
Constructors' World Titles:	0	Best: 7th 1993
Drivers' World Championships:	0	Best: 10th 1994
Most Points in a Season:	7	1993
Total Constructors' Cup Points:	28	
Average Points/Grand Prix:	0.12	

That Minardi continue to turn out race after race is a credit to the effort the team put in, operating as they do on what is probably the smallest budget in F1. Perhaps the pressure isn't there for them because, frankly, no one expects them to achieve any more than they actually do. When they pick up points, or finish just outside the top six, it is often highlighted more than any other team. But the ambition is there and burns bright. Indeed the team signalled what they hoped would be a new dawn in their history by producing a completely new car for the 1999 season. They signified the fact by moving from the M198 specification of the 1998 model to the M01 designation for the 1999 machine. Technical Director Gustav Brunner hoped to achieve a number of objectives in the new design by lowering the centre of gravity, lowering the weight and producing a smaller, simpler and hopefully therefore more reliable chassis. They had mixed results.

In 1999 they achieved the one championship point that had eluded them in 1998 – that sixth place being achieved by rookie Marc Gene at the European Grand Prix. The M199 was again powered by a Ford V10 and it and the car proved reliable enough. Gene in his first season finished more races than he retired in while Badoer was one short of that goal.

What the team didn't have was those vital seconds to make a difference that often left them trailing. In the six races that Luca Badoer finished he was at least one lap down on the winner and it was almost an identical position for Gene, who managed to stay on the same lap as the winner in Brazil – only his second Grand Prix.

Luca finished only one of his first four races, although rookie Stephane Sarrazin stepped into the breech for the Brazilian meeting when the Italian injured himself. Five completions from six in the middle of the season boosted his and Minardi's hopes but a succession of mechanical problems hampered Badoer in the final stretch.

The team will have been reasonably pleased with Gene's contribution in his first season of F1 and one improvement they did make was to get both drivers across the finishing line in five of the season's races. Qualifying was always about getting past the 107% mark to ensure they lined up on the grid. This was normally on the last two rows but Gene did managed to push himself up to a 15th place start in Germany.

Cash will no doubt continue to be tight for the team in 2000 although their main sponsors Telefonica have agreed an extension of one year and are reported to be paying close on $10 million for the privilege.

Drivers and Results 1999

Driver	Races	Com	Ret	Dnq	HP	Pts	Psn	Comp%
Gene, M.	16	10	6	0	6	1	17/24	62.50
Badoer, L.	15	6	9	0	8	0	–	40.00
Sarrazin, S.	1	0	1	0	–	0	–	0.00
Aggregate	32	16	16	0	6	1	9/11	50.00

		Marc Gene			**Luca Badoer/Sarrazin***	
	Grand Prix	*Gd*	*P*	*Details*	*Gd*	*P*	*Details*
1	Australian	22	r	spin	21	r	gearbox
2	Brazilian*	20	9	1:37:02.116	18	r	accident
3	San Marino	21	9	3 laps down	22	8	3 laps down
4	Monaco	22	r	accident	20	r	gearbox
5	Spanish	21	r	gearbox	22	r	spin
6	Canadian	22	8	1 lap down	21	10	2 laps down
7	French	19	r	spin	20	10	1 lap down
8	British	22	15	2 laps down	21	r	gearbox
9	Austrian	22	11	1 lap down	19	13	3 laps down
10	German	15	9	1:23:46.912	19	10	1 lap down
11	Hungarian	22	17	3 laps down	19	14	2 laps down
12	Belgian	21	16	1 lap down	20	r	suspension
13	Italian	20	r	accident	19	r	accident
14	European	20	6	1:42:59.468	19	r	gearbox
15	Malaysian	19	9	1 lap down	21	r	overheating
16	Japanese	20	r	gearbox	22	r	engine

Minardi M02 Specifications

Engine — **Fondmetal**
Cylinders: V10 – 4 valves per cylinder
Dimensions: Length: 607 mm Width: 540 mm Height: 530 mm

Car
Chassis: Carbon fibre monocoque
Suspension: Carbon push-rod with torsion bars; steel wishbones; F/S shock absorbers
Brakes: Brembo callipers with six pistons front and rear Carbone Industrie carbon fibre discs; hydraulic brake balance adjuster
Cooling System: Water radiators (x2), oil radiator (x1)
Gearbox: Minardi longitudinal in magnesium, six-speed plus reverse, semi-automatic with Magneti Marelli electronic control with Minardi software.

Differential:	Minardi viscous	
Clutch:	Sachs	
Dimensions:	Length: 4420 mm	Width: 1800 mm
	Front track: 1452 mm	Rear track: 1420.7 mm
Sponsors:	Telefonica, Fondmetal, PDP	

Engines 1985-99

1985-87: Motori Moderni Turbo. 1988-90: Ford Cosworth. 1991: Ferrari. 1992: Lamborghini. 1993-96: Ford Cosworth. 1997: Hart. 1998-99: Ford.

Drivers 1989-99

1989: P.Martini, L.Perez Sala & P.Barilla. 1990: P.Martini, P.Barilla & G.Morbidelli. 1991: P.Martini, G.Morbidelli & R.Moreno. 1992: G.Morbidelli, C.Fittipaldi & A.Zanardi. 1993: C.Fittipaldi, F.Barbazza, P.Martini & J-M.Gounon. 1994: P.Martini & M.Alboreto. 1995: P.Lamy, L.Badoer & P.Martini. 1996: P. Lamy & T.Inoue. 1997: U.Katayama & J.Trulli. 1998: S.Nakano & E.Tuero. 1999: M.Gene & L.Badoer.

Constructors' Cup Record

Year-Position/Points: 1988-10/1; 1989-10/6; 1991-7/6; 1992-11/1; 1993-8/7; 1994-10/5; 1995-10/1; 1999-9/1.

Grand Prix Best Performance

4th position three times: 1991 San (Martini), Por (Martini); 1993 SA (Martini).

Prost

Equipe Prost Peugeot

Technopole de la Nievre, 58470 Magny-Cours, France
Tel: +33 3 86 60 62 00   Fax: +33 3 86 21 22 96

Owner:	Alain Prost
MD:	Bruno Michel
Chief Mechanic:	Robert Dassaud
Chief Designer:	Loic Bigois
Drivers:	Jean Alesi (1st year)
	Nick Heidfeld (1st year)

Brief History

1976: Ligier enter F1 at the end of the 1976 season. Jacques Laffite takes pole and sets the fastest lap in Italy. 1979: Laffite wins the opening two Grands Prix in Argentina and Brazil. 1980: Ligier finish second in the Constructors' World Championship behind Williams. 1983: Ligier fail to score a point in the season for the first time in their history. 1996: Tom Walkinshaw leaves for Arrows. 1997: Alain Prost takes control of Ligier and renames team to Prost Grand Prix. 1998: Secure Peugeot engine for cars.

Grand Prix Record

Contested:	(326/49)	375	as Ligier and Prost
Cars Started:	(577/96)	673	Completed: 372 Retired: 301
Victories:	(9/0)	9	
Pole Positions:	(9/0)	9	
Fastest Laps:	(9/0)	9	
Constructors' World Titles:		0	Best: 2nd 1980
Drivers' World Championships:		0	Best: 4th 1979, 1980, 1981
Most Points in a Season:		66	1980
Total Constructors' Cup Points:		419	Toleman: 388 Prost: 31
Average Points/Grand Prix		1.12	

Review

Alain Prost's team came into the 1999 season with a re-designed car – the AP03. The hope was that it would be a significant improvement on the AP02 that had been plagued by gearbox and suspension problems throughout the 1998 season. The problems though persisted with a number of gearbox problems meaning early retirements for both its drivers. The Peugeot V10 engine was not looking as competitive as in previous years, in what was its first year in the Prost, having set a winning pace in its final season at Jordan in 1998.

The only real light out of the Prost tunnel from last season was the form of Jarno Trulli – a driver they have lost for the 2000 season. Trulli produced some real gutsy drives throughout the season culminating with a terrific second place finish at the European Grand Prix. If Trulli was good then Olivier Panis was bad. Two years ago, in these pages, I expressed a view that I thought he needed a new challenge, but he failed to move when the takers were there and now the team will line up for the 2000 season, having discarded his services and with two new drivers wearing team colours.

The sort of season that lay in wait for the team was rather typified by the retirement of Olivier Panis in his first race of the season. An horrendous 20th place on the grid simply previewed the misery when the driver had to retire after 23 laps when he had to stop after a locked wheel nut meant that he couldn't change tyres at his first pit stop. A better qualifying run and a sixth place helped boost confidence for Panis but then followed three dnfs down to mechanical problems. Jarno Trulli failed to finish his first three races following two accidents and an engine failure but from the Monaco Grand Prix onwards he showed the sort of consistency that had the other teams sitting up and taking note. His qualifying performances were also streets ahead of his more experienced team-mate, although the numbers in terms of who out-qualified who were pretty even by the end of the season.

The best qualifying run came from Panis who secured a third place on the starting grid for his home Grand Prix in amongst the rain that rather turned the grid on its head. The best Trulli could manage was seventh, that coming in Monaco.

After a poor start Olivier put in a sequence of consistent finishes – nine in succession starting from the Canadian race. The best finish came in Germany where he collected his single point, but generally he was way off the pace and in three of those completions he finished a lap down on the race winner. In the same nine races Trulli produced six finishes, but was generally better placed, two sevenths, an eighth and a ninth culminating in his attrition-assisted second place at the Nurburgring.

The final two races of the season pretty much mirrored the start of the season but this time neither driver was able to record a finish. Panis went out of both races early on, suffering engine and gearbox failures while Trulli bowed out with engine problems – the first of these coming on the formation lap in Malaysia.

Alain Prost sold 10% of his team's parent company Prost Development to luxury goods corporation LVMH. The aim is to produce a merchandising arm for the team – and they will be hoping for an improvement in fortunes on the track to help generate enthusiasm from the French fans. Behind the wheel the team have an all new line-up for 2000, with the experienced Jean Alesi partnering rookie and McLaren F3000 Champion Nick Heidfeld, who spent the tail end of the 1999 season helping with the development of an all-new Peugeot A20 engine. An engine much smaller than previous incarnations, so much so that the team have had to redesign a special mounting to secure it to the chassis.

Driver	Races	Com	Ret	Dnq	HP	Pts	Psn	Comp%
Panis, O.	16	11	5	0	6	2	15/24	68.75
Trulli, J.	15	8	7	1	2	7	11/24	53.33
Aggregate	31	19	12	1	2	9	7/11	61.29

		Olivier Panis			**Jarno Trulli**		
	Grand Prix	Gd	P	*Details*	Gd	P	*Details*
1	Australian	20	r	locked wheel nut	12	r	accident
2	Brazilian	12	6	1:37:13.388	13	r	gearbox
3	San Marino	11	r	engine	14	r	accident
4	Monaco	18	r	engine	7	7	1:50:05.845
5	Spanish	15	r	oil pressure	9	6	1:34:24.028
6	Canadian	15	9	1 lap down	9	r	accident
7	French	3	8	1:59:22.874	8	7	1:59:22.114
8	British	15	13	1:33:50.636	14	9	1:33:42.189
9	Austrian	18	10	1 lap down	13	7	1 lap down
10	German	7	6	1:22.28.473	9	r	engine
11	Hungarian	14	10	1 lap down	13	8	1 lap down
12	Belgian	17	13	1:27:24.600	12	12	1:27:19.211
13	Italian	10	11	1 lap down	12	r	gearbox
14	European	5	9	1 lap down	10	2	1:42.16.933
15	Malaysian	12	r	engine	18	dns	engine on formation lap
16	Japanese	6	r	gearbox	7	r	engine

Prost AP03 Specifications

Car

Chassis:	Carbon fibre composite monocoque manufactured by Prost Grand Prix
Suspension:	Double wishbone and push-rod made of carbon composite – front and rear
Brakes:	Prost Grand Prix specification. Brembo one-piece callipers and Prost master cylinders with Carbone Industries carbon fibre discs
Transmission:	Longitudinal semi-automatic six-speed gearbox. Multi-plate clutch
Fuel System:	ATL rubber fuel cell mounted within the monocoque structure behind the cockpit
Oil System:	Eight-litre capacity oil tank

Cooling System: Separate water radiators in each side pod plus oil
                   radiator on right-hand side of engine
Details based on 1999 AP02 car specifications.

Engines 1976-00

1978-78: Matra. 1979-80: Ford. 1981-84: Matra. 1984-86: Renault Turbo.
1987: Megatron Turbo. 1988: Judd. 1989-90: Ford. 1991: Lamborghini.
1992-94: Renault. 1995-97: Mugen-Honda. 1998-00: Peugeot.

Drivers 1989–00

1989: R.Arnoux & O.Grouillard. 1990: P.Alliot & N.Larini. 1991:
T.Boutsen & E.Comas. 1992: T.Boutsen & E.Comas. 1993: M.Brundle &
M.Blundell. 1994: E.Bernard, O.Panis, J.Herbert & F.Lagorce. 1995:
M.Brundle, A.Suzuki & O.Panis. 1996: P.Diniz & O.Panis. 1997: O.Panis
& S.Nakano. 1998-99: O.Panis & J.Trulli. 2000: J.Alesi & N.Heidfeld.

Constructors' Cup Record

Year-Position/Points: (Ligier) 1976-5/20; 1977-8/18; 1978-6/19; 1979-
3/61; 1980-2/66; 1981-4/44; 1982-8/20; 1984-10/3; 1985-6/23; 1986-
5/29; 1987-11/1; 1989-13/3; 1992-7/6; 1993-5/23; 1994-6/13; 1995-5/24;
1996-6/15; (Prost) 1997-6/21; 1998-9/1; 1999-7/9.

Grand Prix Wins

1977 Swe (Laffite); 1979 Arg (Laffite), Bra (Laffite), Esp (Depailler);
1980 Bel (Pironi), Ger (Laffite); 1981 Aut (Laffite), Can (Laffite); 1996
Mon (Panis).

Sauber

Red Bull Sauber Petronas
Team Sauber Formel 1
Wildbachstrasse 9, CH 8340 Hinwell, Switzerland
Tel: +41 75 232 77 64   Fax: +41 75 232 77 47
Team Principal: Peter Sauber
CEO: Heinz Haller
COO: Jost Capito
Technical Director: Leo Ress

Engine Director:	Osamu Goto
Team Manager:	Beat Zehnder
Chief Designer:	Sergio Rinland
Chief Mechanic:	Urs Kuratle
R&D:	Andrew Tilley
Track Engineering:	Tim Preston
Drivers:	Mika Salo (1st year)
	Pedro Diniz (2nd year)
Race Engineers:	Remi Decorzent (Salo)
	Gabriele Delli Colli (Diniz)
Test Driver:	Enrique Bernoldi
Sponsors:	Petronas, Red Bull, Parmalat

Brief History

1993: Sauber record a scoring finish in their first Grand Prix with J.J. Lehto taking fifth in South Africa. The team end the season sixth in the Constructors' World Championship with twelve points. 1995: Achieve first podium finish when Frentzen finishes third at Monza. 1996: Herbert finishes third at Monaco. 1997: Herbert finishes third in Hungary.

Grand Prix Record

Contested:	113	
Cars Started:	223	Completed: 116 Retired: 107
Victories:	0	Best Finish: 3rd – four times
Pole Positions:	0	
Fastest Laps:	0	
Constructors' World Titles:	0	Best: 6th 1993, 1998
Drivers' World Championships:	0	Best: 8th 1994
Most Points in a Season:	18	1995
Total Constructors' Cup Points:	84	
Average Points/Grand Prix:	0.75	

Review

Sauber celebrated their 100th Grand Prix last year. It was a year in which McLaren celebrated their 100th pole position. Such is the difference between the new boys and the established heavyweights. However, you can't help but admire what the Swiss team have done in just seven years of Formula One. They remain in what could be called the third division of F1, and their near-term aim must be to gain promotion to the middle order. It is something that is not beyond them and even given their fledgling nature, it is perhaps disappointing they haven't already done so.

In recent seasons they have had some excellent drivers through their ranks and a deal with Ferrari has seen Sauber running earlier models of the engine. But they haven't been able to build on the performances of 1997 – probably their best season to date.

Sauber started the 1999 season using the Ferrari engine that had won the Italian Grand Prix in 1998. Sauber designer Leo Ress described the C18 as a natural evolution on the previous year with the biggest change coming in lowering the car's centre of engine. Something aided by the Petronas-badged engine. Development throughout the course of the season was probably the team's biggest challenge but was aided by the arrival of ex-Jordan aerodynamist Seamus Mullarkey. In retrospect though the team struggled on low-down force circuits suggesting last year's C18 suffered from either high-drag or poor mechanical grip.

Internal wrangling also seems to have been a problem, with the relationship between Sauber and Jean Alesi seemingly going from bad to terrible with him indicating a long way before the end of the season that he would not be returning. It was a shame because it was Alesi who was the most consistent of finishers.

After a disappointing start to the season, Alesi managed to get the car classified in all but two of the final set of nine races. His team-mate Diniz, who had been brought in to replace Johnny Herbert, was facing his first season as a paid driver, as opposed to bringing sponsorship money to the team for his drive. He had a terrible season, managing only four finishes from his 16 starts – ironically though the first three of those completions were all sixth-placed points earners. It was also a situation where it was difficult to blame car reliability. Twice gearbox failures were recorded as reasons for dnfs, the rest were either spins or accidents. Diniz, who was so often vilified in the early part of his career when he seemed to be buying his place in the team with sponsorship monies, had destroyed the burgeoning good reputation of the past two years. His starting position was invariably in the back end of the grid, his best performance coming in the rain at France where he started 11th.

Transmission and gearbox failures had hampered Alesi's start to the season, but a sixth-place in San Marino was encouraging. Car problems produced another two dnfs, each was disappointing in Spain where the Frenchman had qualified fifth. He did better in France where he used the weather conditions to perfection to start in second place – only Alesi himself had managed this in a Sauber before, in Austria the previous year. A spin on lap 25 in the changeable conditions only accentuated the emotions he was feeling and then in Austria he ran out of fuel after failing to hear the call to pit and re-charge.

The anger of Jean Alesi continued to surface and at the German race he qualified a terrible 21st, but managed to get the car home eighth. Indeed it marked a good run for the Frenchman who was being linked with the Prost team, and although he was generally a mid-order qualifier he only failed to finish once in the final seven races, that at the Nurburgring. Alesi ended the season and his Sauber career with a sixth placed point in Japan where Diniz was classified 11th and a lap down.

For 2000 Diniz will be partnered by a re-vitalised Mika Salo and the team have extended its deal with Ferrari by paying a reputed £11 million for the hardware. In addition the experienced F1 designer Sergio Rinland has joined the team and will work under current technical director Leo Ross as the team's chief designer. Rinland's addition will have a positive effect on the team as he brings 20 years of experience working for a number of F1 teams including Ferrari, Benetton and Dallara.

Drivers and Results 1999

Driver	Races	Com	Ret	Dnq	HP	Pts	Psn	Comp%
Alesi, J.	16	8	8	0	6	2	15/24	50.00
Diniz, P.	16	4	12	0	6	3	13/24	25.00
Aggregate	32	12	20	0	6	5	8/11	37.50

			Jean Alesi			Pedro Diniz	
	Grand Prix	Gd	P	*Details*	Gd	P	*Details*
1	Australian	16	r	transmission	14	r	gearbox
2	Brazilian	14	r	gearbox	15	r	accident
3	San Marino	13	6	1:34:33.056	15	r	spin
4	Monaco	14	r	accident	15	r	accident
5	Spanish	5	r	electrics	12	r	gearbox
6	Canadian	8	r	accident	18	6	1:41:39.438
7	French	2	r	spin	11	r	drive shaft
8	British	10	14	1 lap down	12	6	1:33:23.787
9	Austrian	17	r	out of fuel	16	6	1:29.23.371
10	German	21	8	1:23:09.885	16	r	accident
11	Hungarian	11	16	out of fuel	12	r	spin
12	Belgian	16	9	1:26:56.905	18	r	accident
13	Italian	13	9	1:17:45.121	16	r	spin
14	European	16	r	transmission	13	r	accident
15	Malaysian	15	7	1:37:32.902	17	r	spun-out
16	Japanese	10	6	1 lap down	17	11	1 lap down

Sauber Petronas C19 Specifications

Engine:	**Sauber-Petronas SPE 03A**
Type:	V10
Valves:	40
Valve Mechanism:	Pneumatic
Management:	Magneti Marelli
Car	
Chassis:	Carbon fibre monocoque
Suspension:	Upper and lower wishbones, combined spring/damper units (Sachs), mounted inboard with pushrod actuation
Brakes:	Six-piston callipers (Brembo) front and rear; carbon pads and discs (Carbone Industrie/Hitco)
Transmission:	Semi-automatic, longitudinally mounted, seven-speed transmission (Sauber), carbon clutch (Sachs)
Dimensions:	Length: 4410 mm Width: 1800 mm
	Height: 1000 mm Wheelbase: 2980 mm
	Front Track: 1470 mm Rear Track: 1410 mm

Engines 1993-00

1993: Sauber. 1994: Mercedes. 1995-96: Ford. 1997-00: Petronas.

Drivers 1993-00

1993: K.Wendlinger & J.J. Lehto. 1994: K.Wendlinger, H-H.Frentzen, J.J.Lehto & A.de Cesaris. 1995: H-H.Frentzen, J-C.Boullion & K.Wendlinger. 1996: J. Herbert & H-H.Frentzen. 1997: J.Herbert & N.Larini. 1998: J.Herbert & Jean Alesi. 1999: J.Alesi & P.Diniz. 2000: M.Salo & P.Diniz.

Constructors' Cup Record

Year-Position/Points: 1993-6/12; 1994-8/12; 1995-7/18; 1996-7/11; 1997-7/16; 1998-6/10; 1999-8/5.

Grand Prix Best Performance

3rd position four times: 1995 Ita (Frentzen), 1996 Mon (Herbert), 1997 Hun (Herbert), 1998 Bel (Alesi).

Williams

Williams F1

Williams Grand Prix Engineering Ltd
Grove, Wantage, Oxfordshire, OX12 0QD
Tel: +44 (0)1235 777700   Fax: +44 (0)1235 764705

MD:	Sir Frank Williams
Tech. Director:	Patrick Head
Chief Designer:	Gavin Fisher
Aerodynamicist:	Geoff Willis
Race Team Mgr:	Dickie Stanford
Test Team Mgr:	Bryan Lambert
Senior Ops Eng:	James Robinson
Chief Mechanic:	Carl Gaden
Drivers:	Ralf Schumacher (2nd year)
	Alex Zanardi – tbc – (2nd year)
Race Engineers:	Craig Wilson (Schumacher)
	Greg Wheeler (Zanardi)
Test Driver:	–

Brief History

1972: Entered British GP as Williams-Motul. 1973: Entered Formula 1 under the name of Frank Williams Racing using ISO chasssis. 1978: Williams Grand Prix Engineering founded. Australian Alan Jones signed to drive. 1979: Clay Regazzoni wins in Britain for Williams' first Grand Prix victory. 1980: Alan Jones wins the Drivers' World Championship with Williams taking the Constructors' title for the first time. 1986: Frank Williams seriously injured in a car crash and confined to a wheelchair. 1992: Nigel Mansell becomes the first driver to win the opening five rounds of a season and achieves a record of nine victories in total as Williams take the Drivers' and Constructors' World Championships. 1993: Alain Prost wins his fourth world title and announces his retirement from the sport. 1994: Williams record their seventh Constructors' Championship victory to bring them level with Lotus in the all-time record. 1996: Williams win eighth Constructors' Championship, Damon Hill wins first Drivers' World Championship, Jacques Villeneuve runner-up in first season. 1997: Williams win ninth Constructors' Championship, Jacques Villeneuve wins first Drivers' World Championship in only his second season. 1999: Frank Williams knighted in New Year honours list.

2000: BMW supply engines. Rothmans do not renew sponsorship for season.

Grand Prix Record

Contested:	403	349 as Williams Grand Prix
Cars Started:	768	Completed: 497 Retired: 271
Victories:	103	
Pole Positions:	108	
Fastest Laps:	111	
Constructors' World Titles:	9	1980, 1981, 1986, 1987, 1992, 1993, 1994, 1996, 1997
Drivers' World Championships:	7	1980, 1982, 1987, 1992, 1993, 1996, 1997
Most Points in a Season:	175	1996
Total Constructors' Cup Points:	1989.5	
Average Points/Grand Prix:	4.94	

Review

The start of the 2000 season represents another one of change for the Williams team. Gone are their long term sponsors Rothmans and gone are the Renault engines that provided much of their mid-nineties success. Powering their cars will be BMW engines who will look to be strong in their battle to out-gun German rivals Mercedes. Just how competitive the power-packs are, certainly in the first phase of the season, will remain to be seen. Reliability will probably be the biggest hurdle they have to overcome. All the testing in the world cannot substitute for race conditions. Just ask the BAR team.

The changes for the commencement of the 1999 season were also major. They welcomed the arrival of two new drivers in Ralf Schumacher – younger brother of Michael – and Champ Car Champion Alessandro Zanardi. They also made a major design change on their new FW21 car, re-introducing a longitudinal gearbox for the first time since 1979 as the team totally re-thought the design of the car.

By the end of the year there were mixed fortunes from all this. 1999 was the second successive season in which Williams had failed to win a Grand Prix. Never before had the team gone more than one season without celebrating a victory. If that was a disappointment for the team, then the form and performances of Ralf Schumacher were the perfect pick-me-up and led to many independent observers picking him as their driver of the season. Although his performances in qualifying were not consistent, his finishes in the points were and one wonders, on reflection what Williams might have achieved had they kept the services of Frentzen to pair with the younger Schumacher. That tells the tale of Ralf's partner who probably arrived as the senior of the two. As it was, Zanardi simply failed to get to grips with the car or the F1 circuits bar a couple of races near the end of the season. The Italian had arrived at Williams, just as Villeneuve had a few years earlier, as Champ (CART) Car Champion but failed to transform that type of form into even one championship point throughout the season. Indeed his performances reflected his previous spell in Formula One as a driver for three different teams at the start of the Nineties.

As far as the performance of the FW21 goes, there would seem to be mixed reactions. On the one hand Ralf only suffered one retirement due to reliability – an engine failure at Imola – while Alex seemed to be the brunt of them almost every other race. Bad luck or driving style – the choice is yours. What it did mean though was that Williams finished out of the top four of the Constructors' Cup for the first time since 1990 and that will not have pleased Sir Frank and the pressure will be on Zanardi to produce finishes and results more comparable with those of Schumacher Junior.

While Zanardi started the season with two dnfs at Melbourne and Interlagos, Ralf secured seven points with a third place in Australia followed by a fourth place in Brazil. The roles were reversed in the next two races with Ralf failing to complete the course in San Marino or Monaco while Alex finished his first race in a Williams, this at Imola and improved on his 11th place in the next race in Monaco by finishing eighth. Frank Williams might have hoped for a better performance from his two drivers as he celebrated his 30th anniversary of his debut as a team in F1.

The team's fourth decade in F1 did get off to a great start though. Fifth, two fourths and a second third of the season, established any lingering doubts anyone might have had about Ralf's credentials as he turned disappointing grid positions into successive points finishes in Spain, Canada, France and England. Alex though had a hat-trick of mechanical problems, suffering two gearbox failures and a blown engine in the first three of those venues. His 11th place at Silverstone would prove to be his only completion in a seven-race period with further retirements coming in the three races following the British GP. The Silverstone race had marked the 20th anniversary of the Williams team's first ever win in Formula 1, but there was never any chance of that success being repeated this time around.

Nevertheless the results had started to show a distinct improvement, especially for Ralf – a fact which was credited to the team who made tweaks to the car that improved its aerodynamics especially at the rear.

Ralf used the British meeting to start making improvements in his qualifying position and by the time of the European Grand Prix managed a place on the second row with a season's best fourth. His best performance though came a race earlier when he produced a tremendous drive in Italy to finish second. Notably that was Williams' highest placing since Frentzen came second in Japan in what was the penultimate race of 1997.

Looking for a way to break out of his rut, Zanardi switched to using steel brakes for the German GP, arguing that the greater consistency they provide under braking would help him through the corners, even though they are not as durable and are also heavier than the normal carbon ones generally used in F1.

For the penultimate race of the season, the Williams team introduced a new sidepod design they hoped would help improve downforce and provide their drivers with greater stability on the new circuit. Ralf spun out after seven laps and Alex finished a lap down on a weekend when Sir Frank was forced to wear Tartan trousers to honour a bet he had with Jackie Stewart earlier in the year, in which he said the Scottish team would not achieve a Grand Prix win in the season! The season finished as it had started really. Zanardi having an electrical failure on his first lap to bring his season to a sad end, but with Ralf driving to score two points in Japan with a fifth place finish.

When it was all over the rumours centred on the Italian Alex Zanardi and whether he would remain with the Williams team for the year 2000 or whether Jenson Button, third in the 1999 British F3 championship, would come through pre-season testing with the teams and complete the most dramatic of leaps in recent history.

Drivers and Results 1999

Driver	Races	Com	Ret	Dnq	HP	Pts	Psn	Comp%
Schumacher, R.	16	12	4	0	2	35	6/24	75.00
Zanardi, A.	16	6	10	0	7	0	–	37.50
Aggregate	32	18	14	0	2	35	5/11	56.25

			Ralf Schumacher			**Alex Zanardi**	
	Grand Prix	Gd	P	Details	Gd	P	Details
1	Australian	8	3	1:35:08.671	15	r	accident
2	Brazilian	11	4	1:36:22.860	16	r	differential
3	San Marino	9	r	engine	10	11	spin
4	Monaco	16	r	accident	11	8	1:49:49.514
5	Spanish	10	5	1:35:40.873	17	r	gearbox
6	Canadian	13	4	1:41:38.119	12	r	gearbox
7	French	16	4	1:59:09.818	15	r	engine

8	British	8	3	1:32:57.555	13	11	1:33:47.268
9	Austrian	8	r	spin	14	r	out of fuel
10	German	11	4	1:22:11.403	14	r	differential
11	Hungarian	16	9	1 lap down	15	r	differential
12	Belgian	5	5	1:26:31.124	8	8	1:26:50.079
13	Italian	5	2	1:17:06.195	4	7	1:17:30.970
14	European	4	4	1:42:33.822	18	r	accident
15	Malaysian	8	r	spun-out	16	10	1 lap down
16	Japanese	9	5	1:32:58.279	16	r	electrics

Williams FW22 Specifications

Engine: **BMW**
Car
Chassis: Carbon Aramid epoxy composite, manufactured by Williams
Transmission: Six-speed Williams transverse semi-automatic
Clutch: AP Racing
Suspension: Williams with Williams-Penske dampers
Cooling system: Two Secan water radiators either side of chassis; two IMI oil radiators
Brakes: Carbone Industrie discs and pads operated by AP callipers
Lubricants: Castrol
Fuel: Petrobras
Instrumentation: Williams digital data display
Dimensions: Length: 4450 mm   Wheelbase: 3050 mm
Front Track: 1460 mm   Rear Track: 1400 mm
• *Details based on 1999 FW21 car specifications.*

Engines 1973-00

1973-83: Ford. 1984-87: Honda Turbo. 1988: Judd. 1989-97: Renault. 1998-99: Supertec. 2000: BMW.

Drivers 1989-00

1989: T.Boutsen & R.Patrese. 1990: T.Boutsen & R.Patrese. 1991: N.Mansell & R.Patrese. 1992: N.Mansell & R.Patrese. 1993: A.Prost & D.Hill. 1994: A.Senna, D.Hill, D.Coulthard & N.Mansell. 1995: D.Hill & D.Coulthard. 1996: D.Hill & J. Villeneuve. 1997-98: J.Villeneuve & H-H.Frentzen. 1999-00: A.Zinardi & R.Schumacher.

Constructors' Cup Record

Year-Position/Points: 1973-10/2; 1974-10/4; 1975-9/6; 1978-9/11; 1979-2/75; 1980-1/120; 1981-1/95; 1982-4/58; 1983-4/36; 1983-11/2; 1984-6/25.5; 1985-3/71; 1986-1/135; 1987-1/137; 1988-7/20; 1989-2/77; 1990-4/57; 1991-2/125; 1992-1/164; 1993-1/168; 1994-1/118; 1995-2/112; 1996-1/175; 1997-1/123; 1998-3/38; 1999-5/35.

Grand Prix Wins

1979 GB (Regazzoni), Ger, Aut, Hol, Can (all Jones); 1980 Arg (Jones), Mon (Reutemann), Fra, GB, Can, USA (all Jones); 1981 Long Beach (Jones), Bra (Reutemann), Bel (Reutemann), Las Vegas (Jones); 1982 Swi (Rosberg); 1983 Mon (Rosberg), 1984 Dallas (Rosberg); 1985 Detroit (Rosberg), Eur (Mansell), SA (Mansell), Aus (Rosberg); 1986 Bra (Piquet), Bel, Can, Fra, GB (all Mansell), Ger (Piquet), Hun (Piquet), Ita (Piquet), Por (Mansell); 1987 San, Fra, GB (all Mansell), Ger (Piquet), Hun (Piquet), Aut (Mansell), Ita (Piquet), Esp (Mansell), Mex (Mansell); 1989 Can (Boutsen), Aus (Boutsen); 1990 San (Patrese), Hun (Boutsen); 1991 Mex (Patrese), Fra, GB, Ger, Ita (all Mansell), Por (Patrese), Esp (Mansell); 1992 SA, Mex, Bra, Esp, San, Fra, GB, Ger, Por (all Mansell), Jap (Patrese); 1993 SA, San, Esp, Can, Fra, GB, Ger (all Prost), Hun, Bel, Ita (all D.Hill); 1994 Esp, GB, Bel, Ita, Por, Jap (all D.Hill), Aus (Mansell); 1995 Arg, San, Hun (all D.Hill), Por (Coulthard), Aus (D.Hill); 1996 Aus, Bra, Arg (all D.Hill), Eur (J.Villeneuve), San, Can, Fra (all D.Hill), GB (J.Villeneuve), Ger (D.Hill), Hun (J.Villeneuve), Por (J.Villeneuve), Jap (D.Hill). 1997 Bra (J.Villeneuve), Arg (J.Villeneuve), San (Frentzen), Esp, GB, Hun, Aut), Luxembourg (all J.Villeneuve).

Grand Prix Circuits 2000

Indianapolis 500

1950	Parsons	Kurtis Kraft
1951	Wallard	Kurtis Kraft
1952	Ruttman	Kuzma
1953	Vukovich	Kurtis Kraft
1954	Vukovich	Kurtis Kraft
1955	Sweikert	Kurtis Kraft
1956	Flaherty	Watson
1957	Hanks	Epperly
1958	Bryan	Epperly
1959	Ward	Watson
1960	Rathmann,J.	Watson

US Grand Prix

1959	McLaren	Cooper-Climax
1960	Moss	Lotus-Climax
1961	Ireland	Lotus-Climax
1962	Clark	Lotus-Climax
1963	Hill,G.	BRM
1964	Hill,G.	BRM
1965	Hill,G.	BRM
1966	Clark	Lotus-BRM
1967	Clark	Lotus-Ford
1968	Stewart,Jackie	Matra-Ford
1969	Rindt	Lotus-Ford
1970	Fittipaldi,E.	Lotus-Ford
1971	Cevert	Tyrrell-Ford
1972	Stewart,Jackie	Tyrrell-Ford
1973	Peterson	Lotus-Ford
1974	Reutemann	Brabham-Ford
1975	Lauda	Ferrari
1981	Jones	Williams-Ford
1982	Watson	McLaren-Ford
1983	Alboreto	Tyrrell-Ford

1985	Rosberg	Williams-Honda
1986	Senna	Lotus-Renault
1987	Senna	Lotus-Honda
1988	Senna	McLaren-Honda
1989	Prost	McLaren-Honda
1990	Senna	McLaren-Honda
1991	Senna	McLaren-Honda

US East Grand Prix

1976	Hunt	McLaren-Ford
1977	Hunt	McLaren-Ford
1978	Reutemann	Ferrari
1979	Villeneuve,G.	Ferrari
1980	Jones	Williams-Ford

US West Grand Prix

1976	Regazzoni	Ferrari
1977	Andretti	Lotus-Ford
1978	Reutemann	Ferrari
1979	Villeneuve,G.	Ferrari
1980	Piquet	Brabham-Ford
1981	Jones	Williams-Ford
1982	Lauda	McLaren-Ford
1983	Watson	McLaren-Ford

Ceasars Palace Grand Prix

1982	Alboreto	Tyrrell-Ford

Dallas Grand Prix

1984	Rosberg	Williams-Honda

Detroit Grand Prix

1984	Piquet	Brabham-BMW

A1-Ring

A1-Ring
Austrian Grand Prix – 16 July 2000
Lap Distance: 2.684 miles/4.321 km – Clockwise
Race Distance: 190.564 miles/306.808 km – 71 laps

The A1-Ring is an updated and redesigned version of the famous old Österreichring. It lies in a green, hilly area of Austria known as Styria, roughly central in a triangle formed by the cities of Vienna, Salzburg and Graz.

Originally built in 1968, a total of 18 Grands Prix were held there between 1970 and 1987, with the final event needing three starts to get it underway! It came back on to the calender in 1997 after £17 million had been spent on it to turn the circuit into one of the most modern in the world. The circuit has a square feel to it and combines a number of long straights with tight and sweeping corners that will test drivers and keep teams on their toes when it comes to car set-ups. This is because the circuit has very low grip, although during the course of the weekend this increases as the rubber is laid down. Most of the corners are relatively slow although towards the end of the lap there are a couple of quite challenging faster corners. The other notable thing about the circuit are the changes in elevation. In setting the car up it is necessary to maximise grip particularly in terms of traction – heavy braking is required as cars go from fast straights into tight corners. This results in the engine being highly stressed with the throttle fully open here more than for most other circuits.

The Circuit

The starting line and grid are located in front of the medical centre and are at the bottom of a hill from where the cars power their way down past the garages in top gear at 180 mph. Changing down and braking hard, the bumpy Castrol Kurve is a sharp right-hand turn that is taken in 2nd gear at 45 mph. Once through the turn the cars come out on to the fastest part of the circuit and a near straight that is over half a mile in length. At a top speed of 180 mph, the stands of the Naturtribune West flash past on the left as the track curves slightly out to the left.

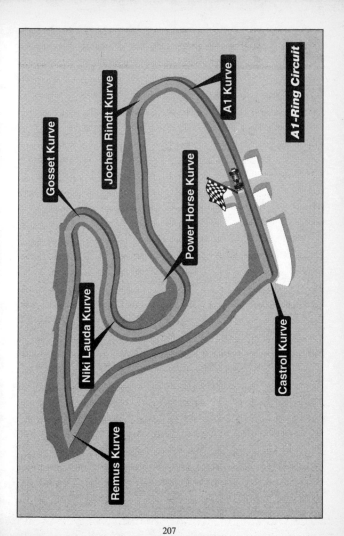

A1-Ring Circuit

A1 Kurve

Jochen Rindt Kurve

Gosset Kurve

Power Horse Kurve

Niki Lauda Kurve

Remus Kurve

Castrol Kurve

At the end of the straight the Remus Kurve looms and also marks the highest point on the circuit – very tight, it takes the cars through 150 degrees. It is the hardest braking point in the circuit with drivers pulling -3.6 g as they decelerate hard to 40 mph at the apex of the corner. By getting the braking right, overtaking is a possibility at this point. Out of here is another long straight, only slightly shorter than the one leading into the Remus Kurve and just as fast as it passes in front of the Naturtribune Nord stands at around 170 mph. The end of this straight marks the entry to the most curvaceous part of the circuit which swings inside and out.

The Gosset Kurve is a double right-hand turn, the 50 mph 2nd-gear entry being slower than the shallower exit which can be negotiated in 4th gear at 110 mph. The Niki Lauda Kurve is an open sweeping turn around to the left, taken at 95 mph in 4th gear, and leading into another similar turn called the Power Horse Kurve which is marginally faster at 100 mph.

Out on to a shorter straight, the cars run parallel to the Start-Finish line at 175 mph as they approach the Jochen Rindt Kurve. This is an open right-hand turn that is taken in 4th gear at 125 mph and leads into a short straight from where cars can re-enter the pit lane. The A1 Kurve slows the cars down through 3rd gear at 95 mph as they turn right before accelerating out downhill along the straight across the Start-Finish line.

3-Year Record

Year	1st	2nd	3rd	4th	5th	6th
1997	Villeneuve (Williams)	Coulthard (McLaren)	Frentzen (Williams)	Fisichella (Jordan)	R.Schum'r (Jordan)	M.Schum'r (Ferrari)
1998	Hakkinen (McLaren)	Coulthard (McLaren)	M.Schum'r (Ferrari)	Irvine (Ferrari)	R.Schum'r (Jordan)	Villeneuve (Williams)
1999	Irvine (Ferrari)	Coulthard (McLaren)	Hakkinen (McLaren)	Frentzen (Jordan)	Wurz (Benetton)	Diniz (Sauber)

Pole Positions

1997	1998	1999
Villeneuve (Williams)	Fisichella (Benetton)	Hakkinen (McLaren)
1m 10.304s (dry)	1m 29.598s (wet)	1m 10.954s (dry)

Barcelona

Circuit de Catalunya
Spanish Grand Prix, Barcelona – 7 May 2000
Lap Distance: 2.937 miles/4.727 km – Clockwise
Race Distance: 191.69 miles/307.255 km – 65 laps

Located 12 miles north-east of Barcelona, Catalunya is one of five circuits to play host to the Spanish Grand Prix. Held here since 1991, the circuit continues to be improved and upgraded on an annual basis, making it one of the most advanced circuits in the world. Despite that, it remains bumpy and the track surface has ripples on it. It has some very exciting high speed corners and coupled with these corners there is quite a long straight, a very long corner plus a couple of quite low speed corners. In fact it represents every sort of condition normally encountered. As the circuit contains so many varying features, the set-up of the car is a compromise between good speed on the straight and high grip in the low speed corners, in addition a good balance must be maintained in the fast corners to get a good lap time. Generally, a neutral chassis setting is opted for which helps with understeer in the long corners. Tyre wear is high due to the abrasive nature of the track surface and requires a relatively hard tyre.

Most Formula One teams use Barcelona for testing more than any other single circuit these days, including Silverstone, and therefore it is a circuit that the teams know well. It is a circuit with few overtaking opportunities and race strategy is often the key to the race.

The Circuit

From the starting line cars accelerate downhill at 190 mph to Elf. The approach to Elf is downhill until almost the corner itself when it rises to the left. Braking hard at -3.8 g, this corner is taken in 3rd gear at 85 mph on the inside so that the car can drift out to the left for the next bend taken in 4th at around 100 mph. Curvone Renault is the first long, sweeping 180-degree right-hander, entered in 4th gear at 100 mph with 140 mph attained during its course it provides tyres with their toughest test. Out of Renault and accelerating to about 180 mph before the circuit loops back on itself at Revolt Repsol. Entered in 2nd gear at 85 mph, cars catapult out up to 155 mph and in 5th gear along a short straight to Revolt Seat. Hard on the brakes, this tight left-hand hairpin drops the cars downhill at around 60 mph through a gentle left-handed sweep at 160 mph before braking again to enter Revolt Würth. Here, the track takes a sharp left-hand turn which is almost 90 degrees and is entered in 2nd gear at 85 mph. On exit, the circuit turns slightly right as 5th gear and 155 mph is reached.

Revolt Campsa is a blind right-hander but can be navigated safely in 5th gear at 135 mph. Then it's down the short straight called Nissan in top gear at 185 mph, on the run into 180-degree hairpin Revolt La Caixa, which is taken in 2nd gear at 65 mph as it climbs to the right into the two 100-degree bends at Banc Sabadell. Entered in 3rd at 80 mph, it is exited in 5th gear as the car accelerates towards the penultimate corner, another right-hander that turns into a short straight leading to the final bend which is taken in 5th gear at about 140 mph. On to the Start-Finish straight where cars reach a maximum of 190 mph on the kilometre-long straight.

3-Year Record

Year	1st	2nd	3rd	4th	5th	6th
1997	Villeneuve (Williams)	Panis (Prost)	Alesi (Benetton)	M.Schum'r (Ferrari)	Herbert (Sauber)	Coulthard (McLaren)
1998	Hakkinen (McLaren)	Coulthard (McLaren)	M.Schum'r (Ferrari)	Wurz (Benetton)	Barrichello (Stewart)	Villeneuve (Williams)
1999	Hakkinen (McLaren)	Coulthard (McLaren)	M.Schum'r (Ferrari)	Irvine (Ferrari)	R.Schum'r (Williams)	Trulli (Prost)

Pole Position

1997	1998	1999
Villeneuve (Williams)	Hakkinen (McLaren)	Hakkinen (McLaren)
1m 16.525s (dry)	1m 20.262s (dry)	1m 22.088s (dry)

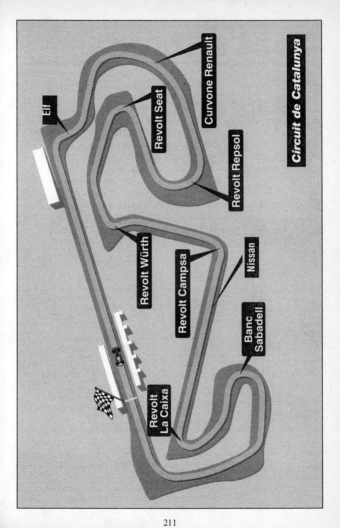

Circuit de Catalunya

Curvone Renault

Revolt Seat

Elf

Revolt Repsol

Revolt Würth

Revolt Campsa

Nissan

Banc Sabadell

Revolt La Caixa

Hockenheim

Hockenheimring
German Grand Prix – 30 July 2000
Lap Distance: 4.239 miles/6.829 km – Clockwise
Race Distance: 190.755 miles/309.305 km – 45 laps

Located some 50 miles south of Frankfurt and 15 miles west of
Heidelberg, the circuit was originally built as a test circuit for Mercedes
cars. The German Grand Prix has been staged here since 1986 and it is,
for the majority, an open circuit that is very fast throughout. The
exception to this is the stadium complex near the starting grid where the
track twists back and forth through 360 degrees in front of the
grandstands. At over four miles in length, it is one of the longest Grand
Prix circuits, and it is often more infamously remembered as the circuit
that took the life of Jim Clark in April 1968. Weather is often very
changeable as the circuit winds its way through dense pine forests
which can create dangerous patches of fog and mist.

To gain a good lap time and to maintain overtaking possibilities it is
necessary to run an extremely low level of drag but the consequent low
level of downforce makes the car extremely difficult to drive in the
stadium section. It is also necessary to have good chassis settings to
achieve the highest possible level of mechanical grip and maintain a
good ride over the kerbs of the chicanes. Tyre wear is high and one of
the tasks of the drivers is to keep this to a minimum. The track itself is
narrow but overtaking is possible due to the very long braking distances
into the chicanes and the opportunities for slipstreaming by the car
coming up from behind.

The Circuit

From the Start-Finish line, cars approach Nord Kurve, a fast right-
hander that is taken in 4th gear at 125 mph and exited in 5th ready to
move up to top gear and accelerating to around 210 mph for the long
run to the first chicane. The posthumously named Jim Clark Kurve
slows cars to 2nd gear as they brake hard at -3.2g, decelerating to 60
mph before accelerating back up to 200 mph deep into the forest.

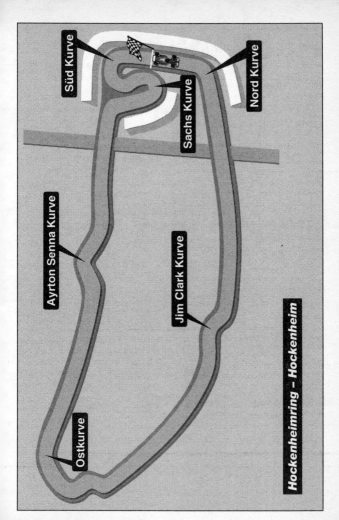

Süd Kurve

Nord Kurve

Sachs Kurve

Ayrton Senna Kurve

Jim Clark Kurve

Ostkurve

Hockenheimring – Hockenheim

Before the Ostkurve, the drivers get busy. The previous straight turns into a sharp right-left turn taken in 2nd gear at 50 mph before it becomes a long right-hand bend about 350 metres before Ostkurve is entered – a chicane which is a right-left taken in 2nd gear leading into a long, fast right-hander and on to the next straight. The Ayrton Senna Kurve, which is also known as Bremskurve 3, is approached down the back straight at 205 mph. The left-right turn slows the cars drastically to 60 mph as it's taken in 2nd gear and then it's full-power as the cars accelerate back up to 195 mph before the stadium complex begins to come into view.

The Agip Kurve is a fast right-hander that is taken in 4th gear at 105 mph and leads quickly into the Sachs Kurve as drivers shift down to a 60 mph 2nd gear for the hairpin that has a well-earned reputation for being slippery. The final section in the stadium complex that leads back to the start line, the Süd or Opel Kurve, is a double-apex hairpin with both right-handers taken in 3rd gear at an average of 90 mph and leading into the finishing straight where cars can accelerate to 175 mph.

3-Year Record

Year	1st	2nd	3rd	4th	5th	6th
1997	Berger	M.Schum'r	Hakkinen	Trulli	R.Schum'r	Alesi
	(Benetton)	(Ferrari)	(Benetton)	(Mclaren)	(Prost)	(Benetton)
1998	Hakkinen	Coulthard	Villeneuve	Hill	M.Schum'r	R.Schum'r
	(McLaren)	(McLaren)	(Williams)	(Jordan)	(Ferrari)	(Jordan)
1999	Irvine	Salo	Frentzen	R.Schum'r	Coulthard	Panis
	(Ferrari)	(Ferrari)	(Jordan)	(Williams)	(McLaren)	(Prost)

Pole Position

1997	1998	1999
Berger (Benetton)	Hakkinen (McLaren)	Hakkinen (McLaren)
1m 41.873s (dry)	1m 41.838s (dry)	1m 42.950s (dry)

Hungaroring

Hungaroring
Hungarian Grand Prix – 13 August 2000
Lap Distance   2.465 miles/3.968 km – Clockwise
Race Distance   189.805 miles/305.586 km – 77 laps

Just 12 miles to the north-east of Budapest, Hungaroring is a modern Grand Prix complex that has been created with F1 in mind. It has hosted the Hungarian Grand Prix since 1986 but is not the best liked of tracks among the drivers. Bumpy and slippery, there is limited scope for overtaking with no fast corners, which can make the race rather processional in nature. After Monaco it is the slowest track on the calendar and is also one of the shortest. Race day is traditionally extremely hot and due to the slow average speed of the circuit and the need to run very high front wing angles, overheating is one more problem the teams have to contend with.

The circuit is one of the worst for overtaking and often leads to races that are won and lost in qualifying and pit stops. Grid position is therefore all important, as is a high downforce, and the circuit is second only to Monaco in this respect. Despite all this, because the circuit is situated in a natural bowl, it is one of the most enjoyable to watch.

The Circuit

From the Start-Finish line it's full power to Turn 1 with speeds approaching 175 mph. Turn 1 is a long, right-hand downhill bend taking the drivers through 180 degrees, entered in 3rd gear at 75 mph, exited in 4th at 135 mph. The camber on this corner can also catch drivers out or, at the very least, see them slipping out of the drive line and into the dirty sections of the track, which does not benefit their tyres or subsequent grip. Entry and exit positions are also important as the corner is blind. A short straight brings the cars into Turn 2 and then Turn 3 and here there is a choice of two lines, but whether the car turns in early or late makes little difference to the amount of oversteer experienced as this long left-hander begins to sweep right. Turn 2 is entered at 135 mph, slowing to 70 mph before accelerating out of Turn 3 at 115 mph.

215

Cars approach Turn 4 leaving the straight at around 170 mph, changing down from top to 4th gear while braking to 110 mph before climbing uphill on the approach to Turn 5 – another long right-hander negotiated in 3rd gear at 80 mph and accelerated out of in 4th gear to 150 mph.

Turn 6 leads to the highest part of the circuit and is a right-left chicane that is entered in 2nd gear at 55 mph and exited in 5th at 115 mph. Turn 7 comes quickly and the approach to this left-hander is bumpy. Third gear maintained throughout, 75 mph being the slowest point at the apex of the curve. Turn 8 is a right-hander and is taken in 3rd gear at 85 mph with the left-hander taken flat out. A curving straight forms Turn 9 and leads into Turn 10 which is not as fast as it looks as the corner suddenly tightens. It is taken in 4th at 110 mph.

Turn 11 is an off-camber and downhill right-left chicane which always seems to gather particles of grit, while a high kerb awaits the unsuspecting at the second apex. It is taken in 3rd gear at 90 mph. Turn 12 is almost a hairpin-like corner directly behind the pits and it's taken in 2nd at 60 mph. A long right-hander marks Turn 13, which mirrors Turn 1. Through it, the cars first oversteer, turning to understeer by the time they exit on to the straight via the kerb. Around 80 mph sees the cars through the apex of the curve from which they power towards 175 mph as they flash across the Start-Finish line.

3-Year Record

Year	1st	2nd	3rd	4th	5th	6th
1997	Villeneuve (Williams)	Hill (Arrows)	Herbert (Sauber)	M.Schum'r (Ferrari)	R.Schum'r (Jordan)	Nakano (Prost)
1998	M.Schum'r (Ferrari)	Coulthard (McLaren)	Villeneuve (Williams)	Hill (Jordan)	Frentzen (Jordan)	Hakkinen (McLaren)
1999	Hakkinen (McLaren)	Coulthard (McLaren)	Irvine (Ferrari)	Frentzen (Jordan)	Barrichello (Stewart)	Hill (Jordan)

Pole Position

1997	1998	1999
M.Schumacher (Ferrari)	Hakkinen (McLaren)	Hakkinen (McLaren)
1m 14.672s (dry)	1m 16.973s (dry)	1m 18.156s (dry)

NB: At the time of going to press there was some talk about modifying the circuit to produce a shorter race distance. This may or may not have happened for the 2000 race.

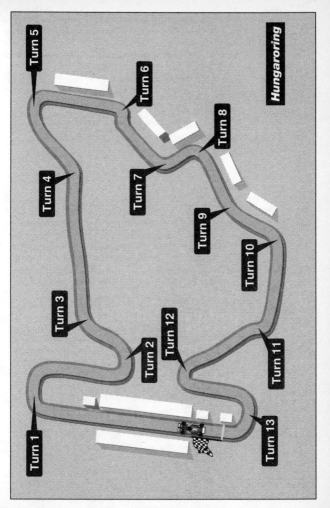

Hungaroring

Turn 1
Turn 2
Turn 3
Turn 4
Turn 5
Turn 6
Turn 7
Turn 8
Turn 9
Turn 10
Turn 11
Turn 12
Turn 13

Imola

Autodromo Enzo and Dino Ferrari
San Marino Grand Prix – 9 April 2000
Lap Distance: 3.063 miles/4.931 km – Anti-clockwise
Race Distance: 189.906 miles/305.749 km – 62 laps

Located in north-central Italy in the principality of San Marino, Imola provides one of the most atmospheric race days anywhere in the world. Major modifications have been made to the very fast circuit in the wake of the 1994 event in which Ayrton Senna and Roland Ratzenberger lost their lives. This brought revision to Tamburello, Villeneuve and Variante Bassa which have now made the circuit a low-to-medium speed track which requires a lot of heavy braking. Medium to high downforce is required with emphasis put on making the car responsive, getting good traction and smooth engine characteristics. To help achieve this teams usually have stiffer than normal settings for stability when braking; as such, this can hinder grip. Brake performance is always a major concern. Overtaking opportunities at Imola are somewhat limited although late-braking into Tosa is a favourite spot for most drivers to try!

The Circuit

Tamburello is the first corner from the start and cars brake heavily at its entrance. The corner is a left-handed S-bend which is entered in 3rd gear at 75 mph and exited in 4th gear at 125 mph as cars power up the straight to Villeneuve. This is a second S-bend that slows the approach to the forthcoming hairpin and slows cars down from 130 mph to 105 mph in 4th gear. Accelerating quickly up to 150 mph, cars almost immediately brake for Tosa, a tight hairpin from right to left taken in 2nd gear at around 55 mph. On exit, cars accelerate to 175 mph and climb towards Piratella. This is a somewhat blind left-hander that pulls -3.5g as drivers brake at its entrance; it is taken in 4th gear at 100 mph and accelerated away from at 160 mph. Despite its nature it is a corner well liked by most drivers.

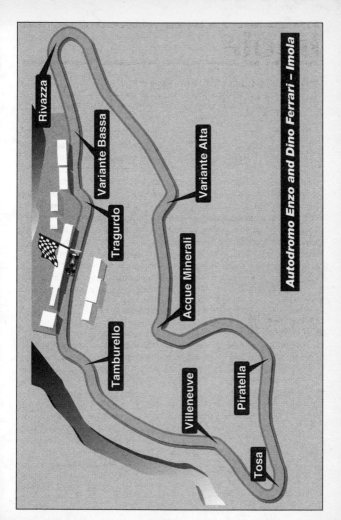

Autodromo Enzo and Dino Ferrari – Imola

Rivazza

Variante Bassa

Tragurdo

Variante Alta

Acque Minerali

Tamburello

Villeneuve

Piratella

Tosa

219

The approach to Acque Minerali is downhill at 165 mph. Slowing down to 4th gear at 125 mph the cars turn to the right and after a short straight turn right again through 90 degrees at 65 mph. The track then turns slightly to the left as cars accelerate through 105 mph in 4th gear.

Variante Alta is next and, coming off a short straight, it is a fast chicane that can be tackled in 3rd gear – it certainly requires a 3rd-gear exit. It is entered in 6th gear at 170 mph and speeds of 75 mph are maintained through it. Drivers tend to take more chances at this chicane because it does have a safe run-off area.

Out of the chicane and the track plunges downhill through some stunning countryside, arriving at a sharpish double left-hander called Rivazza which swings the cars through 180 degrees. This requires very hard braking, down from 6th (180 mph) to 3rd gear (60 mph) at its entrance where a massive -3.8 g really tests the driver's strength. Shifting up briefly before changing down to tackle the final turn, which is taken at 80 mph, the cars arrive on a curving right-hand line and fly through the Variante Bassa, accelerating all the time up to 170 mph. The Tragurdo then looms up as a left-right chicane that feeds the pits and is taken in 2nd gear at around 55 mph. Cars then accelerate to 185 mph across the Start-Finish line.

3-Year Record

Year	1st	2nd	3rd	4th	5th	6th
1997	Frentzen	M.Schum'r	Irvine	Fisichella	Alesi	Hakkinen
	(Williams)	(Ferrari)	(Ferrari)	(Jordan)	(Benetton)	(McLaren)
1998	Coulthard	M.Schum'r	Irvine	Villeneuve	Frentzen	Alesi
	(McLaren)	(Ferrari)	(Ferrari)	(Williams)	(Williams)	(Sauber)
1999	M.Schum'r	Coulthard	Barrichello	Hill	Fisichella	Alesi
	(Ferrari)	(McLaren)	(Stewart)	(Jordan)	(Benetton)	(Sauber)

Pole Position

1997	1998	1999
Villeneuve (Williams)	Coulthard (McLaren)	Hakkinen (McLaren)
1m 23.303s (dry)	1m 25.973s (dry)	1m 26.362 (dry)

Indianapolis

Indianapolis Motor Speedway
USA Grand Prix – 27 September 2000
Lap Distance: 2.55 miles/4.20 km

Formula One racing returns to Indianapolis for the first time since 1960. The home of the famous Indy 500 race, fans of the American event will see a major change at the circuit when the Indianapolis 500 is run on May 28, four months before the Grand Prix itself.

The cars will race north on the main straightaway and then negotiate 13 turns on a 2.55-mile track which will wind through the north infield, then south. The cars will then turn east just north of the Hall of Fame Museum and exit back on to the Speedway's oval near Turn 2. The cars will then run clockwise on the oval. The F1 course will utilise about one mile of the existing 2.5-mile Indy oval. The first turn is right-handed, just before the exit of the oval's Turn 4. Eight more right-handed and four left-handed turns follow before the cars return to the oval.

Computer imaging has predicted that an F1 car can circle the circuit in 73 seconds, a speed average of 127 mph, reaching 195 mph at the Yard of Bricks and a top speed of 200 mph just before the entrance to Turn 1. The drivers will have to gear down to 55 mph at Turn 9, a right-hand turn just south of the golf course and will re-enter the oval over Tunnel 3, located at the entrance of Turn 2, at 100 mph and begin accelerating.

New additions to the renovated circuit, including 36 garages, topped by 12 suites plus a new 400-seat press building, will be constructed near the north end of the main straight.

Grand Prix racing was staged at Indianapolis for 11 years from 1950 to 1960. However, it ran to different regulations and and attracted very few European participants, and conversely very few American participants in the Indy 500 appeared on the European F1 circuit. The last F1 race to be staged in the USA was in 1991 when Ayrton Senna won the fifth out of six successive races there! The start to this Circuit section contains a list of races staged in the USA and their victors.

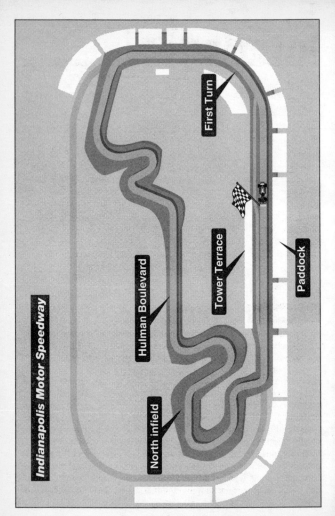

Indianapolis Motor Speedway

First Turn

Paddock

Tower Terrace

Hulman Boulevard

North infield

Interlagos

Autodromo Jose Carlos Pace
Brazilian Grand Prix – 26 March 2000
Lap Distance: 2.667 miles/4.292 km – Anticlockwise
Race Distance: 192.023 miles/309.024 km – 72 laps

Located ten miles south of central Sao Paulo, the track is named after Carlos Pace who won here in 1975. It has staged the Brazilian GP since 1991. The track was resurfaced for the 1995 season and reworked for the 1997 race, but the majority of drivers complain that it is still extremely bumpy. It remains one of the most tiring circuits that taxes even the fittest of drivers, not least because it undulates throughout its course. Cars will generally be set with a medium amount of wing, with downforce settings ranging from medium to high. Teams play with soft suspension settings to find that extra grip that might make the difference in the race. The high humidity and track temperatures during March normally ensure that cars are set to maintain maximum grip on the track. Nevertheless the sudden onset of heavy rainfall can spice things up! The circuit is one of the better ones for overtaking.

The Circuit

At the start, the cars race downhill to the left. It is approached in top gear at about 180 mph. Then braking very hard (-3.3 g), the cars approach the 'S' do Senna – a left-right-left section which begins with Curva 1, one of just two places where you might get to see overtaking manoeuvres as they try to out-brake one another. Cars take this corner in 2nd gear at 60 mph changing up to 3rd gear and accelerating through 100 mph towards the final turn in the sequence (Curva do Sol) and a 4th gear 140 mph. Hard on the throttle, cars accelerate to 180 mph along the Reta Oposta straight in top gear at 180 mph.

  The Descida do Lago is a tight left-hand corner to which there is a bumpy entrance, which often throws rash drivers into a spin. Those who get through it take it in 3rd gear at 85 mph, having braked hard at its entrance. Drivers who get it right can often get past those who don't at this point. After a short straight, another left-hander (135 mph in 4th gear) swings the cars back on themselves as they accelerate to 170 mph before braking hard at the entrance to Ferradura.

The Ferradura is a sweeping, double apex right-hander with an extremely bumpy entrance. Probably the most difficult corner on the circuit as it is approached downhill and at speed – 5th gear at 165 mph. After going through the first apex in 3rd gear at around 100 mph, the car drifts out for the second apex and, on exiting at the top in 3rd, another right-hander is on top of you almost immediately as Pinheirinho approaches and is taken in 2nd gear at about 55 mph.

The Pinheirinho is a very tight left-hander that is only taken in 2nd gear at 60 mph, exited in 3rd gear, and then it's up to 4th for the approach to another tight corner, this time with a right-hand turn. The Cotovêlo is taken in 2nd at just over 45 mph and exited in 3rd gear, climbing to 5th as the car makes for a left-hander prior to turning for Mergulho. This sweeping corner is taken in 4th gear at 145 mph before accelerating along to the 3rd gear Junção.

Subida do Boxes marks the entrance to two left-handed curves, both banked and going uphill. The first is approached at 110 mph and is followed by Arquibancadas, which is taken in 5th gear at 160 mph. Acceleration continues as the Start-Finish line straight comes into view and is crossed at about 185 mph.

3-Year Record

Year	1st	2nd	3rd	4th	5th	6th
1997	Villeneuve	Berger	Panis	Hakkinen	M.Schum'r	Alesi
	(Williams)	(Benetton)	(Prost)	(McLaren)	(Ferrari)	(Benetton)
1998	Hakkinen	Coulthard	M.Schum'r	Wurz	Frentzen	Fisichella
	(McLaren)	(McLaren)	(Ferrari)	(Benetton)	(Williams)	(Benetton)
1999	Hakkinen	M.Schum'r	Frentzen	R.Schum'r	Irvine	Panis
	(McLaren)	(Ferrari)	(Jordan)	(Williams)	(Ferrari)	(Prost)

Pole Position

1997	1998	1999
Villeneuve (Williams)	Hakkinen (McLaren)	Hakkinen (McLaren)
1m 16.004s (dry)	1m 17.092s (dry)	1m 16.568s (dry)

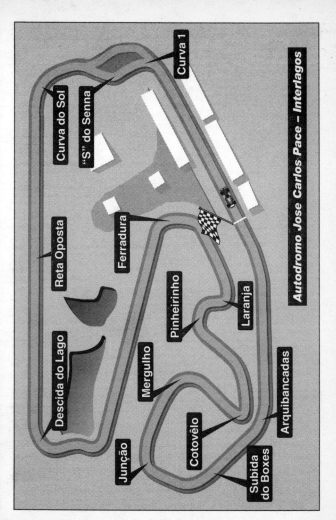

Autodromo Jose Carlos Pace – Interlagos

Curva 1
Curva do Sol
"S" do Senna
Reta Oposta
Ferradura
Descida do Lago
Pinheirinho
Mergulho
Laranja
Cotovêlo
Junção
Arquibancadas
Subida do Boxes

225

Magny-Cours

Circuit de Nevers
French Grand Prix – 2 July 2000
Lap Distance   2.641 miles/4.25 km – Clockwise
Race Distance   190.08 miles/306.029 km – 72 laps

Located about halfway between Paris and Lyon, Circuit de Nevers was opened to Grand Prix racing in 1991 following a massive refurbishment. Its smooth 'billiard table' surface makes it a favourite with the drivers but it is often difficult for teams to set the car up, simply because there is no other circuit like it with its mixture of very low-speed hairpins, some medium-speed corners and fast chicanes. Teams therefore normally opt for medium downforce with a lower than normal ride height, which helps to increase downforce while producing minimal drag. The circuit itself offers a good overtaking opportunity into the Adelaide hairpin and this is where much of the action takes place. The circuit is quite hard on the cars and great emphasis has to be put on reliability under the hot conditions to achieve a good finishing position.

The Circuit

From the starting grid, cars accelerate up to 170 mph before entering Grande Courbe, a long, left-hand bend which is driven in 5th gear at 165 mph. Drivers take great care to get the right line out of the curve into Estoril, which is a sweeping right-hand turn that goes through 180 degrees. Here, 4th gear is maintained at a speed of 110 mph. Understeer can be a real problem for drivers and time can be lost if the entry into Golf is not right. Golf itself is very nearly a straight but has a gentle curve to the right throughout its length. As such, it is taken full-out in top gear with speeds around 170 mph.

Adelaide is a 2nd-gear hairpin that brings the drivers back to earth. Braking hard at -3.2 g, and at 35 mph, it turns through 180 degrees and takes the vehicle back in the direction from which it has just come with the track immediately to the right. This leads straight into a fast right-left that is cleared in 4th and which leads to Nurburgring, a chicane that wriggles the cars left and right – not as tight as Adelaide but,

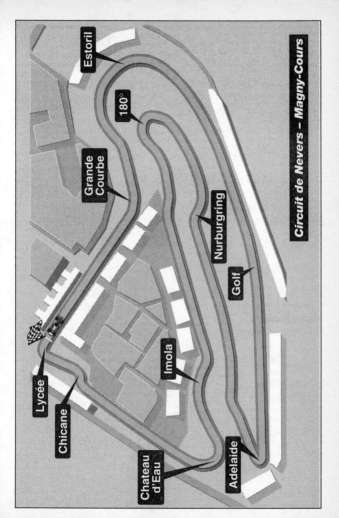

Circuit de Nevers – Magny-Cours

227

nevertheless, tricky because it closes up in the middle. Hard on the throttle, cars approach 150 mph and brake hard at the entrance to 180 Degrees. This is another hairpin and again brings the cars through 180 degrees and back upon themselves – taken in 2nd gear at 50 mph.

From the 180 it's up quickly through the gears to 6th and 170 mph before changing down to meet the challenge of Imola at 110 mph, a right-left that protects the Chateau d'Eau, a virtual 90-degree turn entered in 4th and exited in 2nd at 55 mph on to a straight that allows the car to accelerate to 155 mph towards the 2nd-gear Chicane. This is a very tight right-left turn where drivers have to be very careful to avoid the kerbs, especially on the second part of the corner. Immediately following the Chicane is the sharp Lycée right-hander taken in 2nd gear as the cars slow to 40 mph. Positioning for exit out of Lycée is important as it affects the driver's ability to get on the throttle quickly to ensure maximum speed down the straight. The corner also provides the entry to the pit lane.

3-Year Record

Year	1st	2nd	3rd	4th	5th	6th
1997	M.Schum'r (Ferrari)	Frentzen (Williams)	Irvine (Ferrari)	Villeneuve (Williams)	Alesi (Benetton)	R.Schum'r (Jordan)
1998	M.Schum'r (Ferrari)	Irvine (Ferrari)	Hakkinen (McLaren)	Villeneuve (Williams)	Wurz (Benetton)	Coulthard (McLaren)
1999	Frentzen (Jordan)	Hakkinen (McLaren)	Barrichello (Stewart)	R.Schum'r (Williams)	M.Schum'r (Ferrari)	Irvine (Ferrari)

Pole Position

1997	1998	1999
M.Schumacher (Ferrari)	Hakkinen (McLaren)	Barrichello (Stewart)
1m 14.548s (dry)	1m 14.929s (dry)	1m 38.441s (wet)

Notebook

Rubens Barrichello secured only his second career pole position here in 1999 when torrential rain turned the grid on its head and produced one of the best races of the season. Michael Schumacher has won four out of the last six races here which is the record number of victories at this circuit. The barren years were in 1996 when neither Ferrari managed to finish and last season when he finished fifth.

Melbourne

Albert Park Grand Prix Circuit
Australian Grand Prix – 12 March 2000
Lap Distance: 3.274 miles/5.269 km – Clockwise
Race Distance: 189.89 miles/305.6 km – 58 laps

Melbourne hosts its fifth Grand Prix in 2000. A street circuit situated in a park, the track is a combination of fast corners and tight hairpins along with sweeping curves. It is quite hard on the brakes and has few overtaking possibilities. Not particularly challenging as a race circuit, but most drivers do consider it among their favourites. The approaches to some of the corners are a little bumpy and can create problems for the drivers. Expect to see cars with a high wing level to produce maximum downforce. The circuit can be heavy on tyres so teams often opt for soft set-ups that will prolong tyre life.

The Circuit

From the start, cars accelerate to 185 mph as they reach the Fangio Stand. Flanked by the Fangio and Brabham Stands are two 45-degree right- and left-handers – Turns 1 and 2. Turn 1 is the hardest braking point in the circuit pulling -3.5 g. A change down to 2nd gear sees the first turn taken at 70 mph before a short acceleration into Turn 2, which is taken at 100 mph. Turn 2 and Turn 3 mark the bumpiest parts of the circuit. From here the cars accelerate to 180 mph before braking hard again (-3.4 g) towards a sharp right-left S-bend, taking Turn 3 in 2nd gear at around 55 mph. Accelerating again the cars catapult out through Turn 4 at 80 mph, accelerating past the Whitford Stand in 5th gear at 170 mph.

A short, sharp right-hander marks Turn 6 with cars again braking hard (-3.0 g) and slowing to 70 mph. The circuit then loops round to the right, negotiating Turn 8 at 155 mph, and then past the Clark Stand at 175 mph. The Fittipaldi Stand is at Turn 9 where cars brake hard again (-3.3 g) before setting off to a long, inner-loop curve turning the cars left at a speed of 160 mph. They slow to 90 mph and swing right, past the Waite Stand and changing up to 5th and 140 mph before passing the Hill Stand at 160 mph. Braking hard again (-3.5 g) the cars change down to 3rd gear and enter the right-hand Turn 13 at 80 mph. Accelerating to 100 mph in front of the Stewart Stand, Turn 14, another right-hander, is taken in 3rd gear at 100 mph.

The Prost Stand marks the entrance to the most difficult section of the circuit with the cars turning through two sharp 90-degree turns, going first left (Turn 15) and then right (Turn 16). Cars approach Turn 15 at 130 mph, braking hard and changing down from 4th to 2nd to negotiate the near hairpin turn at 50 mph. Turn 16 is less demanding but still requires 2nd gear with cars accelerating in front of the Senna Stand from 80 mph on to the finishing straight. The longest section of straight on the circuit, cars can go flat out in 6th gear at 180 mph as they flash across the Start-Finish line.

3-Year Record

Year	1st	2nd	3rd	4th	5th	6th
1997	Coulthard	M.Schum'r	Hakkinen	Berger	Panis	Larini
	(McLaren)	(Ferrari)	(McLaren)	(Benetton)	(Prost)	(Sauber)
1998	Hakkinen	Coulthard	Frentzen	Irvine	Villeneuve	Herbert
	(McLaren)	(McLaren)	(Williams)	(Ferrari)	(Williams)	(Sauber)
1999	Irvine	Frentzen	R.Schum'r	Fisichella	Barrichello	de la Rosa
	(Ferrari)	(Jordan)	(Williams)	(Benetton)	(Stewart)	(Arrows)

Pole Position

1997	1998	1999
Villeneuve (Williams)	Hakkinen (McLaren)	Hakkinen (McLaren)
1m 29.369s (dry)	1m 30.010s (dry)	1m 30.462s (dry)

Notebook

Since the track was only opened in 1996 it has recorded different winners in each year. Eddie Irvine took the honours last year following in the wake of Hill, Coulthard and Hakkinen. Pedro de la Rosa scored his first Grand Prix point here last season in his very first Formula One race while Heinz-Harald Frentzen came second in his first race for Jordan. Meanwhile Michael Schumacher has only managed to finish in the points here once, that was in 1997 when he finished second.

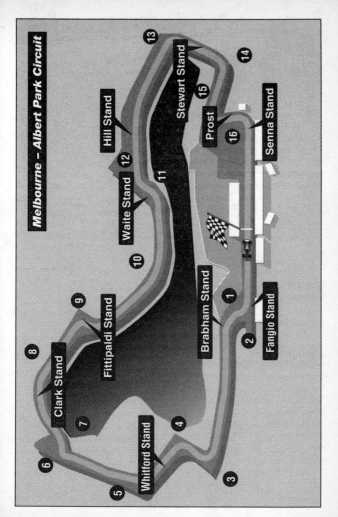

Melbourne – Albert Park Circuit

Stewart Stand
Hill Stand
Waite Stand
Fittipaldi Stand
Clark Stand
Whitford Stand
Brabham Stand
Prost
Senna Stand
Fangio Stand

1 2 3 4 5 6 7 8 9 10 11 12 13 14 15 16

Monaco

Circuit de Monaco
Monaco Grand Prix Monte Carlo – 4 June 2000
Lap Distance: 2.082 miles/3.352 km – Clockwise
Race Distance: 162.24 miles/261.478 km – 78 laps

Probably the most famous Grand Prix circuit in the world, taking its macadam from the busy city streets and harbour front of Monte Carlo in the south of France. A tight, demanding circuit, there is little room on the track with overtaking a near impossibility – as such, pole position can be decisive and much of the teams' efforts are directed in this area. The circuit is not hard on the engines as they are never operating at full power; it is demanding on the drivers, however – a typical lap of the circuit requires 36 gear changes, and that's over 2800 per race! Teams look for maximum downforce as mechanical grip is vital because the roads are very slippery and highly cambered in places which makes the setting of the suspension very complex. In addition, the circuit contains two very slow hairpins at which the car tends to understeer strongly. So the set-up needs to enable the car to get round this type of corner and the engine characteristics have to be such that the power delivery is very smooth. Suspension settings are soft with increased ride height to avoid the bumps. The working conditions for teams at Monaco are always very difficult as the pits are also temporary!

The Circuit

The start of the Monaco Grand Prix is all about getting to, and through, the very first corner safely. Do that and you have a chance! The Virage de Sainte Devote is a near 90-degree right-hander that is approached from the Start-Finish line at 170 mph. Then, it's a hard brake at -3.6 g and down to a 2nd gear 55 mph for cornering. The Montée du Beau Rivage is a short straight that takes the cars past what used to be the site of the world-famous Rosie's Bar (RIP) in 6th gear at 165 mph and then it's over the crest of the hill and down to 4th gear as Virage Massenet beckons. A long left-hander, the car must be kept close to the inside kerb in 3rd gear at 80 mph. The cars then come to Virage Casino which is a quick right-hander that is taken in 2nd gear at 70 mph.

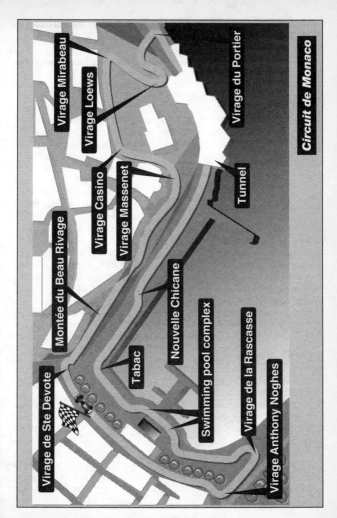

Circuit de Monaco

Virage Mirabeau
Virage Loews
Virage du Portier
Virage Casino
Virage Massenet
Tunnel
Montée du Beau Rivage
Nouvelle Chicane
Virage de Ste Devote
Tabac
Swimming pool complex
Virage de la Rascasse
Virage Anthony Noghes

Coming out of Casino the cars get a chance to accelerate briefly along a short straight before they enter one of the most complex sections of the course. The Virage Mirabeau is approached downhill in 4th at 130 mph, requiring fast gear changes to get into 2nd gear for this bumpy right-hander, taken slowly at 30 mph. Out of this comes the short approach to the Virage Loews, a left-hand hairpin negotiated in 2nd gear at about 20 mph with the steering turned full lock, then right – this is one of the most famous TV and photographic views in F1. The turns are ended by the Virage du Portier, another sharp right-hander cleared in 2nd gear at 50 mph. Coming out of the turns, the cars start on a long sweep through the Tunnel. Noise and sparks fly as the cars change up to 5th gear and 145 mph. Once out of the tunnel, left-right Nouvelle Chicane is approached at 175 mph before drivers change down to 2nd gear and a sedate 30 mph.

The most spectacular and glamorous part of the course is Tabac, lying, as it does, alongside the harbour, which is driven through at 95 mph in 4th gear. Piscine or the Swimming Pool Complex provides a short kink in the circuit which pushes the drivers through a succession of gear changes and speeds ranging from 50 mph to 100 mph. This section of the circuit underwent major revision prior to the 1997 Grand Prix to make it safer. Virage de la Rascasse is the slowest part of the circuit with a very tight hairpin that is taken in 1st gear at a crawling 20 mph. Along a very short straight and a faster right-hander, Virage Anthony Noghes, is taken in 2nd at 45 mph before accelerating and climbing upward into the Start-Finish straight.

3-Year Record

Year	1st	2nd	3rd	4th	5th	6th
1997	M.Schum'r (Ferrari)	Barrichello (Stewart)	Irvine (Ferrari)	Panis (Prost)	Salo (Tyrrell)	Fisichella (Jordan)
1998	Hakkinen (McLaren)	Fisichella (Benetton)	Irvine (Ferrari)	Salo (Arrows)	Villeneuve (Williams)	Diniz (Arrows)
1999	M.Schum'r (Ferrari)	Irvine (Ferrari)	Hakkinen (McLaren)	Frentzen (Jordan)	Fisichella (Benetton)	Wurz (Benetton)

Pole Position

1997	1998	1999
Frentzen (Williams)	Hakkinen (McLaren)	Hakkinen (McLaren)
1:18.216 (dry)	1:19.798 (dry)	1m 20.547s (dry)

Montreal

Gilles Villeneuve Circuit
Canadian Grand Prix – 18 June 2000
Lap Distance: 2.747 miles/4.421 km – Clockwise
Race Distance: 189.543 miles/305.049 km – 69 laps

Located on the Ile Notre Dame, the circuit is within easy reach of the
Montreal city centre. It has a picturesque backdrop which includes
views of the Lawrence River and the old Olympic Rowing Basin. The
Canadian Grand Prix has been staged here since 1978 and the track is
part permanent and part street circuit. This is the only race to take place
on the course each year, so the roads collect a great amount of grit
which the wind shifts about causing severe grip problems. It is a high-
speed circuit with equally fast chicanes, but it also has slow corners
which are fed by straights; as such, braking is paramount and brake
performance often proves critical. The conditions make the set-up such
that it is necessary to run relatively low downforce for the straight while
trying to maintain good grip on the smooth surface and responsive
change of direction through the chicanes. Traction is always at a
premium and leads to a relatively high fuel consumption. The circuit
possesses a couple of good overtaking opportunities by out-braking at
very high speed at the corners, especially the final one.

The Circuit

From the starting grid, the cars accelerate to 170 mph and swing quickly
through Turn 1 as the track waves right and left. Once through they
brake heavily, pulling -3.8 g at the entrance to Virage Senna. This
hairpin is marked by a tight 90-degree turn to the left before the hairpin
itself turns the cars through 180 degrees and it is negotiated at 45 mph
in 2nd gear. Cars quickly accelerate to 150 mph and 5th gear as the
track curves gently to the right. A series of bends (Turns 2-6) see the
cars down to 3rd gear and speeds averaging 60 mph as the circuit turns
to the right.

Turn 7 marks the Pont de la Concorde which occupies about a third
of the track length. This is a long straight, broken up by a quick right-
left turn – Turn 8 and Turn 9 – that can be negotiated in 3rd gear.

Decelerating from 170 mph, the right bend is entered at 50 mph and then exited at 65 mph.

The lead-up to Turn 10, which marks the Virage du Casino, is done at full throttle with a top speed of around 170 mph. This hairpin comes at a point where the entrance and exit run side by side, and so it gives the drivers a chance to see who is behind them. It is a relatively wide portion of the track and it is common to see overtaking manoeuvres here as cars try to out-brake one another. It is also the slowest part of the track, with cars braking down from 180 mph to around 40 mph.

Patients in the nearby hospital get a good view of the cars accelerating up through the gears along the Casino Straight. This is the fastest section of track with cars hitting speeds of 190 mph in top gear. Turn 11 marks the hardest braking point on the circuit with drivers experiencing -3.8 g. This was modified for the 1996 Grand Prix, from the Casino Bend (Turn 12 and Turn 13) which used to be a chicane, slowing the cars down into the final straight. Now it is much shallower, with cars swinging through it at around 60 mph before accelerating again as they cross the Start-Finish line.

3-Year Record

Year	1st	2nd	3rd	4th	5th	6th
1997	M.Schum'r (Ferrari)	Alesi (Benetton)	Fisichella (Jordan)	Frentzen (Williams)	Herbert (Sauber)	Nakano (Prost)
1998	M.Schum'r (Ferrari)	Fisichella (Benetton)	Irvine (Ferrari)	Wurz (Williams)	Barrichello (Stewart)	Magnussen (Stewart)
1999	Hakkinen (McLaren)	Fisichella (Benetton)	Irvine (Ferrari)	R.Schum'r (Williams)	Herbert (Stewart)	Diniz (Sauber)

Pole Position

1997	1998	1999
M.Schumacher (Ferrari)	Coulthard (McLaren)	M.Schumacher (Ferrari)
1m 18.095s (dry)	1m 18.213s (dry)	1m 19.298s (dry)

Notebook

Mika Hakkinen took the win last season – it was the first time in three years he managed to get in the points at Montreal. Giancarlo Fisichella managed his second successive second at the circuit.

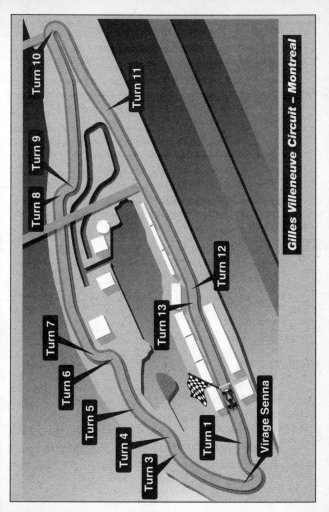

Gilles Villeneuve Circuit – Montreal

Turn 10
Turn 11
Turn 9
Turn 8
Turn 12
Turn 13
Turn 7
Turn 6
Turn 5
Turn 4
Turn 3
Turn 1
Virage Senna

Monza

Autodromo Nationale di Monza
Italian Grand Prix – 10 September 2000
Lap Distance: 3.585 miles/5.772 km – Clockwise
Race Distance: 191.005 miles/305.908 km – 53 laps

Fifteen miles north-east of Milan, Monza was built in 1922. The modern-day autodromo combines fast, sweeping corners and long straights, with Parabolica and Lesmo two of the more famous. The Italian Grand Prix has been staged here for all but one year since the World Championship was introduced in 1950. Downforce requirements are normally low with stiff settings on the car to help ride some of the big bumps that the circuit is notorious for. The low wing levels make grip poor in the low-speed turns, which can create problems for drivers who brake too late into them. This is countered somewhat by cars having stiff set front ends. In short the requirements of the car are to have high power, low drag and very efficient brakes as this circuit is the hardest on brakes of any of the current Grand Prix venues. In addition, particularly at the first chicane, it is essential to have a car that can ride the kerbs well, especially in qualifying, as this is paramount to a good lap time. The main overtaking opportunity is into the first chicane and this is where much of the action will take place, especially at the start.

The Circuit

The Rettifilio Tribune is the long start straight and leads to the Variante Goodyear (also known as Variante del Rettifilio). This is approached in top gear at around 205 mph and it is marked by the wide pit straight that precedes it. It is a very fast but bumpy left-right-left-right 2nd gear chicane that's entered in 2nd at 60 mph and exited at 80 mph. Almost immediately after is Curva Grande, which is a very bumpy, longish right-hander that is hard work on the steering. Entered in 4th gear at 160 mph, drivers invariably use the kerb at its exit at 185 mph and then it's along the back straight where 200 mph is touched.

The Variante della Roggia is also known as 2A Variante. The braking area prior to entering this left-right chicane is both bumpy and slippy. Approached in top gear, it is negotiated in 2nd at 60 mph and exited in

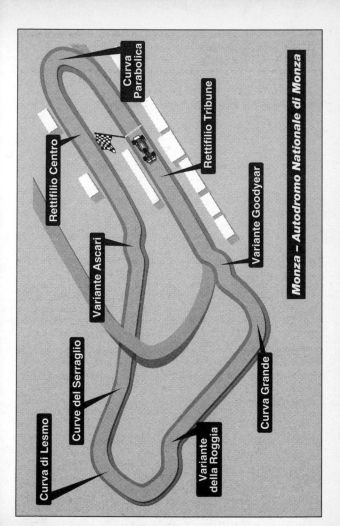

Monza – Autodromo Nationale di Monza

3rd at 85 mph. Curva di Lesmo is a contentious sharp right-hander – invariably taken fast, shifting between 4th and 3rd gears, with speeds ranging between 150 mph and 95 mph. Coming out of the turn, the cars rocket down Curve del Serraglio, a long straight that means the driver approaches the next chicane at speeds approaching, and often exceeding, 200 mph.

Drivers hope their brakes are in good order as they approach Curva del Vialone, a left-hander, braking from 200 mph in 6th gear to 4th gear at the 100-metre board. Then, on to Variante Ascari, the second part of the chicane, quickly flicking right, then left and changing down into 2nd gear at 85 mph. Exited in 4th gear at 135 mph, cars accelerate on to the Rettifilio Centro straight and attain 205 mph on the approach to the final curve.

The Curva Parabolica is a long, looping right-hander that is important to lap times as the entry and exit to it determine how quickly drivers can get on the gas as they come out on to the longest straight on the circuit. Braking hard at 3.2 g, cars decelerate to 100 mph and 3rd gear at its apex. As the curve opens out it is exited in 5th gear at 175 mph as the cars arrive in the long Rettifilio Tribune straight, before applying full throttle and crossing the Start-Finish line.

3-Year Record

Year	1st	2nd	3rd	4th	5th	6th
1997	Coulthard (McLaren)	Alesi (Benetton)	Frentzen (Williams)	Fisichella (Jordan)	Villeneuve (Williams)	M.Schum'r (Ferrari)
1998	M.Schum'r (Ferrari)	Irvine (Ferrari)	R.Schum'r (Jordan)	Hakkinen (McLaren)	Alesi (Sauber)	Hill (Jordan)
1999	Frentzen (Jordan)	R.Schum'r (Williams)	Salo (Ferrari)	Barrichello (Stewart)	Coulthard (McLaren)	Irvine (Ferrari)

Pole Position

1997	1998	1999
Alesi (Benetton)	M.Schumacher (Ferrari)	Hakkinen (McLaren)
1m 22.990s (dry)	1m 25.298s (dry)	1m 22.432s (dry)

Nurburgring

Nurburgring (Germany)
European Grand Prix – 21 May 2000
Lap Distance   2.831 miles/4.568 km – Clockwise
Race Distance   190.079 miles/306.027 km – 67 laps

The circuit, which is located about 55 miles south-west of Cologne, was opened for Grand Prix action in 1984, when Alain Prost won the European event. This was followed by the German Grand Prix, which was the last for some time. Then, after ten years of Grand Prix inactivity, the circuit was used for the European Grand Prix in 1996. In 1998 it staged what was laughingly called the Luxembourg Grand Prix, despite it being situated in Germany.

Amid beautiful countryside, the Nurburgring is both fast and forgiving with wide run-off areas and large gravel traps. Its 12 corners and curves make for an exciting race. The long slow corners tend to lead to understeer problems which can make handling problematic. Medium downforce settings are normally employed with a degree of stiffness that still allows the driver to attack the last chicane, which has steep kerbs. The circuit is generally easy on tyres but the race location and time of year can invariably see the onset of rain and the need to run 'wets'.

The Circuit

Out of the blocks and into top gear at 180 mph towards the Castrol 'S' bend and hard on the brakes at the entry to the right-left at 80 mph in 3rd gear. The curve is exited at 100 mph as drivers change up. Quickly up to 6th gear and accelerating to 170 mph for the approach to Ford Kurve which is taken at 110 mph in 3rd gear and leads directly into the Ford Kurve at 65 mph in 2nd gear. Then, hard on the throttle, the cars approach the Dunlop Kurve at 175 mph in 6th gear.

The Dunlop Kurve is a right-hand 190-degree loop, making it the second slowest part of the circuit taken at 50 mph in 2nd gear. Provided cars have managed a good line through the loop, they can get on to the gas quickly and through 155 mph as the track swings gently left and right. Out of here the approach to the RTL Kurve sees the cars in top gear at 170 mph, which is almost halved to 3rd gear at 95 mph through the near

90-degree left-hand turn. Having swept left, the Bit-Kurve sweeps another 90 degrees through a right-hand turn, again in 3rd gear at around 105 mph.

On to the straight, taken full-out in top gear at 180 mph, slowing to 165 mph as they sweep right through ITT-bogen – up to 180 mph – before braking hard to the Veedol 'S' which is negotiated at 60 mph. Sweep left and then right in 2nd gear, before accelerating to 135 mph in 4th gear. Out of here comes the sharp left-hand turn through 160 degrees which marks the Coca-Cola Kurve. This is taken in 2nd gear at 70 mph before accelerating out into the finishing straight at top speed.

3-Year Record

Year	1st	2nd	3rd	4th	5th	6th
1997	Villeneuve (Williams)	Alesi (Benetton)	Frentzen (Williams)	Berger (Benetton)	Diniz (Arrows)	Panis (Prost)
1998*	Hakkinen (McLaren)	M.Schum'r (Ferrari)	Coulthard (McLaren)	Irvine (Ferrari)	Frentzen (Williams)	Fisichella (Benetton)
1999	Herbert (Stewart)	Trulli (Prost)	Barrichello (Stewart)	R.Schum'r (Williams)	Hakkinen (McLaren)	Gene (Minardi)

* Luxembourg Grand Prix.

Pole Position

1997	1998	1999
Hakkinen (McLaren)	M.Schumacher (Ferrari)	Frentzen (Jordan)
1m16.602s (dry)	1m 18.561s (dry)	1m 19.910s (damp)

Notebook

Last season's race was run in very changeable conditions. Johnny Herbert was the surprise victor, taking advantage of the attrition around him to record a popular win. In qualifying Heinz-Harald Frentzen took the number one position on the grid for the first time in his career. Marc Gene secured what was to be Minardi's only point of the year. A win for Mika Hakkinen in 2000 would equal the total of three wins achieved here by Jackie Stewart and Juan Manuel Fangio. Not bad company!

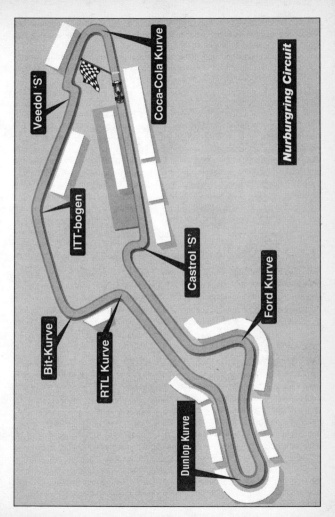

Nurburgring Circuit

Veedol 'S'

Coca-Cola Kurve

ITT-bogen

Castrol 'S'

Bit-Kurve

RTL Kurve

Ford Kurve

Dunlop Kurve

Sepang

Malaysian Grand Prix – 22 October 2000
Lap Distance: 3.443 miles/5.542 km
Race Distance: 192.855 miles/310.362 kms – 56 laps

The Sepang Circuit is located about 40 miles from the capital city of
Kuala Lumpur and about 10 miles from the Kuala Lumpur International
Airport (KLIA). The main grandstand has a capacity of 30,000, with
room to cram another 80,000 into the rest of the circuit. It opened for
business in December 1998 just one month after being completed at a
cost of $120 million and staged its first Formula One race in 1999.

The circuit has three very slow corners, four 3rd gear corners, four 4th
gear corners and two high speed 5th gear corners. In addition there are
two quite long straights of around 800 m each. These present an
interesting challenge for the engineers as speed on these straights is
essential because they both lead to overtaking opportunities whereas
much of the rest of the circuit will require high downforce and maximum
grip. The optimum downforce level then is in the medium to high range,
somewhere close to Silverstone and Barcelona. The race is staged in the
Rainy Season and this adds to the flavour of the event.

The Circuit

The Start-Finish line is located two thirds of the way along the opening
straight to enable teams to make a blistering start towards the first turn.
The cars arrive at Turn 1 doing around 185 mph in 6th gear and it
follows directly into Turn 2. Both are taken in second gear at about 60
mph and although they are very tight they have a high positive camber,
and provide good overtaking opportunities. Turn 3 is a more gentle curve
that can be taken flat out in dry conditions with cars approaching 155
mph in 5th gear. Turn 4 comes up quickly and is taken at 75 mph and in
3rd gear.

Turns 5 and 6 are quite demanding high speed corners taken in 4th and
5th gear respectively with the cars touching on 140 mph. Turns 7 and 8
are not quite right-handers but effectively form one double apex taken at
110 mph in 4th gear. This leads into a short straight where cars accelerate

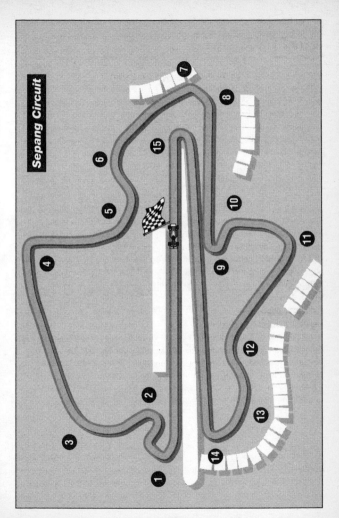

Sepang Circuit

to 170 mph before hitting a near hairpin at Turn 9. Cars almost come back on themselves dropping to 2nd gear and 55 mph.

After the hairpin, turns 10, 11 and 12 are fairly straightforward, as the cars arch right and then left. Cars enter 10 at 135 mph and brake to 90 mph to take Turn 11 before accelerating through Turn 12 at 155 mph. Braking into Turn 13 can create problems as they enter it at around 13 mph and exit at 80 mph, but this provides another good place for overtaking. This leads into the back straight which is just slightly shorter than the main straight. The two straights are joined by a 65 mph 2nd gear hairpin (Turn 15) which is approached at 185 mph along the straight. Out of the hairpin the cars accelerate across the Start-Finish line for another lap.

3-Year Record

Year	1st	2nd	3rd	4th	5th	6th
1999	Irvine	M.Schum'r	Hakkinen	Herbert	Barrichello	Frentzen
	(Ferrari)	(Ferrari)	(McLaren)	(Stewart)	(Stewart)	(Jordan)

Pole Position

1999
M.Schumacher (Ferrari)
1m 39.688s (dry)

Notebook

Last year's race was shrouded in post-race controversy when the two Ferrari cars were disqualified for having what were at the time deemed to be illegal bargeboards. This happened a couple of hours after the race, and effectively elevated Hakkinen to first, a position that would have won him the World Championship. On appeal, six days later Ferrari were re-instated to keep the championship alive to the final race.

Silverstone

Silverstone Circuit
British Grand Prix – 23 April 2000
Lap Distance: 3.194 miles/5.142 km – Clockwise
Race Distance: 191.634 miles/308.52 km – 60 laps

Silverstone is Britain's longest continually used race circuit and staged the first ever British Grand Prix in 1926. Although not used for all British Grands Prix, it has held the event since 1987. The circuit is located in the Northamptonshire countryside near the village of the same name. Operated and owned by the British Racing Drivers' Club, Silverstone held the first ever round of the World Championship in 1950. It has undergone design revisions in recent years, with changes made to a number of corners.

Silverstone provides quite a challenge to both the drivers and the race engineers in that it features many different types of corner. Some of these, for example the final corners, are rather slow 'point-and-squirt' corners. Others, such as the Becketts series of curves, Copse and Bridge, are among the best corners of any circuit in the world.

Overtaking opportunities are limited, so a good qualifying position is essential. The circuit is quite hard on tyres and the effect of high fuel loads is greater than at most circuits. Therefore a fine balance has to be achieved. Reliability is also important due to high average throttle openings and engine speeds during the race.

The Circuit

From the grid, cars pull away and the straight allows speeds of 175 mph to be reached on the approach to Copse. This right-hand corner is blind but, at 145 mph, very fast; so fast in fact that drivers don't normally brake – just change down a gear. Switching back up, cars thunder on towards Maggotts at 180 mph and shift down twice as they wave their way first through Maggotts and then Becketts – as the track wiggles left-right, left-right, slowing down to 100 mph before Chapel ends the series of left-right bends and is accelerated through, coming out at 145 mph in 5th gear.

The Hanger Straight is the fastest part of the circuit, at 190 mph in top gear, before braking hard into Stowe, a right-hand turn that can be taken in 4th gear and speeds of 105 mph maintained. Vale is a quick straight in which the cars go through at something like 160 mph with a 2nd-gear, sharp left into Club, a right-hand corner taken at 50 mph and then accelerated through as the cars swing back on themselves at 130 mph. Both Vale and Club present good overtaking opportunities, not least because they are tricky to negotiate and understeer comes into play. Up through two gears into 6th and 170 mph towards Abbey, a 3rd gear, 75 mph corner which flips into Farm at 100 mph and up to 160 mph along this straight.

Bridge marks the entrance to the 'Complex', a section of the track containing bends at Priory, Brooklands and Luffield. The corners at Bridge and Priory are fast, entering the first at 150 mph and exiting the second at 100 mph. Priory, along with Brooklands, steer the car through 180 degrees. Brooklands, along with Luffield, again turns the car around and both are negotiated in 2nd gear at 50-80 mph. Luffield used to be two corners called Luffield 1 and Luffield 2 prior to 1996. On exit, it's a quick dash through Woodcote at 165 mph and a smooth turn to the right before hitting the Start-Finish straight at 175 mph. At the start of 1998 Silverstone renamed the sequence of corners from Priory to Luffield as 'The Grandstand' but the individual corners are still referred to by name.

3-Year Record

Year	1st	2nd	3rd	4th	5th	6th
1997	Villeneuve (Williams)	Alesi (Benetton)	Wurz (Benetton)	Coulthard (McLaren)	R.Schum'r (Jordan)	Hill (Arrows)
1998	M.Schum'r (Ferrari)	Hakkinen (McLaren)	Irvine (Ferrari)	Wurz (Benetton)	Fisichella (Benetton)	R.Schum'r (Jordan)
1999	Coulthard (McLaren)	Irvine (Ferrari)	R.Schum'r (Williams)	Frentzen (Jordan)	Hill (Jordan)	Diniz (Sauber)

Pole Position

1997	1998	1999
Villeneuve (Williams)	Hakkinen (McLaren)	Hakkinen (McLaren)
1m 21.598s (dry)	1m 23.271s (dry)	1m 24.804s (dry)

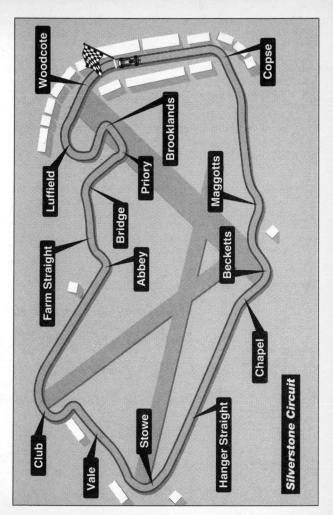

Silverstone Circuit

Woodcote · Copse · Brooklands · Priory · Luffield · Maggotts · Bridge · Becketts · Farm Straight · Abbey · Chapel · Stowe · Vale · Club · Hanger Straight

Spa

Circuit de Spa-Francorchamps
Belgian Grand Prix – 27 August 2000
Lap Distance: 4.33 miles/6.971 km – Clockwise
Race Distance: 190.527 miles/306.7375 km – 44 laps

Lying 30 miles south-east of Liege, Spa-Francorchamps is located in central Belgium. It was first used in 1985 and, at 4.33 miles in length, it is the longest circuit in use in the World Championship. A temporary circuit that makes use of public roads, it remains a firm favourite with most drivers, not least because of its picturesque setting, and because it is demanding enough to present a difficult challenge to those racing. It has a mixture of long straights and some challenging fast corners with a minimum number of slow chicanes. The corner Eau Rouge is probably the most famous corner on any race track in the world and due to its high speed and extreme elevation changes, it provides a supreme challenge to both the drivers and the engineers. Low to medium downforce settings are used to enable drivers to cope with varied high- and low-speed sections and a number of corners which are all the faster for being downhill. The start is always very tricky at Spa as the first corner, which is a very short distance from the start line, is an extremely tight hairpin. Both cars and engines experience very high stresses at this circuit and as always reliability is of paramount importance.

The Circuit

From the start, the corner at La Source comes very quickly and is a hairpin that is taken in 2nd gear at around 40 mph after which drivers have two long straights that are separated by Eau Rouge – which amounts to a small kink in the circuit. Accelerating to 180 mph along the first section, Eau Rouge can be taken in 6th gear with only a slight loss of speed (165 mph) as it goes downhill and then uphill left, right, and left. Cars exit at Raidillon and then encounter the fastest part of the course along the Kemmell straight at 190 mph.

As the track bears round slowly to the right, there exists good overtaking possibilities at Les Combes due to the wide run-off areas.

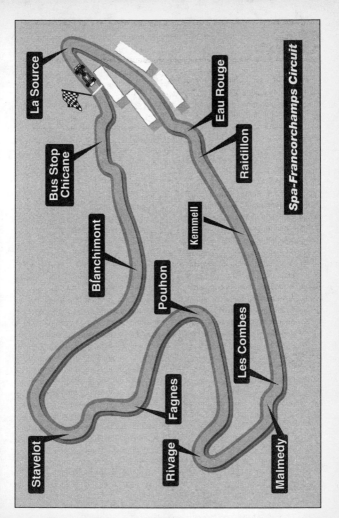

Spa-Francorchamps Circuit

La Source
Eau Rouge
Raidillon
Bus Stop Chicane
Kemmell
Blanchimont
Pouhon
Les Combes
Fagnes
Stavelot
Rivage
Malmedy

251

The right-left combination chicane is taken in 3rd gear and 85 mph and is exited at Malmedy, which is a right-hander taken at 100 mph.

Rivage is a virtual hairpin which, due to being off camber and downhill, causes cars all sorts of steering problems. It is approached in 4th gear at 155 mph, taken in 2nd at 60 mph and exited in 3rd at 110 mph. Out of Rivage the cars sweep along a short straight at 155 mph before the track veers left at 90 mph and on to Pouhon at 100 mph, a double left-hander. Also off camber, it is entered and exited in 4th gear at an average of 140 mph. On exit, cars power through the gears to 180 mph before slowing at Fagnes – a right-left chicane which is taken in 3rd gear at 100 mph.

Stavelot is a double right-hand loop, turning the cars through 180 degrees as they go downhill. Entered in 3rd with 4th (135 mph) being engaged in the middle, but it is bumpy and cars tend to skip about a bit as cars speed up to 150 mph on exit. Blanchimont is a long, sweeping left-hander taken full-out in 6th gear at 185 mph. With the Start-Finish line almost in sight, Bus Stop Chicane appears, a sharp right-left-right chicane that slows the cars right down to a 2nd gear 45 mph before they emerge on to the pit straight at 170 mph.

3-Year Record

Year	1st	2nd	3rd	4th	5th	6th
1997	M.Schum'r (Ferrari)	Fisichella (Jordan)	Frentzen (Williams)	Herbert (Sauber)	Villeneuve (Williams)	Berger (Benetton)
1998	Hill (Jordan)	R.Schum'r (Jordan)	Alesi (Sauber)	Frentzen (Williams)	Diniz (Arrows)	Trulli (Prost)
1999	Coulthard (McLaren)	Hakkinen (McLaren)	Frentzen (Jordan)	Irvine (Ferrari)	R.Schum'r (Williams)	Hill (Jordan)

Pole Position

1997	1998	1999
Villeneuve (Williams)	Hakkinen (McLaren)	Hakkinen (McLaren)
1m 49.450s (dry)	1m 48.682s (dry)	1m 50.329s (dry)

Suzuka

Suzuka International Racing Course
Japanese Grand Prix – 8 October 2000
Lap Distance: 3.642 miles/5.864 km – Figure of Eight
Race Distance: 193.026 miles/310.772 km – 53 laps

Located between Osaka and Nagoya, south-west of Tokyo, Suzuka has been a regular date on the Grand Prix calendar since 1987. The circuit is unique to the Championship in that it follows a figure of eight pattern with numerous turns and straights, thus providing both clockwise and anti-clockwise movement for the cars. It is one of the most technical circuits on the calendar and the 130 R corner is perhaps the most challenging found anywhere. Setting up the cars is difficult as drivers have to balance between aerodynamic downforce and mechanical grip. The track requires low grip but has some bad bumps in it. Thus drivers normally opt for medium to soft settings for the smooth surface with stiff suspension to take in the various bumps.

The Circuit

The start is downhill and this can help cars get away. Indeed, in 1988, it helped Ayrton Senna get away after he stalled just before the go signal. Once away, the cars approach First Curve flat out in top gear at speeds of up to 190 mph with a change down to 5th and 150 mph into the bend and into a second curve that is much tighter than the first and can only be negotiated in 3rd with speed dropping to 95 mph.

The S Curve is a left-right-left-right combination that severely taxes any car that is not well balanced. It can usually be taken all the way through in 4th. The sequence is entered at 135 mph, dropping to 85 mph on exit of the final curve. On exiting, the S Curve's 4th gear is maintained for the approach to the Dunlop Curve. This long left-hander is extremely bumpy with plenty of understeer at 135 mph.

Accelerating to 160 mph, the Degner Curve is a tight right-hander that is taken in 4th gear at 120 mph, down to 3rd as the second part of the corner becomes tighter still, and then generally exited with the use of the kerb. Then it is up to top gear at 170 mph to go under the bridge where the course crosses itself to the Hairpin Curve. This is guarded by a short right-hander which slows the cars, but then they have to get down very quickly to 2nd gear for the 45 mph hairpin. Out of the hairpin the circuit curves to the right and on completion of the curve the majority of cars will be in top gear at 170 mph.

Spoon Curve awaits at the end of the looping right-hander. It is negotiated in 3rd gear, with speeds dropping from 105 mph on entry to 85 mph on exit. Then it's full on the throttle and it's a 185 mph straight-screamer over the Crossover to 130 R, a very fast left-hander which forces a slight deceleration to 155 mph. The Casino Chicane (also known as Triangle Chicane or Casino Triangle) guards the entrance to the finishing straight. The right-left combination is taken in 2nd gear at 40 mph, with the cars having to brake hard from 175 mph as they approach it. Once through, the cars swing right at 120 mph and on to the Start-Finish straight for the next lap.

3-Year Record

Year	1st	2nd	3rd	4th	5th	6th
1997	M.Schum'r	Frentzen	Irvine	Hakkinen	Villeneuve	Alesi
	(Ferrari)	(Williams)	(Ferrari)	(McLaren)	(Williams)	(Benetton)
1998	Hakkinen	Irvine	Coulthard	Hill	Frentzen	Villeneuve
	(McLaren)	(Ferrari)	(McLaren)	(Jordan)	(Williams)	(Williams)
1999	Hakkinen	M.Schum'r	Irvine	Frentzen	R.Schum'r	Alesi
	(McLaren)	(Ferrari)	(Ferrari)	(Jordan)	(Williams)	(Sauber)

Pole Position

1997	1998	1999
Villeneuve (Williams)	M.Schumacher (Ferrari)	M.Schumacher (Ferrari)
1m 36.071s (dry)	1m 36.293s (dry)	1m 37.470s (dry)

Notebook

Mika Hakkinen secured his second successive Drivers' Championship here last year, thanks to a terrific start in which he shot off in front of Michael Schumacher who held a second successive pole position at the circuit. Eddie Irvine, the only other challenger for the title, finished third. With both Ferraris in a good points-scoring formation, Ferrari took the Constructors' Cup title. Hakkinen ties Schumacher Snr, Senna and Gerhard Berger with two wins at the circuit.

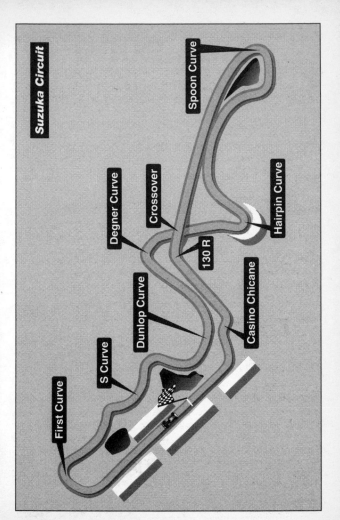

Suzuka Circuit

Spoon Curve

Degner Curve

Crossover

130 R

Hairpin Curve

Dunlop Curve

Casino Chicane

S Curve

First Curve

Race 2000

Listed below are provisional dates and venues for the 2000 Formula 1 season. They were awaiting final FIA confirmation at the time of going to press. As such dates and start times are subject to change and alteration.

Date	Grand Prix	Circuit	Laps	Start GMT
12 March	Australian	Melbourne	58	0400 hours
26 March	Brazilian	Interlagos	71	1600 hours
9 April	San Marino	Imola	62	1200 hours
23 April	British	Silverstone	60	1300 hours
7 May	Spanish	Catalunya	65	1200 hours
21 May	European	Nurburgring	67	1200 hours
4 June	Monaco	Monte Carlo	78	1300 hours
18 June	Canadian	Montreal	69	1800 hours
2 July	French	Magny-Cours	72	1200 hours
16 July	Austrian	A1-Ring	71	1200 hours
30 July	German	Hockenheim	45	1200 hours
13 August	Hungarian	Hungaroring	77	1200 hours
27 August	Belgian	Spa	44	1200 hours
10 September	Italian	Monza	53	1200 hours
27 September	USA	Indianapolis	tba	
8 October	Japanese	Suzuka	53	0400 hours
22 October	Malaysian	Kuala Lumpur	56	0600 hours